THE GUITAR

The History ★ The Music ★ The Players

Allan Kozinn/Pete Welding/Dan Forte/Gene Santoro

QUILL

New York   1984

A Quarto Book

Copyright ©1984 by Quarto Marketing Ltd.

Library of Congress Catalog Card Number: 83-62354
ISBN: 0-688-01972-2
ISBN: 0-688-01973-0 (paperback)

The Guitar was produced and prepared by Quarto Marketing Ltd.
212 Fifth Avenue, New York, NY 10010

Editor: Gene Santoro

Typeset by Associated Typographers
Color separations by Hong Kong Scanner Craft Company Ltd.
Printed and bound in Hong Kong by Leefung-Asco Printers Ltd.

First Quill Edition

1 2 3 4 5 6 7 8 9 10

COVER DESIGN BY RICHARD BODDY

COVER PHOTO BY JOHN PEDEN

The guitars that appear on the cover are, from front to back:
★ Fender Custom Telecaster (1962) #77522 ★
★ Gibson Les Paul Gold Top (1957) #71200 ★
★ Fender Stratocaster Fiesta Red (1963) #L21506 ★
★ Gibson L-5 archtop (1936) #92584 ★
★ Martin OM-28 14-fret (1931) #46419 ★
All guitars courtesy
Matt Umanov, 273 Bleecker St., New York, NY 10014

CONTENTS

ABOUT THE AUTHORS

Pete Welding is a distinguished critic, an A&R man at Capitol Records, and a regular contributor to *Guitar World*.

Dan Forte is a writer for *Guitar Player* and *Musician* and lead guitarist for Cowabunga.

Allan Kozinn, winner of the ASCAP-DEEMS TAYLOR award for general excellence in articles about music, is a writer about classical guitar for *Frets, High Fidelity, Guitar Player,* and *The New York Times*.

Gene Santoro is a guitarist who has written and edited a range of music and books and articles.

PHOTO CREDITS

FOREWORD
by David Lindley

From childhood the guitar has always had a strange power over me which I have yet to explain. Whenever I enter a room in which there is a guitar the instrument will force me to pick it up, to touch it, hold it. I am sure there are others who share the same affliction. And I know there are others whose eyes glaze over, whose hands sweat as they fumble for the cash to buy what might finally be the ultimate guitar... at long last the instrument that will play itself... only to find that it still takes daily practice and concentration.... And the search goes on.

One of the earliest pictures of a guitarlike instrument was carved into a stone wall of an ancient Hittite building in what is now modern Turkey. It looks like a Martin D-28 uke body fitted with a Persian tambur neck. The guy holding it is smiling. Maybe he has found his ultimate instrument – he definitely has himself a collector's item. Is it an original? What kind of strings did he use? What kind of picks?

There are things constantly being discovered about the long and colorful history of the guitar and those who contributed to the evolution: builders, innovators not only in design and construction but also in various styles and techniques of playing. Instrument builder and player went hand in hand, each feeding the other with new ideas, requirements, dreams. "Sacre bleu, Django! What an ugly guitar!"

Experimentation with various materials brought forth strange and exotic variations. Plastic, metal, unusual woods were tried with varying degrees of success. Even the father of the modern classical guitar, Antonio Torres, tried a body made from paper maché, and with good results. The instrument was a natural for constant change.

As the shape and construction evolved so did the player. Giants appeared: Andrés Segovia, Ramon Montoya, Django Reinhardt, Charlie Christian, Les Paul, and those they took inspiration from and those they inspired. We owe much to early masters. What drove them? Can we put a name to it? Bottle it and O.D. on it? It may be the same thing that makes our eyes glaze over, makes our palms sweat.... Who knows?

We may never reach as high as they did or find the guitar that plays itself, but as the travel agent said, "Half the fun is getting there."

So if you're like me, God forbid, this book is for you, put together by guitar junkies for guitar junkies – pleasant dreams....

The Classical Guitar

by Allan Kozinn

In a sense, the classical guitar is a child of our times, an instrument whose lifeblood and substance are of the 20th century, even if its roots can be traced to antiquity. Only within the past few decades have guitarists at last succeeded in their long quest to be taken seriously as concert artists; and now that most of the world's major conservatories offer the guitar alongside the piano and orchestral instruments, the youngest generations of concert guitarists are displaying both a sparklingly precise performance technique and a more fully informed approach to music-making. Fifty years ago, the novelty of a guitarist playing classical repertoire led the general concertgoing public to overlook certain matters of musicality – today the standards for guitar performance are quite high.

In the same short span, composers who were not themselves guitarists have turned their attention to this comparatively soft-spoken yet eloquent instrument. And, as living composers have kept the repertoire current, a line of players and musicologists – beginning with Emilio Pujol and his colleagues in the 1920s, and continuing with renewed vigor thanks to a breed of determined specialists that emerged in the 1970s – has unearthed a literature more extensive than even Andrés Segovia himself could have imagined.

EARLY PREDECESSORS

The musicologists have also, however, raised questions about letting the 20th century guitar's forceful personality eclipse the voices and styles of its predecessors. They have realized, for example, that the suites of Robert de Visée, or the dances of

Edouard Manet's
The Spanish Singer

Gaspar Sanz, so familiar through concert performances and recordings, were composed for an instrument constructed, tuned, and played very differently from today's guitar, and that today's standard performances of these works sound quite unlike those Visée and Sanz gave. Because of this historical insight, new fields within the guitar world have opened up: just as there are keyboard players who devote themselves to the harpsichord and fortepiano, violinists who use only gut strings and Baroque bows, and flutists who specialize in the recorder, there is now a class of guitarists whose specialty is the Renaissance and Baroque literature, and who use only the four- and five-course guitars of the 16th through 18th centuries.

The Ancients

These instruments are, in fact, the earliest fretted, plucked, stringed instruments that can truly be called guitars – or, at least the earliest for which music, documentation, and actual period instruments

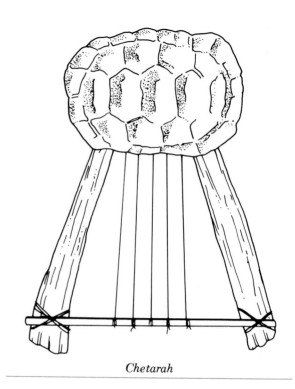

Chetarah

A bas relief of a man playing a nefer

survive. Exactly how remote the guitar's ancestors are remains a matter of conjecture, and since most identifications of ancient guitarlike instruments have been made only through representations in paintings and sculptures, or from poetic and literary references, one must be extremely cautious about claiming direct lines of descent. It must also be kept in mind, when reading ancient descriptions of instruments and players, that instrument names were not applied consistently from one country to the next, or from one century to the next; and that instruments whose names seem to imply etymological ties to the guitar are often not guitarlike at all.

Ancient art works and writings tell, for example,

that the Assyrians had a lyre, or harplike instrument, called a *chetarah*, dating at least 2000 B.C., and that the Egyptian *nefer*, from 1500 B.C., had a long neck and an oval-shaped resonating body, something like an early lute. Sometimes the visual representations offer a rough idea of how the instrument was played, but not always. Many questions remain about playing technique, how the instruments were strung and tuned, what they sounded like, what sort of music was played on them, and what function they served in their musical world.

Nor is there solid evidence of direct evolutionary links between these instruments and the guitar of today. There are, naturally, abundant theories, many of them plausible, if not adequately documented. One theory is that the Greek *kithara*, a lyre with a large wooden sounding-chest, evolved from the Assyrian *chetarah*, and that the Romans carried both the *kithara* and the lutelike *pandoura* to the far corners of their European empire. Another theory has it that the lutelike instruments of ancient Egypt were taken to Europe by merchant ships trading in the Mediterranean. Such explanations would account for the presence of plucked instruments in Europe before the arrival of the Arabic lutes, which were brought to Spain and Italy during the Moorish invasions of the 8th century, and which developed

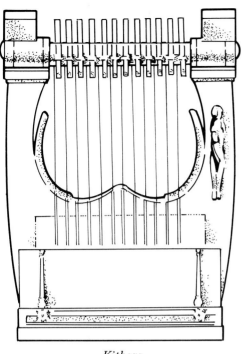

Kithara

Pandoura

into the lute, which remained in use in Europe until the middle of the 18th century.

But must the guitar necessarily have originated in Mesopotamia? And if so, what of the Japanese *samisen*, the Indian *sitar* and its family of related instruments, and the Chinese *p'ip'a*? Must there have been a common ancestor from which all the world's guitar- and lutelike instruments evolved? It is possible, certainly, that these instruments evolved independently around the world, perhaps sharing only the primitive twang of the hunting bow as a common heritage.

There are, after all, basically three paths along which instruments in any culture have evolved. The first is percussive: sound is produced by striking one object with another. Ideally, the struck object will have been large and hollow, and covered by a firm but slightly elastic material – a prototype drum. The second path involves sending a stream of air through a hollow tube, regulating the pitch by making the air current's journey longer or shorter – the flute prototype. Finally, the guitar prototype, in its simplest form, is a taut string that, when plucked, produces vibrations that are recognizable as a tone.

That, obviously, is only the start of the story, and here the paths diverge. If more than a single note is required, an ancient instrument maker could either

add more strings, varying their length and tightness, and playing his tunes by plucking the strings individually (as on a harp); or, he could place a flat board behind the strings, altering the vibrating string length (hence the pitch the strings produce) by pressing the strings against the board with his fingers. He could allow the strings to resonate on their own, unamplified; or he could increase their volume by attaching them to a hollow gourd, a tortoise-shell, or a wooden box, any of which serve admirably as resonating sound chambers. He might choose to set his strings in motion by plucking them, either with his fingers or with a plectrum; or by drawing another taut string, or bow, across them.

In any case, whether the ancestors of the European guitar arrived on a Phoenician trading vessel, or were made independently by astute cavemen in France, some combination of these evolutionary steps would have been taken. The history of the guitar from the 16th through the 20th centuries shows that instrument makers have continued to experiment with these few basic variables of stringed instrument sound production.

The Middle Ages

By the 13th century, literary and pictorial references indicate the use of two main forms of the guitar. The *guitarra morisca*, or *morache*, was an

Guitarra morisca

Guitarra latina

Cittern

oval-bodied instrument with eight strings, a crescent-shaped bridge, and a round pegbox. It was, in all probability, an early version of the Europeanized lute, derived from the Moorish instrument (which still exists in its own right, in the Middle East) called *al'ud*. The *guitarra latina*, or *gittern*, on the other hand, is depicted as an instrument with a flat back, a waisted body, a fretted neck, and four single strings. It was held high, and played from below with a plectrum.

After the 14th century, evidence of the *guitarra latina* is scarce, although the name *gittern* and its derivative, *cittern*, lived on in somewhat different instruments. The *guitarra latina* may have fallen out of use, or with some modification, it may have evolved into the four-course guitar. By the early 16th century, though, there were clearly three distinct kinds of plucked instruments in use, all of which played a part (some directly, some indirectly) in the development of today's classical guitar.

The Lute

The first, and most prominent, was the lute, an instrument that went through a number of radical changes during its millennium as Europe's dominant

14th century miniature of Arabic lutenist

16th century painting of lutenist

contrapuntal instrument. The most significant of these changes was its growth from a small instrument with four double strings (courses), to a much larger one with as many as thirteen or fourteen courses. By the 16th century, the lute was still relatively compact, with six courses. There was, at the time, nothing resembling today's actual pitch. On any of these instruments, the top string would have been tuned to the highest pitch it could hold, and the rest tuned to a standard intervalic relationship. Lute books call the variable top string g', and give the six-course lute's tuning as G-c-f-a-d'-g'.

The lute's literature is a rich one, and a good deal of this music has been transcribed for the modern guitar. Early in this century, Diana Poulton, in England, and Maria Rita Brondi, in Italy, began giving performances on the lute; but the instrument was not fully reborn until Julian Bream took it up in the 1950s. Today, lutenists abound in all countries, and they are in the process of reclaiming their repertoire from the upstart guitar. For delightful as the lute music of Weiss, Baron, Logy, Bach (whose lute works may actually have been composed for a keyboard instrument), and Dowland sounds on guitar

programs, many guitarists admit that the lute's more fragile textures serve the music better.

The *Vihuela*

While the lute thrived everywhere in Europe, the second of the 16th century's plucked instruments, the *vihuela*, was favored only in Spain and Italy. The term *vihuela*, or in its Italian form, *viola*, actually refers generically to several kinds of instruments. The *vihuela de arco* was the form played with a bow, and the *vihuela de peñola* was played with a plectrum. Both instruments can be traced to medieval times. But the instrument that concerns us, the finger-plucked *vihuela da mano*, did not appear in literature or art until the 15th century.

The *vihuela* is a strange instrument in that it is shaped very much like a guitar, with a long body, slightly waisted sides, and a flat back; yet it has six double courses, tuned nearly like those of the lute, the difference being that the lute's lower courses are normally tuned to octaves, while the *vihuela's* are tuned to unisons. The differences between the lute and the *vihuela* seem, in fact, more formal than musical: Besides the difference in basic body style, the *vihuela* has a mildly inclined pegbox, compared with the sharp angle of the lute's; and where the lute has one soundhole – a large central rose – the *vihuela* has several large and small roses positioned at various places.

There is, unfortunately, only one confirmed *vihuela* extant, an instrument from about 1500, in the collection of the Musée Jacquemart-André, in Paris. With its body length of 58.4 cm, and its vibrating string length of 80 cm, it is somewhat larger than today's concert guitar (which has a string length of about 65 cm). It is thought that this was actually a bass *vihuela*, for use in ensembles, and that the solo instrument for which the Spanish and Italian *vihuela* music was composed would have been considerably smaller. None of the smaller variety has yet been positively identified (although one has reportedly been discovered in a church in Quito, Ecuador). Nor are there existing examples of the seven-course *vihuela* described in Antonio Cabezón's *Obras de musica* (1578); or of the eight-course *vihuela napolitano* described in a 1599 manuscript of Francisco Pachero, and in Scipione Cerreto's *Della prattica musicale* (1601).

Vihuela Literature

The surviving body of music composed for the *vihuela* includes more than 700 works, most of them contained in seven books published in Spain between

1536 and 1576. All this music, as well as that composed for the lute and the early forms of the guitar, was set down in tablature, a system of notation that shows the player which frets to finger (rather than which pitches to fret for, as in modern notation). In tablature, the lines of the staff correspond to the strings of the instrument. There would, therefore, be six lines in the *vihuela* and lute tablature, and

15th century love song, notated in the shape of a heart

four or five (depending on when the tablature dates from) in early guitar music. In Spain, the lowest line of tablature represented the highest-pitched string, yielding a direct physical correspondence between the instrument (when held in playing position) and the music on the printed page. In Italy and France, the system is slightly more abstract, and more akin to the form of tablature used in some popular music arrangements today: the highest line represents the highest-pitched string. In Italian and Spanish tablatures, numerals represent the frets; French tablature employs letters instead. Rhythms and note values are indicated by a series of flags printed above the course lines.

Although the *vihuela* must be considered a relative, rather than an ancestor, of the guitar, its literature has played a central part in the guitar's history. For one thing, several of the *vihuela* books contain music intended for the early guitars, included in the collections as adjuncts to the main bodies of music. Also, many of the *vihuela* works sit well on the mod-

ern guitar, despite its single strings and its lower pitch; and in the early years of this of this century, when guitarists were researching the instrument's heritage, the *vihuela* literature offered an ideal solution – magnificent contrapuntal fantasies, stately pavans, and involved variation sets that had been left unplayed for centuries, and which were composed for an instrument not too distant structurally from the guitar itself.

The pioneering work in the modern rediscovery of the *vihuela* and the translation of its literature into modern notation was done by the musicologists Oscar Chilesotti, Felipe Pedrell, and the Conde de Morphy. Most guitarists, however, have become familiar with the *vihuela* composers and their music through the editions of Emilio Pujol. Pujol began researching and transcribing in 1922, and soon thereafter undertook a series of recitals consisting entirely of his transcriptions. In 1936, he identified the odd-looking guitar in the Musée Jacquemart-André as a *vihuela*, and by the end of that year, he had acquired a modern copy of the instrument, giving the *vihuela* its 20th-century debut at the Second Congress of the International Society of Musicology, held in Barcelona.

Pujol continued transcribing *vihuela* works, making them accessible to players with only a modern

15th century notation using black and white notes

*14th century began use of
black and white to indicate note duration*

concert guitar at their disposal. However, in the introduction to his collection *Hispanae Citharae Ars Viva* (1956), he suggests that the ideal way to play this music on a modern instrument is to approximate the *vihuela*'s tuning (by taking the third string down half a step, and using a capo on the third fret), and reading the music directly from the original tablature.

Thanks in part to Pujol's work, the *vihuela* composers are more than simply shadowy historical names, and selections from their seven books still figure on recital programs. Chronologically, the seven books are: Luis Milán's *El Maestro* (1536); Luis de Narváez's *Los seys libros de Delphin de Música* (1538); Alonso Mudarra's *Tres libros de música en cifras para vihuela* (1546); Enrique de Valderrábano's *Silva de sirenas* (1547); Diego Pisador's *Libro de música de vihuela* (1552); Miguel de Fuenllana's *Orphenica Lyra* (1554); and Esteban Daza's *El Parnasso* (1576). In addition, several books not devoted exclusively to the *vihuela* nevertheless included a few pieces for it.

The music of these collections was arranged in ascending order of difficulty, and included an extraordinary variety of styles. Among these are intabulations of polyphonic vocal works (including French *chansons*, Italian madrigals, and mass movements in the Franco-Flemish style); *fantasias* that were at first based on vocal polyphony, but which later developed into more strongly imitative (as opposed to harmonic) counterpoint; *canciones*, in which the *vihuela* accompanied the voice; and two thoroughly Spanish forms, *villancicos* and *romances*. *Villancicos* are essentially love songs, while *romances* are somewhat weightier, derived from the heroic or historical epic poems of the middle ages. In the *vihuela* books, the composers often give instrumental forms of the old *romance* melodies, substituting variations (*diferencias*) for

the narrative of the text. Among the best known of these today are Mudarra's setting of *Conde Claros*, and Narváez's variations on *Guárdame las vacas*.

What seem to be missing from the *vihuela* literature are dance forms, the sole exception being the courtly pavan, sometimes paired with a galliard. Otherwise, the music of the *vihuela* is quite like that composed for the lute. Indeed, publications of the late 16th century show that the lute and *vihuela* repertoires were virtually interchangeable. Why should two similarly tuned, similarly played instruments that could take on each other's literature be in fashion at the same time? One particularly romantic and possibly overstated explanation offered is that the very shape of the lute symbolized the hated Moors, to the Spanish, and that the *vihuela* had the dual advantage of being, first of all, a native instrument, and second, one whose shape suggested a cruciform to Catholic Spain.

Jan Vermeer's A Guitar Player

Method Books

These *vihuela* books are not merely anthologies, but also tutors, designed to take the player from beginning to advanced stages. As such, they are a rich repository of information about performance styles. Most discuss the problems of choosing strings, tell the player how to tune, and explain tablature. Some provide enlightening technical details. Milán, for instance, tells us that scales and quick passages may be played either by the index finger alone (*dedillo*), or by alternating the thumb and index, or index and second finger (*de los dedos*). Fuenllana includes a section on playing cleanly (*tañer con limpieza*), in which he tells us that the use of the right hand's fingernails led to "imperfection" in tone production, and that "only the finger, the living thing, can communicate the intention of the spirit."

The popularity of the new five-course, or "Spanish," guitar toward the end of the 16th century led composers to devise short-hand systems by which the not-too-ambitious strummer could learn the basics without going to too much trouble. One such system is found

Early Italian lute tablature used numbers to indicate which frets to stop

in Juan Carlos Amat's treatise *Guitarra española de cinco órdenes* (1596). In this basic tutor, Amat (who was a doctor by profession) used drawings of a hand upon a fretboard to indicate the positions of all the basic chords. Each of the chords is assigned a number, so that once the number/chord correlation is memorized, the player could accompany songs by reading a simple form of lead-sheet containing only lyrics, chord numbers, and sometimes a series of lines indicating the rhythm and the direction (up or down) of the right hand's *rasgueado* strokes.

Amat's was a popular tutor, and it remained in print until the 19th century. Ironically, few pieces using his numerical system have survived. The dominant system was the Italian *alfabeto*, a shorthand method similar to Amat's, but using letters (which did not correspond to the pitches of the chords, but were

The Four-Course Guitar

The Spanish had a second native stringed instrument, one that was far more popular throughout lute-dominated Europe than the *vihuela*, although musically somewhat less exalted than either the *vihuela* or the lute. This was the small-bodied four-course guitar – the third of the plucked instruments that has come down to us from the 16th century (with illustrations going back to the 15th), and the first instrument that has direct evolutionary links with today's concert guitar.

Unlike the *guitarra latina*, the four-course guitar is played without a plectrum, with the right hand approaching the strings from above, rather than from below. In fact, the small finger of the right hand normally rested on the table, leaving the thumb and first two fingers to pluck the strings.

There were however, two distinct styles of performance on this guitar: *rasgueado* (called *battente*, in Italy) was a chordal strumming style, used for simple accompaniements; *punteado* (called *pizzicato* in Italy) was the plucked style, used in the performance of polyphonic and more generally complicated music.

The theorist Johannes Tinctoris, in his *Inventione et usa musicae* (1487) provides what is generally accepted to be a description of the four-course guitar, calling it "the instrument invented by the Catalans, which some call the guiterra and others the ghiterne. It is obviously derived from the lyre, since it is tortoise-shaped (though much smaller) and has the same stringing and method of tuning." At least one performer-musicologist (James Tyler) has suggested that Tinctoris's description pertains to the used only as symbols) instead of numerals. The first mention of this system is found in a 1595 manuscript by Francisco Palumbo, a Spaniard working in Italy. The first published *alfabeto* method, however, was Girolomo Montesardo's *Nuova inventione d'intavolatura per sonare li balletti sopra la chitarra spagnuola, senza numeri e note* (1606).

Like the old *vihuela* books, Sanz's *Instrucción de música sobre la guitarra española* (1674) was partly a tutor, and partly a graded collection of pieces. Like Amat, Sanz supplies a chart showing chord fingerings, and the first group of pieces is in the old *alfabeto* style. For this *rasgueado* music, which Sanz calls "*música ruidosa*," or "noisy music," the suggested tuning is: AA-dd-gg-bb-e′; or, with an octave doubling on the fourth and fifth courses, A/a-d/d′ etc. Later in the book, he gives a re-entrant tuning (one in which the bottom strings are pitched higher than fourth and the third courses) that he considers more refined, and more suitable for contrapuntal music, and for the Spanish dances he provides. This tuning — aa-dd-gg-bb-e — makes the fifth course higher in pitch than the third, and the fourth course just a step lower than the top string.

Later in this inclusive volume Sanz discusses embellishment, showing how his ornaments are executed, and suggesting that players add trills to his music (even where they are not specifically indicated) an their own discretion. There is even a section in *Instrucción* devoted to the realization of a figured bass on the guitar, the organ, the harp, and other instruments.

Sanz's book was a popular tutor, and was published in eight editions, the last appearing in 1697. Three years before this final edition, another important tutor appeared, Francisco Guerau's *Poema harmonica*. Guerau did not intend his book for beginners, and includes a set of *passacalles* in every key, as well as arrangements of popular pieces with florid variation in the repeats. He does, however, also provide recommendations designed to help the player improve upon certain points of technique. With regard to right-hand fingering, for instance, he suggests that "the index and middle fingers of the right hand should be alternated, because if the same finger plays too many consecutive notes, the playing will not be as fast and clean" — a recommendation that contrasts with Milán's *dedillo* style, but which is not unlike the right-hand technique taught today.

11th century manuscripts, using neumes

Letter from medieval manuscript displaying period instruments

lute-related *mandora*, rather than to the guitar. If it is in fact the guitar Tinctoris is describing, though, his reference to its "tortoise shape" would have applied to this guitar's rounded, ribbed back. The stringing he refers to seems to imply the seven-string Greek lyre: the four-course guitar did have seven strings, the top being a single string and the bottom three courses doubled.

There were two tunings in use during the 16th century, both of which are given in the earliest source of printed guitar tablature, Alonso Mudarra's *vihuela* book, *Tres libros de música en cifras* (1546). Along with his *vihuela* pieces, Mudarra includes four fantasias, a pavan, and a setting of *Guárdame las vacas*, for the four-course instrument. One of the *fantasias* is to be played in what Mudarra calls the "old" tuning (*a los viejos*) of cc′-ff-aa-d′ (the fourth

course is doubled with a thicker gut string called a *bourdon* and tuned an octave lower than its companion). The other three are for the "new" tuning, B♭′/B♭-f/f-a/a-d′. Mudarra also describes the guitar as an instrument with ten frets. Those frets, however, were not the fixed variety we know today, but rather, movable frets made out of gut and tied around the neck (just as those used on contemporary lutes and *vihuelas* were). The number of frets used, apparently, depended on the use to which the instrument was put. For *rasgueado* playing, four frets were considered sufficient; for more complex music, at least eight frets were required.

Early Spanish works for the four-course guitar are also found in Melchiore de Barberiis's lute collection, *Opera intitulato contina* (1549), which contained four *fantasias* that prove to be lightweight dance pieces. More interesting are the nine pieces Fuenllana includes in *Orphenica Lyra* (1554) – six *fantasias*, the *romance*, *Passeavase el Rey Moro*, and the *villancico*, *Covarde Cavallera*, and a *Crucifixus est*.

Popularity of the Four-Course Guitar

If the *vihuela* never attained a foothold in France, the four-course guitar did so with a vengeance, all but displacing the lute (if only temporarily) in court circles by 1550. The instrument's lofty connections can be traced back to the French court of circa 1530, and it is said that King Henry II – who may have first heard the instrument during his four years as a hostage in Spain – was particularly devoted to it. There was, on the other hand, some resistance in musical circles. Simon Gorlier, in *Le Troysieme Livre* (1551) takes time in his preface, and again before certain of his intabulations, to apologize for publishing a collection for "such a small instrument (by which I mean 'small' in both senses of the word)" which, he says, "does not merit the labor I have devoted to it."

Even so, there was apparently a thriving market for guitar music in France, and the brief spell between 1551 and 1555 yielded four collections by Adrien Le Roy, three by Guillaume Morlaye, and one by Grégoire Brayssing, in addition to Gorlier's. The French publications were largely devoted either to intabulations of *chansons*, or to collections of popular dance forms such as the *branle* (a country dance, of which there are some twenty varieties), the *allemande* (a German dance, at a moderate tempo), the *galliard* (a lively Italian dance in triple time), and the more staid *pavan* and *passamezzo*.

The four-course guitar caught on outside France too. In the Netherlands, Pierre Phalèse and Jean Bellère, partners in a publishing enterprise, brought out *Selectissima elegantissimaque gallica, italica et latina in guiterna ludenda carmina* (1570), an anthology of 182 guitar solos and accompanied songs, many of them pirated from Le Roy and his colleagues. Le Roy's guitar tutor, *Briefve et facile instruction pour apprendre—la guiterne* (1551) turned up in an English translation by James Rowbotham (1568), but both the original and the translation have been lost.

In mid-16th century England, the guitar and its distant cousin, the cittern, were both fashionably foreign and fashionably new. The guitar vogue was not overwhelming – after all, the golden age of the English lute was on the horizon – but samples of guitar music have turned up in English manuscripts devoted primarily to lute and keyboard music. The last English publication intended for the four-course guitar is John Playford's *A Booke of New Lessons for the Cittern and Gittern* (1652). The guitar section, in French tablature, contains settings of forty-one ballads and popular tunes.

Playford's book arrived at an extraordinarily late date, for by 1652, the four-course guitar had been out of use for more than half a century in the rest of Europe. The end of the 1500s saw some significant changes in the plucked instrument situation: the lute had returned to dominance in France, and its position was stronger than ever everywhere in Europe – except, of course in Spain. Even in Spain, though, nothing more was heard from the *vihuela*.

The Five-Course Guitar

As for the guitar itself, the short-lived four-course instrument underwent a series of alterations in the last quarter of the 16th century that transformed it into a new instrument and gave it a form that it would retain for the next 200 years. The first part of this change was the addition of a fifth course, tuned a fourth lower than the fourth course. There was a precedent of sorts: Fuenllana, in *Orphenica Lyra* (1554), includes a few works for what he called a "*vihuela* with four courses," noting that others called the instrument a guitar); and Juan Bermudo, in his *Declaración de instrumentos musicales* (1555) also speaks of a five-course guitar. Both, however, were referring to an instrument whose new course was added a fourth above the first string, rather than below the last – a variation of the instrument that never attracted a substantial following.

The addition of the lower fifth course is credited, by several 16th-century Spanish writers, to Vicente Espinel, a poet and musician born around 1550. With the addition of this lowest string, the guitar's body was enlarged, from an average string length of about 55.5 cm to one of about 63 cm, nearly that of the modern guitar. Several tunings came into use during the lifespan of the five-course guitar; but the first one recorded, in Juan Carlos Amat's *Guitarra española de cinco órdenes*, (1596) is A/a-d/d'-g/g-b/b-e'/e', with the top string doubled, and the bottom courses tuned to octaves.

EARLY GUITAR MUSIC

It would seem likely that the expansion of the guitar by an extra course would have inspired guitarists to reach for new heights of contrapuntal development.

*Front and rear view of guitar attributed
to Jakob Stadler, c. 1625*

Ornate Five-course Guitars:

If the guitar music of the Baroque era reached a new height of elegance, guitar makers and their clients seem to have had a parallel desire for instruments that pleased the eye. From the late 16th century through the start of the 19th, guitars became increasingly ornate — or, at least, so we are led to believe from the considerable number of surviving decorative instruments. It could be, of course, that these instruments survived simply because the artistry embodied in their pearl-inlayed fingerboards and picturesque soundboxes led their owners (and their heirs) to keep the instruments as art objects long after their usefulness as instruments was over, while plainer guitars were discarded as uninteresting valueless objects.

Designs and embellishment styles varied almost along nationalistic lines. Matteo and Giorgio Sellas, working in Venice during the first half of the 17th century, produced guitars that were either remarkably florid, or in some cases, that offered a veneer of geometric designs. The Italians often used tortoise-shell, ebony, and ivory to adorn their instruments, and some existing examples show astoundingly complex designs and illustrations. On the other hand, the few extant guitars of Antonio Stradivari are quite simple: only the three frets at the junction of the table and the fretboard show even the barest hint of artwork, while the back and face are entirely plain. Even the rosette, a carved, swirling pattern, seems a picture of simplicity compared with the layered parchment rosettes of other instruments of this period.

In Germany, the dominant luthier was Joachim Tielke, several of whose guitars have survived. Tielke was also fond of ebony and

Front and rear view of chitarra battente by G. Sellas

Front and rear view of guitar by Rene Voboam

ivory marquetry, and his instruments show an extraordinary range of designs — from floral patterns to hunting scenes to tableaux from Genesis.

In France, both Paris and Lyons flourished as centers of guitar production, and the best luthiers benefited from the patronage of Louis XIV and his court. Perhaps dominant among Parisian luthiers were Alexandre, Jean, and René Voboam, whose instruments showed a mixture of simplicity and elegance. One of the Voboams' trademarks was an ebony and ivory purfling that circumscribed the edges of the table, and extended along the sides of the fingerboard — a design that was modestly decorative, but which also served a protective function. While the Voboams often left the guitar's face comparatively unhindered, they had a fondness for geometric patterns on the front and/or back of the neck, and on the back of the instrument's body.

Sizes and shapes of five-course guitars varied, but a few general principles prevailed. In most cases, the fingerboards were long enough to support only eleven frets, which would normally have been made of gut. Toward the end of the five-course guitar's reign, the practice of building instruments with fixed frets began; these would have been made of ivory or brass. The tables of these instruments are normally of thin, delicate spruce, and extend a few frets up the fingerboard — which, unlike those on today's guitars, were fastened at the same level as the table, not higher. The bodies of the guitars were less broadly waisted than today's, the common proportion being 7:6:8 (upper bout, waist, lower bout). The strings are fastened to a bridge that sits low on the body; although by the middle of the 18th century, the bridge had moved closer to the soundhole. And, while both flat and rounded backs flourished in the early part of the five-course guitar's lifespan, later instruments were predominantly of the flat-back variety.

Front, side, and rear view of guitar by Stradivari

That, however, is not what happened – at least, not at first. Instead, guitarists headed off in the opposite direction, seeking the simplest possible music for their newly enlarged instrument. Stringing only four or five frets around the neck, guitarists devoted themselves to the simple *rasgueado* style of chord strumming. Among the general population, guitaring was quite popular, as it was fairly easy to learn the chords required to accompany popular songs. But among real musicians – lutenists in particular – the guitar was held in disdain. As one commentator, the lexicographer Sebastion de Covarrubias Oroco, wrote in 1611: "The guitar is no more than a cowbell, so easy to play, especially *rasgueado*, that there is not a stable lad who is not a guitarist."

By 1630, nearly seventy books of Italian and Spanish dances, popular tunes, and accompanied songs were published. Little of this music has made its way into the modern guitar repertoire, since on the surface, at least, it has little to offer, and because historians have, until recently, dismissed it as ephemera. But according to James Tyler, a British guitarist who specializes in Renaissance and Baroque guitar music, and whose performances on early instruments have helped give this music new life, the problem may not be that the music is too inherently simple, but that we have lost the tradition. In his concise but detailed study, *The Early Guitar: A History and Handbook* (1980, Oxford), Tyler suggests that the published scores represent skeletons, embellished and varied by an imaginative player.

Still, if contemporary accounts are to be believed, there were as few performers with the imagination required to elevate this music in the 17th century as there are now. In France, where the four-course guitar was a favorite, the five-course instrument was at first held in low esteem. Which wasn't to say that people didn't play it: the French theorist Pierre Trichet, in his *Traité des instruments de musique* (c.1630) condemns the Spanish guitarists whose "thousand gestures and bodily movements are as grotesque and ridiculous as their playing is bizarre and confused," and writes scornfully of French courtesans and ladies who ape the Spaniards," by taking up the guitar. For Trichet, "the lute is right for and familiar to the French (and is) the most agreeable of all instruments."

Contrapuntal Guitar Works

By the time Trichet wrote this, currents in the guitar literature were beginning to change. The first ripples took place in Italy, but the wave would make its way to France, England, the Netherlands, and Spain within the next few decades, and before the end of the century, the contrapuntal style would be reestablished as the province of guitar music. The first sign of this change can be seen in a book by Giovanni Paolo Foscarini, who called himself "Il Furioso." Foscarini had worked as a guitarist, lutenist, and theorboist, first in Italy, and later in Brussels, where his patron was the Archduke Albert, the Hapsburg ruler of the Spanish Netherlands. When Albert died in 1621, Foscarini returned to Italy and began publishing his music. From the evidence of his *Intavolatura de chitarra spagnola, libro secundo* (1629), this was simple music in the *alfabeto* tradition. But in *Il primo, secondo e terzo libro della Chitarra Spagnola* (1629-30), "Il Furioso" makes an important departure: he combines *alfabeto* chords with more complex, contrapuntal textures, notated on five-line tablature.

Foscarini, in his preface, is almost apologetic about including these almost lutelike works in his guitar book, but other composers soon saw the light, among them Giovanni Battista Granata, Domenico Pellegrini, and Ludovico Roncalli, each of whom composed suites, dances, and variations that are rarely performed today, but which may be worthy of reexamination.

Francesco Corbetta

The guitar's next watershed was reached in the music of Francesco Corbetta. Born in Pavia, Italy, around 1615, he began teaching in Bologna, where he published his first collection, *Scherzi Armonici* (1639) before attaining a post at the court of Mantua. His *Varii Capricci per la Chittara Spanuola* (1643), composed at Mantua, and the *Varii Scherzi di Sonate per la Chitara Spagnola* (1648), composed in Brussels, show Corbetta proceeding toward a more sophisticated style. Strummed chords are retained, but only as textural variation within dance movements that are largely contrapuntal.

During his stay in Brussels, Corbetta's playing style influenced the guitarists working there, who adopted his contrapuntal approach, and set it down in collections and publications of their own. One such collection is *Princes An's Lute Book*, which, despite its title, is a collection of dance pieces in five-course guitar tablature, owned by Anna of Hannover, wife of William IV of Orange. Here too, the role of *rasgueado* is diminished, although not absent. The Belgian guitarist Francois LeCocq further crystallized the style for his colleagues in the Low Countries with printed collections of his own work, and with an anthology of music by Granata, Corbetta, Visée, and others, published in 1729.

Corbetta's influence was even greater in Paris, where he worked from 1656 to about 1662. In French court circles, Corbetta had come to know England's exiled Charles II, who had become an enthusiastic guitarist. King Charles returned to England in 1660, and Corbetta followed two years later. Although English commentators were inclined to dismiss the guitar, Corbetta's artistry led many doubters to revise their opinions. Among those not entirely convinced was the diarist Samuel Pepys, who observed, of the guitar, "methinks it but a bauble." Pepys preferred the lute, and even after he heard Corbetta, in 1667, he wrote that the guitarist played "most admirably – so well that I was mightily troubled that all the pains should have been taken upon so bad an instrument." Nevertheless, by the time Corbetta left England, in 1670, the guitar had replaced the lute there as the favored instrument, both at court and among amateurs.

Upon his return to France, Corbetta found that a French school grounded in his style had blossomed. Corbetta himself continued to reign supreme, and his last two books, both entitled *La Guitarre Royalle*, were dedicated to his two royal patrons in England and France. The first (1671), dedicated to Charles II, is the more rewarding, as it continues in Corbetta's advanced style. The second (1674) may indicate that its dedicatee, Louis XIV, was a guitarist of more modest talents, and includes simpler works, more heavily peppered with *rasgueado* chording.

Robert de Visée

When Corbetta died, in 1681, he was succeeded as court guitarist by one of his pupils, Robert de Visée. Visée was born in about 1660, and is first mentioned as a court theorboist in 1680, two years before he published his first collection, the *Livre de Guitarre dedié au Roy*. By the time he died, in 1724, he had become one of the King's chamber players, as well as his guitar tutor; and he had published two books of guitar music and two of lute and theorbo works. Visée's music – like that of his French contemporaries, Remy Médard and Francois Campion – was more delicately constructed than Corbetta's, and even more concerned with melodic and contrapuntal clarity.

Performance Problems

Several of Visée's suites, particularly the one in D minor from his *Livre de pièces pour la guitarre* (1686), are favorites of today's guitarists. They are, however, most often heard in an anachronistic guise, played in a style that makes them sound more like lute works of the German High Baroque than the elegantly textured guitar pieces they are. On the most basic level, one must keep in mind that Visée's guitar sounded nothing like today's concert models. Not only would it not have had the broad spread between the highest and lowest voices that one finds in today's transcriptions and performances, but his tunings most likely included higher octave doublings on the fourth (D) and fifth (A) courses – a configuration that yielded an effect that cannot be achieved on the modern, single-strung guitar.

There are also some matters of performance style that often go unheeded in today's performances of Visée-era guitar music. While Visée's retreat from the *rasgueado* style was even more pronounced than Corbetta's, he did not renounce the effect entirely, and his printed music includes occasional indications showing the direction of the strum. Today, chords in Visée's music are normally plucked, all the notes at once, rather than strummed, as they would have been in Visée's time. Nor do today's performances (or editions) usually include the ornate embellishment the pieces (particularly the slower dances) require. This will undoubtedly change in time: there are already a few recordings that present Visée suites on period guitars, and even a few nicely embellished modern guitar versions.

Gaspar Sanz

Similar problems pertain to the music of Spain's most significant 17th-century composer, Gaspar Sanz. Born in Calenda, around 1640, Sanz studied theology at the University of Salamanca, and then traveled to Italy to study the organ. He apparently worked as an organist in Rome, but also studied the guitar there, having met Foscarini, Granata, and Corbetta. After his return to Spain, Sanz published his single, remarkable collection of works, *Instrucción de música sobre la guitarra española* (1674). (See box on instruction books, p. 24)

In his *Instrucción*, Sanz voices a clear preference for the *punteado* style, and suggests a reentrant tuning without bass doublings on the fourth and fifth courses. This tuning creates an unusual effect when applied to his lively Spanish dances: The bass lines that often adorn modern editions and performances (exciting as they admittedly often are), although suggested in the tablature, are done away with by the high tuning. Sanz himself would probably not have heard them, although the tonality changes they suggest remain in the music. Rather than providing a bass underpinning, though, these lines become what Sanz calls *"campanelas,"* or "little bells," which ring out within the textures of the upper melodic lines.

LATER DEVELOPMENTS

The period following Sanz's *Instrucción* yielded comparatively few guitar publications, and it was clear by the middle of the 18th century that yet another change was in the wings. In 1714, Santiago de Murcia put together a collection of works that is significant on two counts. First, where Sanz's collection and its successors (Lucas Ruiz Ribayaz's *Luz y norte musical*, of 1677, and Francisco Guerau's *Poema harmonica*, of 1694) concentrated on Spanish national dance forms and popular songs, Murcia's *Resumen de acompañar la parte con la guitarra* was a cosmopolitan collection of suites, with all the current European dance movements (*allemandes, courantes, gigues, sarabandes*, and so on) as well as several Spanish *passacalles*. Secondly, *Resumen* was the last Spanish collection written in tablature. For amateurs, the *alfabeto* system would prevail; for professionals the tablature system would soon be supplanted by written staff notation, borrowed from that of the violin.

A Change of Style

Beyond the guitar's sphere, musical styles were changing. The great contrapuntal edifices of J.S. Bach and his predecessors were considered, by the time he died, in 1750, needlessly complicated and hopelessly old-fashioned. The new *galant* style, championed by Telemann in his late works and by Bach's sons Johann Christian and Carl Philipp Emanuel, relied on simple melodic charm, with accompaniments unburdened by the fancy details of voice-leading and dissonance resolution.

For guitarists, who had just succeeded in creating a respectably contrapuntal body of literature, these changes were particularly damaging. By the end of the 18th century, the guitar was again reduced to simple accompaniment, its occasional moments of glory coming in the form of parts in innocuous chamber works of minor German composers. Still, as in every period when the guitar has fallen from grace in the loftier musical circles, it continued its life as a popular instrument; and the publications of the late 18th century show a thriving market for

books that would convey the rudiments of chordal playing as quickly as possible.

The 19th Century

As a "professional" instrument, the guitar may have been slow to react to the prevailing musical tides. But its history shows that it is nothing if not adaptable, and the winds of change would soon sweep the guitar forward once again. The key to the guitar's early 19th-century revival was yet another series of structural modifications (see box on construction, p.30) that led to a louder, sturdier instrument with six single strings.

The new guitars held several advantages for the new class of virtuosi that was blossoming in Spain and Italy in the early 19th century. The sixth string – tuned to E, a fourth below the fifth string – again broadened the instrument's chord voicing possibilities, and created a logical symmetry in the instrument's tuning. With its addition, the modern, standard guitar tuning was established as E A D g b e′. The use of single strings solved a number of problems – from finding a pair of gut strings true enough to be tuned perfectly, particularly in the high courses, to the more basic problem of putting the instrument as a whole in tune quickly and efficiently.

The first half of the 19th century turned out to be an extraordinary age for guitar music, a period in which touring composer/virtuosi produced extended multimovement sonatas, concerti and variation sets, and brought their artistry to the far corners of Europe and even the Americas. It is a period about which we still have much to rediscover, with a rich and rewarding literature that is finally being systematically uncovered, reexamined and republished by such musicologists as Brian Jeffery, Thomas F. Heck, and Montanya Ophee, and performed by many of today's more enterprising players.

THE VIRTUOSO TRADITION

The figure whose work instigated at least the Spanish part of this 19th-century guitar renaissance was one Miguel García, a Cistercian monk, also known as Padre Basilio. Originally an organist, García became interested in *punteado* guitar playing, and became a well known soloist in Madrid, as well as guitar tutor to Queen Marie-Louise. It was García who played the guitar parts in some of the quintets composed, albeit grudgingly, by Luigi Boccherini – a composer who was not fond of the guitar himself, but who was employed by a guitar fancier, the Marquis of Benavente-Osuna.

Strings

Between the end of the five-course era, in the 1770s, and the advent of the improved Torres guitars of the 1850s, the art of guitar making was in what we now think of as a transitional phase. During the first years of this period, experimental luthiers took the first steps across the gulf between the five-course and the six-string guitar, some of them offering instruments with six double courses, while others made guitars that had only five single strings.

The more common stepping-stone seems to have been the six-course guitar, which was probably a Spanish invention, and which dates from at least 1780 — the year Antonio Ballesteros published his *Obra para guitarra de seis órdenes*. The year 1799 saw a spate of six-course methods, including Fernando Ferandière's *Arte de tocar la guitarra española*; Antonio Abreu's *Escuela para tocar con perfección la guitarra de cinco y seis órdenes*; Juan Manuel Garcia Rubio's *Arte, reglas armonicas para aprehender a templar y puntear la guitarra española de seis órdenes*; and the work that was to have the greatest musical influence, Federico Moretti's *Principios para tocar la guitarra de seis órdenes*.

It was in Spain, too, that guitar builders began to seriously address the problems of sound production for the first time. Cadiz was a center of guitar construction toward the end of the 18th century, and it was there, in the 1780s, that the luthier Joseph Benedit (sometimes called Benedid, Benedict, or Benediz) introduced the single most crucial structural innovation of the time, internal fan-strutting.

Until then, the guitar's face — its most important resonating part, as Torres would prove a century later — was supported by a series of transverse struts. This method gave the face solid support against the considerable tension exerted upon it by the strings; but at the same time, the transverse struts inhibited the table's response to the vibrations of the strings. Fan strutting, on the other hand, provides the support the table needs, but the struts radiate from the bottom half of the soundhole at angles that leave the grain of the top comparatively uninhibited, thus allowing for more resonance.

Benedit began with three struts under the tables of his six-course guitars, and he may have collaborated with Juan and José Pagés, who built six-course instruments (also in Cadiz) in the 1790s, using three, five, and seven struts.

As for the jump to six single strings, the precise origin of the practice will probably remain a mystery. One German luthier, Jacob Augustus Otto, put in a claim, sharing the honor with J.G. Naumann, the Kapellmeister at Dresden in the late 1780s. According to Otto, the Duchess Amelia of Weimar returned in 1788, whereupon Naumann ordered a six-string instrument from travels in Italy with a five-string instrument from Otto.

It is thought, however, that the six-string guitar has its origins in either Italy or France, and it has been suggested that Naumann, who studied in Italy, may have taken his idea from Italian models. Federico Moretti, in his 1799 *Principios*, noted that in France and Italy, single strings were used instead of double courses. In Spain and Portugal, the six-string guitar was established early in the 19th century; yet, the six-course version lingered until at least the 1830s.

At first, the six-course and six-string guitars retained the narrow bodies of the five-course instrument, although the curvature of the sides eventually became more pronounced as the upper and lower bouts were broadened. Decoration was held to a minimum, and the elegant rosettes of the 18th century gave way to large, open soundholes. The fretboard remained flush with the table, and was fitted with fixed metal frets that sometimes extended over the table to the soundhole, with twelve frets clear of the body. The flat back became standard, and the pegheads were at first simple, with wooden pegs, but later became slightly more ornately carved, the pegs replaced by machine heads.

These instruments also boast a new "pin-bridge" — the strings pass over an ivory saddle and into holes on the bridge and table, into which they are fastened by small wooden pins.

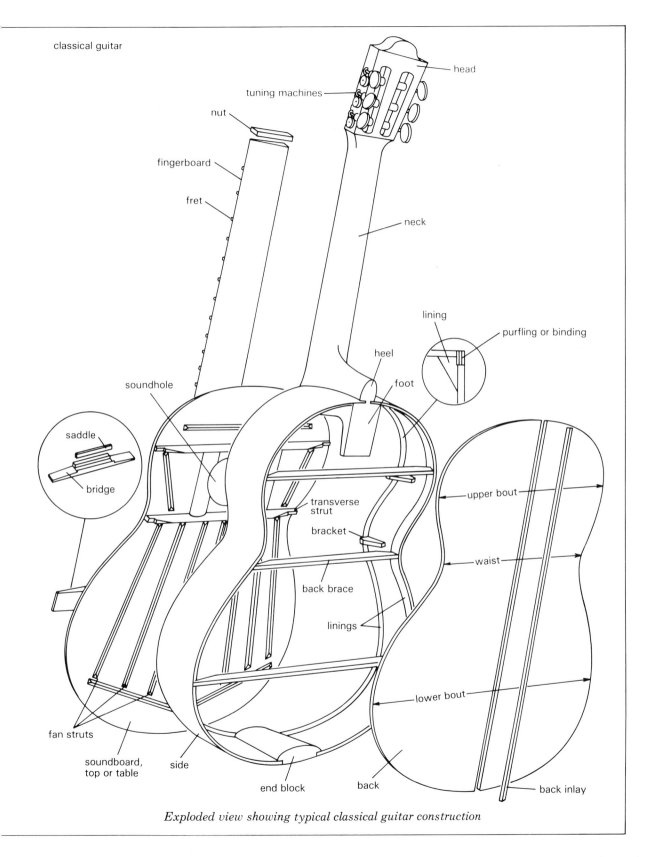

classical guitar

head

tuning machines

nut

fingerboard

fret

neck

lining

purfling or binding

heel

foot

soundhole

saddle

bridge

upper bout

transverse strut

bracket

waist

back brace

linings

fan struts

lower bout

soundboard, top or table

side

end block

back

back inlay

Exploded view showing typical classical guitar construction

*Front and rear view of guitar
attributed to Jean Voboam, c. 1680*

*Front view of guitar
by Giovanni Tesler, c. 1620*

*Rear view of guitar
by Giovanni Tesler, c. 1620*

*Front and rear view of guitar
by Joachim Tielke, early 1700s*

García's students included the authors of two important six-course guitar tutors of 1799, Ferandière and Moretti; and it was Moretti's work, with its discussion of the guitar's part-writing possibilities, that influenced Fernando Sor, the first of the great 19th-century virtuosi. Another of García's students, Dionisio Aguado, went on to codify guitar technique in the *New Guitar Method* (1843), a work whose precepts are central to today's technique.

Fernando Sor

Fernando Sor (born Sors, in 1778, but he later dropped the final s) is, of course, best known as a composer for the guitar, but was actually a versatile artist whose works include two symphonies, two operas, several ballets, a violin concerto, choral music, marches, and examples of virtually all other forms (including idioms that were peculiarly Spanish) addressed by any "general practice" composer of the time. The difference was that the instrument on which he could most fluently express himself was the guitar, and unlike other composers who dabbled with the instrument – among them Berlioz, Gounod, Paganini, and Saint-Saëns – Sor mastered it and gave it the start of a virtuoso repertoire.

Sor was born in Barcelona, and educated at the monastery of Montserrat and later, at a military school. When he was twenty-seven, his opera *Telemaco* was successfully produced in Barcelona, and in 1799, he moved to Madrid. Although he entered the Spanish military to fight against the French, his own republican sentiments led him to support the French after their victory, and he accepted an administrative post. When the French left Spain, in 1813, Sor, like many Spanish intellectuals, was in an awkward political situation, and found it prudent to leave Spain as well. He settled in Paris briefly, but traveled to London, where he performed as a guitarist and, on occasion, as a singer, from 1815 to 1823. In 1823, he traveled to Russia for the Bolshoi premiere of his ballet *Cendrillon* (a work that had been given to great acclaim in London and Paris), giving concerts in Warsaw along the way, as well as in Moscow. By 1827, he had returned to Paris, where he continued to compose, perform, and teach until his death in 1839.

Although he has often been called the "Beethoven of the guitar," Sor's compositional persona is more akin to the refined classicism of Haydn or Mozart, but offers a distinctly Iberic accent. His complete output for guitar, which fills five volumes in the recently published Tecla Editions facsimile series, has its share of short, easy waltzes, divertimentos, and studies for the enthusiastic amateur; but it also contains a body of works that are guitaristic gems, and which can be done justice only by a performer of concert caliber. At the head of the list stand Sor's two full-scale Sonatas, Ops. 22 and 25, as well as several of his extended *Fantaisies* – most notably Ops. 7 and 30, and the exquisite *Fantaisie elégiaque*, Op. 59. These works boast striking melodic characters, and show an inventive sense of development that helps them transcend the instrument's physical limitations. So too do his sets of variations, the best among them including those based on *Folias de España*, Op. 15; *Ye Banks and Braes*, Op. 40, and of course the frequently played paraphrase from Mozart's *Magic Flute*, the *Introduction and Variations*, Op. 9.

The Guitar in Vogue

With Sor in Paris, that city's lapsed love affair with the guitar was revived, and in the early decades of the 19th century, Paris became a center of guitaristic activity. In 1826, Sor was joined by his friend Dionisio Aguado, who is known today more on the strength of his valuable student pieces than for his concert scores. Also based in Paris were Ferdinando Carulli, a Neapolitan cellist and guitarist who settled in Paris, became a popular salon recitalist, and composed some 360 works; and Carulli's young rival, Matteo Carcassi, who arrived in Paris after touring Italy, Germany, and England before making Paris his home. Carcassi and Carulli's studies are still central to the advanced student repertoire, just as their method books remain central to the elementary repertoire; but like Aguado's, their concert works await reevaluation. On the other hand, Napoleon Coste – a student of Sor's who pursued a concert career from 1830 until an accident incapacitated his right hand in 1868 – composed some graceful works that are beginning to enjoy a revival.

Paris was not the only major European city in which the guitar was again in vogue. In Vienna, the instrument had quite a number of devotees, and there was a thriving market for not-too-difficult, lightweight pieces and chamber works involving easy guitar parts. These were supplied by the likes of Leonhard von Call, Anton Diabelli, Josef Kreutzer, and Wenzeslaus Matiegka. Matiegka, in fact, composed a charming *Notturno* for guitar, flute, and viola, to which Franz Schubert later added a cello line. This piece is now often billed as the Schubert Quartet, but is, of course, only one-quarter

Schubert. Schubert did play the guitar, however, and gave it the accompanying role in his *Kantata zur Namensfeier meines Vaters* (1813).

Much has been made of the few works written (or, in the case of the so-called Schubert Quartet, partly written) by the major composers, but these are scant. Carl Maria von Weber used the instrument in a few song accompaniments and in a charming but minor *Divertimento*, Op. 38, for guitar and piano; and of course, Paganini composed a series of fairly easy guitar and violin duets, as well as a few more ambitious ones that make nice guitar solos when the violin and guitar parts are combined. One might even cite the guitar part in the second *Nachtmusik* movement of Mahler's Seventh Symphony, composed toward the end of the Romantic age. But these add up to little. The guitar is used either as a color instrument, or is given simple accompaniment figures. Most composers – at least, until the 20th century – proved the point Berlioz made in his *Treatise on Orchestration* (1856): "It is impossible to write well for the guitar without being a player on the instrument. The majority of composers who employ it are, however, far from knowing its powers; and therefore, they frequently give it things to play of excessive difficulty, little sonority, and small effect." Noting that the instrument has been supplanted by the piano in cultured homes, he adds that "composers employ it but little, either in the church, theater, or concert hall. Its feeble sonority, which does not allow its union with other instruments, or with many voices possessed even of ordinary brilliancy, is doubtless the cause of this. Nevertheless, its melancholy and dreamy character might frequently be made available; it has a real charm of its own, and there would be no impossibility in so writing for it as to make this manifest."

Mauro Giuliani

Still, the only composers of the 19th century who succeeded in making this charm manifest were the guitarist/composers themselves, and it is to them that we inevitably return in the search for the instrument's great literature. In Vienna, there were several composers helping to create this literature, besides those writing easy ditties for mass consumption. Most notable among them was Mauro Giuliani. Born in Bisceglie, Italy, in 1781, Giuliani arrived in Vienna in 1806, and immediately established a career as a virtuoso soloist. He was also celebrated as a chamber musician, and was involved in a series of extremely popular "Dukaten" concerts (a series of

six concerts offered for a ducat) with the pianist and composer Johann Nepomuk Hummel and the violinist Joseph Mayseder, and with the pianist Ignaz Moscheles and Mayseder. Giuliani left Vienna in 1819, apparently under unpleasant legal circumstances. He moved to Rome, and played recitals both on his own and with his daughter Emilia, who later pursued a career as a solo guitarist. He died in Naples, in 1829.

Like Sor, Giuliani left a treasure-trove of works that exploit the guitar's melodic and harmonic resources within a finely crafted late-Classic/early-Romantic style. Single-movement works such as the *Grand Ouverture*, Op. 61, and the *Gran Sonata Eroica*, Op. 150, demand of the guitar a sense of power that strives for an almost orchestral sound; while the more expansive, three-movement *Sonata*, Op. 15 (a work probably contemporary with Sor's Op. 22) contrasts quick, light-spirited outer-movements with a gorgeously tuneful, and rather difficult, slow movement. Giuliani was also a master of the variation form (his Handel Variations, Op. 107 are played as often as Sor's Mozart sets); and composed a series of six lengthy and entertaining tributes to Rossini – the *Rossiniane*, Ops. 119-124 – based on themes from Rossini operas. Crowning these solo works is a set of three concerti, the earliest (aside from lute and mandolin concerto transcriptions) in the guitar's repertoire, as well as the delightful *Introduction, Theme, Variations and Polonaise*, Op. 65, for guitar and strings, the theme being an aria from the Paisiello opera, *La Molinera*.

Viennese Virtuosi

Several other virtuosi flourished in Vienna after Giuliani departed, and their works are only now beginning to return to the repertoire. One such composer is Luigi Legnani, who arrived in Vienna in 1819, toured Germany, Switzerland, and Italy, and left a collection of some 250 numbered works, many in a dazzling bravura style. A much later arrival is the Hungarian-born Johann Kaspar Mertz, who flourished in Vienna from 1840 until his death in 1856. Mertz composed fantasies on opera themes, as well as mazurkas, polonaises, romances, tarantelle, and pieces with Schumann-like titles (such as the *Kindermärchen* from the fifteen volume *Barden-Klänge*, Op. 13). Some of his pieces are light Viennese trifles; others, like the *Fantaisie Hongroise*, Op. 65, No.1, are more extended, and show both a colorful imagination and a command of the guitar's resources.

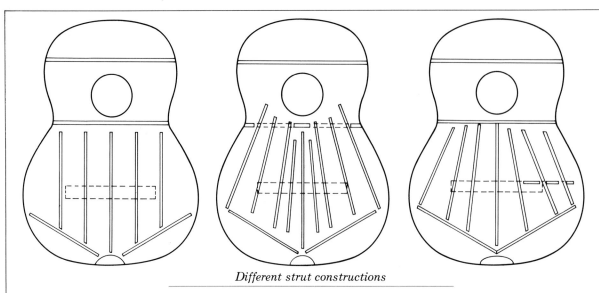

Different strut constructions

Torres and Modern Luthiers

Little is known about the early life or training of Antonio de Torres, and in recent years, certain long-held assumptions have been challenged in the face of seemingly conflicting documentary evidence. Torres was born in 1817, near Almería, and was thought to have begun his study of guitar construction with the luthier José Pernas, in Granada. Whether Torres worked with Pernas is now in dispute; but, by the 1850s, he was building instruments that were championed by Julián Arcas — a composer/virtuoso of the generation before Tárrega, and with whom Tárrega studied. Apparently, Torres's guitar shop did not always do steady business: just after Tárrega acquired his first Torres instrument, in 1869, the luthier began running into financial difficulties, and in the late 1870s, he made his living running a china shop instead of a lutherie. By 1880, he was back in production, and he continued until his death in 1892.

Torres believed firmly that the guitar's table, as its primary resonating surface, was the most cru-cial part of the instrument, and in 1862, he set out to prove this thesis by building a guitar with a back and sides of cardboard, reinforced by wooden strips, but with a table of top quality spruce and Torres's own expanded fan-strutting system. The guitar still exists (in the Instrument Museum of the Barcelona Conservatory), according to published testimony of Domingo Prat, who heard it played, the guitar's sound proved Torres's point.

What Torres did was, first, increase the number of struts to seven, spacing them in a way he believed would allow the six strings to create the optimum amount of resonance. He also added a pair of bars to the sides of the soundhole.

Torres also increased the size of the instrument's body slightly, and widened the fingerboard. He also established the standard string length of 65 cm — two or three centimeters longer than the early 19th-century guitars of Panormo or the French builder Lacote, and a bit shorter than some of the instruments made by some 20th-century builders. It is also often claimed that Torres invented the modern bridge, to which the strings are tied, rather than pegged; but Aguado describes just such a bridge, which he claims to have invented in 1824.

Several Torres instruments have survived, some of them in playable condition, although their age makes them too delicate to be subjected to the rigors of touring.

Torres seems to have had no pupils; but his designs have served as the basis for the concert guitars built by several generations of his successors. After Torres, an important line of luthiers began working in Madrid, the most prominent of whom were Vicente Arias and the brothers José and Manuel Ramirez. José Ramirez is, in fact, responsible for a long tradition that has been passed on not only through the family business — the Ramirez guitar, which is still considered among the finest — but through students who went off on their own. It was José who trained Manuel, who in turn trained Domingo Esteso. José also trained his son, also called José; who in turn trained *his* son José, head of the Ramirez firm today. Among former Ramirez employees who established considerable reputations of their own, also based in Madrid, are Manuel Contreras and Paulino Bernabe; the latter has become the choice builder of ten-string guitars for Narciso Yepes and his students.

Ramirez experiemented with the lengths of the fan struts, and added a diagonal strut, from just under the lower to the upper bout. Ignacio Fleta, of Barcelona, whose

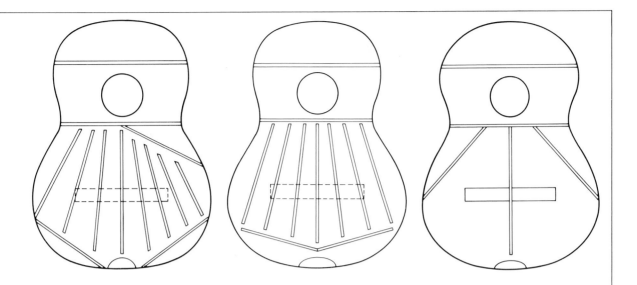

instruments are used by John Williams, also used a diagonal strut, which stopped at the transverse bar under the soundhole. He also used eight struts under the soundhole. But while builders continue to experiment with strutting patterns (some of them quite radical), no post-Torres structural innovation has had as important an effect on the guitar as the introduction of the nylon string, by Albert Augustine, in 1946. Until then, guitarists had been using strings made of catgut—as, of course, guitarists and lutenists had done for centuries. But gut strings posed certain distinct problems. In a recent interview, Andres Segovia reflected on nylon and gut:

"The best gut strings were made by Pirastro, in Germany, and they were torture. When a concert hall was very warm, or very cold, or very damp, they were terrible, and in those days, I used to carry a pair of scissors to cut the little wisps that would splinter from them. Eventually, the strings would just crack. Also, it was very difficult to tune them correctly: the intonation was false at the octave. All these problems disappeared with the introduction of nylon."

Outside Spain, the demand for quality concert guitars has helped create traditions of guitar building everywhere. In Germany, Hermann Hauser built guitars that Segovia used for several years before returning to a Ramirez instrument. After Hauser's death, in 1952, his son carried on the business. In France, Robert Bouchet has long been considered the premier luthier. In England, David Rubio has been producing highly regarded instruments for several years. Also working in England is the Madrid-born luthier José Romanillos, who has established a workshop at Julian Bream's farm, in Dorset. In Japan, where the guitar has a tremendous following, the most prominent builder is Masaru Kohno.

The United States has produced several distinguished luthiers, some of whom have gravitated toward experimental designs. One of these, Richard Schneider, has been collaborating since 1969 with Dr. Michael Kasha, a molecular biophysicist whose approach to guitar construction and acoustics is based on theories of plate mechanics, and involves unusual patterns of strangely sized and placed struts. Dr. Kasha's theories have not yet produced an instrument that concert guitarists have championed (one complaint often noted is that the instruments are too heavy). In New York, Thomas Humphrey has also been working to increase the instrument's volume—in order, as he puts it, to "take the guitar out of its fortepiano stage"—and he too has been formulating unusual design theories. The instruments he builds for concert use, however, make use of more standard designs and materials, and their rich, balanced sound has attracted a strong following among the younger American performers and, in recent years, guitarists around the world.

The question of just what those "standard materials" are, these days, has made for considerable controversy as supplies of instrument building materials have diminished. Humphrey, Rubio, and others have held out for Alpine spruce (for the tables) and Brazilian rosewood (for the sides and back), the traditional materials. But as these woods have become scarce, they have also become expensive; and many of the European builders, including Ramirez, have turned to Western Red Cedar, from California and Oregon, as a substitute for spruce, and Indian rosewood, as a substitute for Brazilian. Those who find the new woods acceptable argue that the cedar produces a sweet, full tone, and that the Indian rosewood has a straighter grain than the Brazilian variety. Of course, if Torres's cardboard guitar experiment actually worked, the variety of rosewood used should not, in itself, have so dramatic an effect.

English Virtuosi

The guitar also flourished in England, where Sor had lived for a spell, and where Louis Panormo was building guitars that incorporated the improved Spanish fan-strutting design. Still, England itself produced few virtuosi. An exception was Madame Sidney Pratten, born Catharina Josepha Pelzer. Her father, Ferdinand Pelzer, was a German immigrant guitarist who published a method in 1830, and began the famous guitar magazine *The Giulianiad* in 1833. Madame Pratten, who lived until 1895 and met Tárrega, published several method books of her own, including an ambitious one that included advanced pieces by Giuliani and Sor. She found, however, that most of her compatriots wanted to learn only the rudiments, and so she published *Learning the Guitar Simplified*, a work that ran to ten editions.

Method Books

During the early 19th century, the composer/virtuosi devoted a good deal of effort toward the codification of technique, and nearly all of them published method books in which they recorded their preferences. That a standard guitar technique had not evolved by the middle of the 19th century can be seen from the considerable number of points on which the methods disagree. Some continued to recommend that the small finger rest on the guitar's table, while others argued for a free hand. Some argued in favor of using the fingernails of the right hand; others, including Sor, insisted on fingertips only. Some argued that the guitar should rest on the right leg, while others preferred the left, and one – Dionisio Aguado, who had invented a tripod to rest the guitar on while playing it – preferred neither.

Dionisio Aguado

Yet, amid this diversity, we find in Aguado's *New Guitar Method* (1843) the seeds of what is now standard technique. Aguado, like Segovia nearly a century later, argued that a combination of fingertip and nail yields the best, most varied sound. Like Tárrega and virtually all who followed him, Aguado places great emphasis on the use of the *apoyando*, or rest stroke. And although he does not insist on alternation of the right-hand fingers as vehemently as today's school does, he provides exercises that develop the ring finger (neglected in methods until then) and even, in one or two instances, the little finger (which is not normally used today, nor was it in Aguado's day). The method, which has recently been translated into English by Brian Jeffery, is quite a thorough document, with fifty lessons, ninety exercises, twenty-two preludes, and twenty-seven studies, as well as a discussion of ornamentation, vibrato, and techniques a guitarist can use to suggest other instrumental colors (including trumpet, harp, cello, violin, and drum).

In the late 19th century, the guitar would see another period of dormancy. Once again, it was unable to keep apace of musical fashion, which by then had turned toward the massive washes of orchestral and keyboard sound, with which the guitar simply could not compete. In Spain, however, the guitar continued to enjoy its position as the country's national instrument, and it was there that it underwent another series of structural improvements. By the time the storms of Romanticism had blown their lasts gusts, the guitar would be ready to burst forth from its Iberic cocoon and claim its place both in the concert hall, and as an increasingly significant voice of the 20th century.

FRANCISCO TÁRREGA

The groundwork for this explosion was laid by two men. One, Antonio de Torres Jurado, was a luthier, whose instruments ushered the guitar into its modern phase. The other, Francisco Tárrega y Eixea, was a concert guitarist and composer who kept the virtuoso tradition alive long enough to inspire a generation of players that would turn his devotion to the instrument into an international crusade. Tárrega was born in Villareal, in 1852, and had developed a substantial technique and repertoire by the time he was ten, when the virtuoso Julián Arcas heard him and agreed to teach him. Tárrega's playing also impressed Torres, from whom he is said to have acquired an especially resonant instrument, in 1869. In 1874 Tárrega entered the Madrid Conservatory, where he studied piano, harmony, and music theory, winning first prize in the Conservatory's harmony and composition contests.

Tárrega began his career as a recitalist in the late 1870s, and performed in Paris and London in 1880. In 1885, he settled in Barcelona, continuing to give concerts around Spain until 1903, when he made a tour of Italy. When his right side became paralyzed in 1906, he was forced to end his concert career, although he continued teaching and composing. In October 1909 in Valencia, he returned to the concert stage once again; but two months later he died.

Compositions

Tárrega's legacy to the guitar was not large in the material sense. Of his eighty compositions, many are miniatures that, delightful and characteristic as they are, are rarely played beyond the student level these days. Which is not to dismiss his creative output out of hand – works like the *Capricho árabe* and *Danza mora*, the *Gran Jota* (after Arcas), and the magnificent tremolo study, *Recuerdos de la Alhambra*, will always remain among the most pleasing and dazzling chestnuts of the Romantic guitar literature. Yet none of Tárrega's works aspire to the scope of the Sor or Giuliani *Sonatas*, on the one hand, or of the extended masterworks of the 20th century, on the other.

Transcriptions

The transcriptions Tárrega labored over – about 150 pieces by composers as diverse as Bach, Beethoven, Boito, Meyerbeer, Gottschalk, Wagner (!), and Tchaikovsky – are also outmoded; some of them considered too fragmentary or otherwise inappropriate for modern guitar performance, and many others replaced by updated arrangements that are more faithful to the original texts. Of course, the vigor with which Tárrega sought works to transcribe served as an example to a younger generation of players who, like Tárrega, were faced with the task of creating a repertoire.

Technique

The standardization of techique is another garland traditionally laid at Tárrega's feet, but which, alas, may also overstate his contribution. As we have seen, many innovations attributed to Tárrega by posterity actually date back as far as Aguado. In fact, Tárrega himself would probably not have claimed to have invented technique: according to Emilio Pujol – a student of Tárrega's, and his biographer – Tárrega was familiar with all the great methods of the 19th-century virtuosi, including Aguado's. The implication is that he did not *create* the modern technique so much as cull the logical precepts of the early players, and mold them into his own style.

Even so, one of the major tenets of the Tárrega style – the belief, shared with Fuenllana and Sor, that the strings should be struck only with the fingertips, never with the nails – cannot be said to have survived. Pujol, in 1960, published a short treatise (*The Dilemma of Timbre on the Guitar*) rationalizing the no-nails approach on philosophical and historical grounds; but the practicalities of modern concert hall performance have rendered this approach less desirable than the Aguado/Segovia combination of flesh and nail.

If the credit for codifying the modern technique

belongs to anyone, it is probably Pujol, who incorporated the principles he learned from Tárrega (and, undoubtedly, some of his own discoveries) in his remarkably thorough method, *La Escuela Razonada de la Guitarra*. The first of the four published volumes of *Escuela* appeared in 1934, and puts forth the very basics of technique; by the fourth volume, which ends with a set of attractive and demanding etudes, Pujol has taken the student to an advanced level by way of a rigid program in which independence of the fingers on both the right and left hands is paramount. A fifth volume, containing only philosophy and theory (with neither etudes nor technical exercises) was in preparation at the time of Pujol's death, in 1980.

Students

If Tárrega's musical and technical contributions were slighter than legend suggests, his inspirational value was, at the turn of the century, incalculable. Pujol, in his *Ensayo biográfico*, paints his master as a priestly mystic whose life was fully devoted to his instrument; Andrés Segovia describes Tárrega as nothing less than a saint.

Tárrega's death did not exactly leave a void in the guitar world. His students – Pujol, Miguel Llobet, Maria Rita Brondi, Pepita Roca, and Daniel Fortea, among them – went on to concertize throughout the world, and to compose, transcribe, teach, and do musicological research. It was Llobet, in fact, who took the next logical step in the development of the literature – that of asking an established non-guitarist composer to provide music for the instrument. The composer was Manuel de Falla, one of the leaders of the Spanish nationalist school, and the work he provided, the haunting *Homenaje pour le tombeau de Claude Debussy* (1920).

ANDRÉS SEGOVIA

But the task of winning the guitar its place in the sun fell not to Tárrega's disciples, but to a self-taught guitarist from Andalusia, Andrés Segovia. Born in Linares, in 1893, Segovia gravitated toward the guitar at age six, and applied himself diligently to it. In 1909, the year of Tárrega's death, Segovia made his public debut in Granada. After a decade of consolidating his repertoire and technique, he left Spain for the first time in 1920, when he undertook a tour of South America.

Performing Career

In retrospect, things seem to have moved quickly from there. In 1924, he made his Paris debut, and in-

Andres Segovia

cluded on the program one of the first pieces composed for him, Albert Roussel's *Segovia*. Other European concerts followed, and in 1925, he toured the Soviet Union. In 1927, he went to London for his first recording sessions, with works of Sor, Bach, and some of the pieces newly composed for him by Torroba and Turina. And in 1928, he made his New York debut.

But it was not an easy conquest. In Spain, he was regarded with suspicion in some circles of the guitar establishment; and outside Spain, even as his reputation grew, he was regarded for many years as a crusader for a lost cause – a brilliant interpreter on an instrument not worth cultivating, and bound to be one-of-a-kind. As late as the 1940s, his manager, Sol Hurok, had trouble booking concerts for him, and had to indemnify promoters against losses. By the 1950s, that was no longer the case, and even through his eighties, Segovia's appearances continued to fill concert halls.

Transcriptions

Segovia's plan of attack was sensibly direct, and first on his list of priorities was a wholesale expansion of the repertoire. Part of this Segovia could accomplish himself, through transcription. Anything that *could* be played on the guitar *would* be played on the guitar, he seemed to decree; and in his early years, he made an enormous number of transcriptions and arrangements. He did not range as far afield as Tárrega had; but among Segovia's editions, we find keyboard works of Frescobaldi, Rameau, Schumann, and Scarlatti, and even some Beethoven and Scriabin. Perhaps the most enduring are his arrangements of the quintessentially Iberic piano works of Albeniz (*Asturias, Granada, Sevilla, Torre Bermeja*) and Granados (*Danzas Españolas* 5 and 10), works that have joined Tárrega's miniatures as guitaristic evergreens.

The centerpieces of Segovia's transcription collection, however, are his selected movements from the violin, cello, and lute works of J.S.Bach. These arrangements clarified the guitar's (and the guitarist's) capabilities for doubtful audiences. Of the set, the work audiences found most astounding when Segovia first played it in 1934 – and which remains the pinnacle of his transcription achievements – is the *Chaconne* from the *Second Partita for Violin Solo*, BWV 1004.

These days, guitarists who perform the works Segovia transcribed usually return to the original pieces and fashion versions of their own. Often, theirs are more literal representations of the composers' scores; for Segovia, like Tárrega, often infused his interpretive personality into his arrangements, leaving a thumbprint that is as recognizable on the printed page as it is in performance.

Performance Style

Segovia's performance style is documented in a series of recordings that span half a century, most of which are still available. His is the style of an age when personalized interpretation (now often seen as Romantic excess) was a performer's stock in trade. Its hallmarks include a generous use of *glissando*; the old-fashioned *rubato*, accomplished by rushing through part of a passage (a scale, for instance) and then compensating by holding the concluding chord just a touch longer than the notation indicates; a penchant for broken chords; and the occasional combination of these elements to create false climaxes. These manipulations, tempered with an expressive vibrato and sensitive use of tonal shading, are often miraculous in Segovia's performances of Spanish Romantic music. In Baroque works, though, we must consider what now seems a lexicon of stylistic error as the fashion of the time, and accept it (as we do similar affectations in the performances of Kreisler, Mengelberg, and Horowitz) on its own terms.

If Segovia's performances of Baroque works seem dated today, his recordings of music composed for him will always stand as vital documents. Realizing that transcription alone was not enough, Segovia began soliciting works from composers in the 1920s. The works he secured – to say nothing of those later composed for other guitarists – represent an avalanche of music, much of it of lasting value. Over the years, dozens of composers have obliged Segovia, if only with a single work – among them, Albert Roussel (*Segovia*, 1925), Darious Milhaud (*Segoviana*, 1959), Joan Manén (the lengthy *Fantasia-Sonata*, 1930), Federico Mompou (the *Suite Compostelana*, 1962), and Albert Harris (*Variations and Fugue on a theme of Handel*).

THE LITERATURE EXPANDS

But the core of the Segovia-inspired literature was produced by six composers who, after their first tentative contributions, in the 1920s and 1930s, returned to Segovia and the guitar time and again, together producing hundreds of works. The six are Joaquín Turina and Federico Moreno Torroba, of arranged and performed scores for several films. Yepes is best known, however, for his tenacious

Spain; Manuel Ponce, of Mexico; Maria Castelnuovo-Tedesco, of Italy; Alexandre Tansman, of Poland; and Heitor Villa-Lobos, of Brazil.

The Spanish School

Turina and Torroba – as well as Joaquín Rodrigo, whose hefty output of guitar music was, for the most part, composed for players other than Segovia – represent a Spanish nationalistic school grounded in the rhythmically vibrant and distinctly modal Iberian folk forms. The works of Turina and Torroba are in many ways quite similar, in that they both rely heavily on the gestures of traditional and flamenco music, molded into classical forms and given a sense of complexity that the folk forms lack. Turina's *Sevillana* (1923) and *Fandanguillo* (1936), for instance, use strummed chords, standard chord progressions, and virtuosic runs, all of which can be found in their popular and flamenco counterparts; the elements Turina adds are formal economy and studied thematic development.

Torroba uses similar raw materials for his *Suite Castellana* (1926), *Madroños* (1954), and other works, but he paints in broader strokes and often uses darker colors. Of the two, Turina contributed more electrifyingly visceral music, while Torroba's works – particularly the gentler, more descriptive movements of his suites – embody greater poetic aspirations.

The Neo-Romantics

Mario Castelnuovo-Tedesco and Alexandre Tansman brought the guitar a body of European neo-Romantic music that offers an important alternative to the literature grounded in popular Iberic roots. Tansman – a Pole who, like Chopin, has spent his life in Paris, and whose compositions reflect both the subtlety of French style and the traditional dance forms of Poland – made his first contribution to Segovia's repertoire in the form of a rather pretty *Mazurka* marked by insistent pedal-point basses, sweet melodies, and unusual harmonic turns. There followed more ambitious but equally atmospheric sets of dance movements, including the almost Baroque-style *Cavatina* (1951) and the ten-movement *Suite in Modo Polonico* (1968).

Castelnuovo-Tedesco became an extremely prolific guitar composer after he met Segovia (and composed a set of *Variazioni* for him), in 1932. There followed a four movement *Sonata* (*Ommagio à Boccherini*), Op.77 (1934); the bravura-style *Tarantella*, Op.87 (1935), the attractive *Quintet*, Op. 143 (1950) for guitar and strings, and the set of twenty-eight pieces of incidental music for *Platero y Yo*. In 1939 – just before the composer fled Mussolini's regime and settled in Los Angeles – he completed the first of his two solo guitar concerti (he also wrote a concerto for two guitars), a work that has the distinction of being the first guitar concerto of the 20th century. It is a work that covers a broad range of moods, with its bouncy *Allegretto* first movement, the bittersweet *Romanza*, and the energetic finale that begins ominously in d minor, but ends triumphantly in D major; but which only hints at the composer's personal upheavals.

Heitor Villa-Lobos

The Brazilian composer Heitor Villa-Lobos began writing for the guitar around the turn of the century – he played the instrument, and a few recordings exist on which he plays his own music. But of those early efforts, only the tuneful *Suite Popolaire Brasilienne* (1908-12; published 1955) and the *Chôros No.1* (1920) have survived. The repertoire he composed for Segovia is compact, comprising only the *Douze Etudes* (1929), *Cinq Préludes* (1940), and a *Concerto* (1951); but each of these works has attained a permanent and important place in the standard repertoire.

Manuel Ponce

But the composer that Segovia considers to have been the finest of his circle (and with good reason) is Manuel Ponce. Like Castelnuovo-Tedesco, Ponce was quite prolific, and gave guitarists an enormous variety of works, some of moderate difficulty (the *Twelve Preludes*, 1930; the *Valse*, 1937; and the *Canciones Populares Mexicanas*, 1928), and some that demand both stamina and virtuosic technique (the *Twenty Variations and Fugue on Folias de España* and several of the sonatas). In Ponce's works, elements of Mexican folk rhythms and melodic contour are blended with European structures and an often French-leaning harmonic feeling. Ponce was a tremendously versatile craftsman, and in his guitar works he was able to capture the spirit of Schubert (in his *Sonata Romantica*, 1928), Sor (in the *Sonata Clásica*, 1928), and even the Baroque lute composers (in his Kreislersque forgery, the so-called "Leopold Sylvius Weiss *Suite*"). He also published several fine variation sets (*Thème Varié et Finale* is frequently played; the beautiful *Variations and Fughetta on a Theme of Antonio de Cabezón* are performed less often), and only his doubts about the sonic balance of guitar and orchestra prevented him from completing his *Concierto del Sur* (started in the late 1920s, completed in 1941) before Castelnuovo-Tedesco's concerto.

Ponce's most extraordinary work is his titanic set of *Folias* variations (1930). Guitarists still debate its merits, some considering it overlong; and indeed, Segovia only recorded ten of the twenty variations. That was, however, in the days of 78rpm discs, and Segovia used the complete score as an example of idiomatic contemorary guitar composition when requesting works from other composers. And a fine example it is: in the course of the work, Ponce leads the guitarist through the gamut of technical and interpretive hurdles without resorting to superficial effects, alluding, along the way, to the works and styles of 19th-century guitarist/composers; to flamenco; and in the closing fugue, to Bach.

THE GUITARISTS EMERGE

While Segovia followed his star, other guitarists around the world followed parallel paths. Rey de la Torre, a Cuban, studied in Spain with Miguel Llobet before embarking on a career as a recitalist and teacher. Regino Sainz de la Maza also earned a reputation as a brilliant soloist early on, and both he and his brother Eduardo composed several virtuosic guitar works that have remained encore favorites. It was for Sainz de la Maza that Rodrigo composed the *Concierto de Aranjuez* (1939), now the most frequently performed and recorded work in the guitar concerto literature. Fifteen years later, Rodrigo wrote a concerto for Segovia, the *Fantasia para un Gentilhombre*, based on Gaspar Sanz themes; and he has composed several more solo and multiple guitar concerti for members of the Romero family guitar quartet. That family's patriarch, Celedonio Romero, began his career as a recitalist in the 1930s.

Agustín Pío Barrios

The most intriguing and enigmatic of the early 20th-century guitarists was Agustín Pío Barrios, an unconventional but inspired South American composer and virtuoso, whose colorful and decidedly original music is now enjoying a belated popularity. Born in Paraguay in 1885, Barrios spent most of his life touring Latin America. He did, however, give concerts and radio performances in Belgium and Germany in the early 1930s, and he was planning a trip to the United States at his death, in 1944.

Barrios was either a genuine eccentric or a crafty promoter: around 1930, he began encouraging the belief that he was descended from Guaraní Indian chiefs. He gave concerts in Indian costume, complete with feather headdress; and he billed himself as Nitsuga Mangoré, "The Paganini of the Guitar from the Jungles of Paraguay," and "The Indian Spirit that Sings in the Guitar."

Fortunately, much more than this bizarre image survives him. Barrios left some eighty manuscripts, as well as dozens of recordings, the earliest of which date to around 1912. These recordings (many of which have been issued on LP by the guitar-oriented El Maestro label) include transcriptions of Bach, Beethoven, and Schumann that, like Segovia's performances of such works, reveal a fund of Romantic mannerism. Most of them, though, contain original works, and show both a complete mastery of the instrument and a broad stylistic palette. There are bouncy waltzes (the fourth and eighth are frequently played today), works in a popular and folk style (*Junto a tu corazón*, *Aire de zamba*, *Danza paraguaya*), and quite a few scores fashioned in a compelling, "European" style (including the rhapsodic *Sueño en la floresta*; the exquisite tremolo work, *El último canto*; the *Romanza en imitacíon al violoncello*; and perhaps the best known of Barrios's works, the sublimely evocative *La Catedral*).

Alirio Diaz

In the 1940s, the post-Segovian guitar revolution began in earnest. Alirio Diaz, a Venezuelan, born in 1923, met Segovia in 1945 and became his student. Diaz championed the music of the Venezuelan guitarist composer Antonio Lauro, bringing another chunk of the Latin American repertoire into the guitar's arsenal. Equally important, Diaz developed a technique in which precision and directness replaced Romantic gestures – a style that John Williams and most of the following generation of players would espouse and extend. Diaz has never achieved the huge following among the general public that he perhaps deserves; but among players, he is considered a guitarist's guitarist.

Narciso Yepes

The 1940s also saw the debuts of Narciso Yepes and Alexandre Lagoya. Yepes, born in Lorca, Spain in 1927, is a self-taught player whose technical development was spurred by the composer Vicente Asencio, whose insistence that the guitar could never produce music as fluid as that of the piano, flute, or violin served as a challenge for Yepes. Since his Madrid debut, in 1947, he has pursued a vigorous touring and recording career; he has commissioned new works from Rodrigo, Leo Brouwer, and Bruno Maderna; he has done a good deal of transcribing; and he has

Odd Stringed Guitars

Although the Torres-style guitar has remained the standard for more than a century, guitar makers — often at the suggestion of players — have continued to experiment with unorthodox designs, particularly new stringing patterns. Actually, this tradition of experimentation goes back centuries, and has produced a gallery of unusual instruments, all designed in the hope of giving the guitarist more flexibility.

Among the earliest of these is the *chitarra tiorbata*, or theorboed guitar (also known as archguitar and harp-guitar), on which an extended peghead accommodates several extra bass strings, which run to the side of the fretboard — that is, constructed along the lines of the theorbo, a large member of the lute family. This kind of instrument dates from around 1640, and although it was never commonly adopted, Giovanni Battista Granata published music for such a guitar (with seven extra bass strings) in 1659; and variations on the free-sitting bass string design continued well into the 19th century.

Another early variant was a guitar with more than one neck. Alexandre Voboam made a double-necked instrument in 1690 by grafting a small five-course guitar onto the treble side of normal-sized instrument. Johann George Staufer worked along similar lines to produce his *Doppelgitarre* of 1807; and in 1829, J.F. Saloman produced a *Harpolyre*, with three necks and twenty-one strings, for which Fernando Sor composed ten pieces. Around the same time, an interest in classical antiquity led to the production of a *Lyre-guitar*, a single-necked instrument with two curved arms emanating from the sound-box and sometimes attached to the neck. Giuliani is known to have given recitals on this instrument.

Among the 19th century's many strange guitar variants, two stand out as particularly bizarre. The first — which was more a theoretical system than an actual production model guitar — was the *Enharmonic Guitar* of the English General T. Perronet Thompson. In 1829, General Thompson published his instructions for a microtonal tuning system in which the octave was divided into fifty-three equal parts. This would have been quite a difficult instrument to play, with its zig-zag fretboard, and not surprisingly, no one seems to have bothered with it. The other instrument was the thirty-five string *Guitarpa* of José Gallegos, of Malaga, in which a guitar, a harp, and a cello were mated.

Somewhat closer to the mainstream are the otherwise standard guitars with wider fretboards and

Napoleon Coste

Narciso Yepes

a modest number of extra strings. These guitars have long been with us, and have often been championed by legendary players. Yet, they have always remained just beyond the fringe of general acceptance. Napoleon Coste, for instance, used a seven-string guitar, with the bottom string tuned to D and sitting clear of the fretboard. A smaller seven-string guitar, tuned D-G-B-d-g-b-d′, was developed by Andreas Ossipovitch Sichra, a Russian virtuoso who popularized this form of the instrument in his homeland, and wrote a method for it. Around the same time, Ferdinando Carulli was using a ten-string guitar, in Paris; while toward the middle of the century, in Vienna, Johann Kas-

par Mertz favored the ten-string instrument.

In the 20th century, the Spanish guitarist Narciso Yepes has returned to the ten-string idea, although his instrument is somewhat heftier than the 19th-century version. Yepes designed his form of the ten-string in the early 1960s, and has used it exclusively since 1963. His tuning, normally, is G^b-A^b-B^b-c-E-A-D-g-b-e′, and his arguments for this instrument revolve around two advantages. First, the lower strings, in Yepes's tuning, provide harmonic (overtone) reinforcement, yielding a fuller guitar tone; and second, the extra strings allow for greater range and greater fingering possibilities in all

music, and for fewer compromises in the transcription of lute music. Until recently, Yepes remained virtually alone in his championship of the instrument, but in the early 1970s, Vincenzo Macaluso began recording with it, and more recently, Janet Marlow, in the United States, and Simon Wynberg, in England, have made recordings with the Yepes style ten-string guitar (although not always using Yepes's tuning system.) In the late 1970s, Göram Söllscher, a young Swedish guitarist, took Yepes's precepts a step further: He uses an eleven-string guitar tuned B-C-D-E-F-G-c-f-a-d′-g′ for Baroque music, and a standard six-string guitar for later works.

Narciso Yepes

championship of the ten-string guitar (see box on unusual guitars, p. 38), which he has been playing since 1963.

Alexandre Lagoya and Ida Presti

Alexandre Lagoya was born in Alexandria, Egypt, in 1929, and is also self-taught. Although he concertized widely in Egypt, he did not come to prominence until 1950, when he moved to Paris and formed a duo with Ida Presti, whom he married. Presti was a child prodigy – she made her first recordings in 1934, at age ten, and they are impressive. Together, Presti and Lagoya refined the difficult art of duo-guitar performance, and paved the way for future duos by creating a repertoire of transcriptions and commissioned works. They are also responsible for several important technical innovations, the most notable being a method of playing trills and other ornaments on two strings, rather than on one. Known as "cross-string" fingering, this technique yields a keyboard-like clarity in Baroque music, and has become standard among today's

younger players. After Presti's death, in 1967, Lagoya spent several years reclaiming his solo repertoire, and today he is again touring and recording on his own.

THE MODERNIST GUITARISTS

Critics of the guitar often ask why Segovia and most of the guitarists mentioned above turned to predominantly conservative composers rather than to the likes of Stravinsky, Webern, and Bartok, music's forward line in the first half of the century. The answer, obviously, is that their tastes did not lie in the modernist direction. But guitarists of the following generation have begun commissioning works that help balance the conservatively weighted repertoire, and which reveal the guitar as an instrument quite well-suited to the demands of the contemporary idiom.

Julian Bream

Among the first of these more adventurous players were Julian Bream, an Englishman, born in 1933, and John Williams, an Australian born in 1941 and now living in London. Bream began as a jazz guitarist and sometime pianist, but gravitated toward the guitar's classical repertoire early in life, also taking up the lute. He was largely self-taught, but by the late 1940s had evolved a good enough technique to give his first recitals and make his first radio broadcasts, and by the mid-1950s, he made the first of what has become an extensive collection of recordings, about half of them on the guitar, and half with the lute.

Bream has, perhaps not surprisingly, devoted much of his energy to encouraging British composers to write for the guitar. Among the first to comply was Malcolm Arnold, who composed a charming *Serenade* (1955) for guitar and orchestra as a study piece to precede his full-length *Guitar Concerto*, Op.67 (1961), a lyrical work inspired by and dedicated to the memory of the French jazz guitarist Django Reinhardt, whose style is paraphrased in the modal, bluesy *Lento* movement. Edging further in the direction of modernity is Reginald Smith Brindle's *El Polifemo de Oro* (1956), a haunting work in which twelve-tone techniques free the instrument from the pervasive sense of tonality implicit in the guitar's tuning and chord structures. This desire to lead the guitar beyond the limits of tonality had a precedent in Frank Martin's *Quatre Pièces Brèves*, composed the year Bream was born, and has become one of the salient features

Julian Bream

of guitar music written since the mid-1950s.

In 1963, Bream received a work that has become one of the most significant 20th-century guitar scores, Benjamin Britten's *Nocturnal*, Op.70. Based on John Dowland's lute song, *Come Heavy Sleep*, this is a set of difficult and picturesque variations, ending with the Dowland theme, and is for guitarists what the Liszt *Sonata* is for pianists.

Bream's encouragement of contemporary composers continues to this day, and among the works he brought into the repertoire in the 1970s are the *Five Impromptus* (1968) and *Concerto* (1970) of Richard Rodney Bennett; William Walton's *Five Bagatelles* (1971); Alan Rawsthorne's final work, the *Elegy* (1971); and extended solo work by the German avant-garde composer Hans Werner Henze, *Royal Winter Musick* (1976), an aggressive, atonal sonata inspired by Shakespearean characters and demanding virtually every kind of "effect."

Bream has also, naturally, addressed the standard guitar literature, beginning with the so-called Segovia repertoire, but soon forging paths of his own. He has published a series of his own transcriptions – including keyboard works of Cimarosa and lute suites of Bach – and has recorded many a work that guitarists of his generation had neglected. Bream was the first, for instance, to record Giuliani's *Rossiniane*, and he has been quick to add newly discovered Romantic works to his repertoire. His lute playing has taken him through most of the works of Dowland and a healthy sampling of other English and Italian lutenists, and he has recently turned his attention to the *vihuela* composers for a recording series in which he plans to document the history of Spanish guitar music.

John Williams

John Williams comes from an entirely different kind of background, and represents a break with the tradition of self-taught players that stretches from Segovia to Bream. At age six Williams was given a

John Williams

guitar by his father, the noted jazz guitarist and arranger, Len Williams, who had taught himself the rudiments of the classical style, and who decided forthwith that he could make a virtuoso out of any bright six-year-old. Williams took to the instrument even more quickly than his father suspected he might; and in 1952, when the family moved to London, Len Williams established the Spanish Guitar Center there, an organization that helped make London a hub of the guitar world. Among the Center's activities was the presentation of concerts and master classes, by Segovia and other soloists. Segovia, impressed with the young Williams's abilities, took him on as a student and worked closely with him for a year. There followed several summers of coaching with both Segovia and Alirio Diaz, in Siena, Italy; and in 1958, Williams made his London debut.

Williams toured regularly during the 1960s, but by the early 1970s he began drastically cutting back on his personal appearances outside London, excepting the occasional tour of Australia, and every few years, a duet tour with Julian Bream. He has, how-ever, continued to learn and record repertoire, and his LPs remain among the best in what is now a growing market for guitar discs. Like Bream, he has recorded virtually the entire standard repertoire, including a tremendous number of concerti. He has also recorded many of his own transcriptions (the Bach lute suites and *Chaconne*, plus a series of Bach works arranged for the unusual combination of guitar and organ; as well as music of Albeniz, Sanz, Granados, Falla, Dowland, and Batchelar); and has sought out guitar music that has not been previously explored (including the guitar and the keyboard sonatas of Rudolf Straube, a student of Bach; and the music of Barrios, to which he devoted a full LP in the late 1970s). And like Bream, he has encouraged composers to write for him. Those who have include Andre Previn and Patrick Gowers, both of whom have provided new concerti; Stephen Dodgson, who has composed two concerti and quite a few solo works for Williams; and several Australian composers.

In the late 1960s, Williams began experimenting with jazz and pop forms, and recorded a series of experimental LPs that lingered somewhere between classical and popular realms. In 1978, he formed a progressive jazz-rock band, called Sky, with which he has recorded several LPs where, again, classical and pop forms mingle. In the context of Sky, he has taken up the electric guitar – he plays it, however, as if it were a nylon-string classical model.

The differences between Bream's and Williams's techniques can be best heard in the duet collaborations, which have resulted in two studio LPs and a recording made during their 1978 concert tour. It is a difference like that between rubies and diamonds: Bream's playing tends toward a more relaxed, delicately shaded sound, hardly as Romantic as Segovia's, but still edging toward the sensual; Williams, by contrast, prefers a sound with sharper edges – also ingeniously shaded, but never yielding its clarity and precision.

THE NEW GENERATION

Looking back from vantage point in the mid-1980s, it seems almost as if Williams and Bream stood as the unchallenged heirs to Segovia's throne. But although their achievements tend to overshadow those of their contemporaries, there were other Segovia desciples in the running during the 1960s. One was Oscar Ghiglia, an Italian guitarist three years older than Williams, and a student of

Segovia's at Siena between 1958 and 1963. In 1963, Ghiglia won the International Competition of the ORTF, in Paris, and the following year, he became Segovia's assistant for a summer master class series at Berkeley.

By the end of the decade, he had embarked in earnest on a concert career, and he made a few recordings for EMI. He was reckoned, at the time, to be a superb technician, with a wide-ranging repertoire and a personal style that was both individualistic and communicative. Indeed, guitarists hold him in high esteem to this day, although he has kept a comparatively low public profile, and has not released a recording in about a decade. Like Diaz, Ghiglia has been influential as model of musical integrity, and as a teacher.

Another Segovia protege who enjoyed a brief moment in the sun was Christopher Parkening, a California-born player who had superstardom virtually handed to him at age twenty, when EMI released three debut recordings simultaneously, accompanied by an unusual amount of publicity fanfare. Parkening had a few things going for him: his quintessentially Californian appearance made life easy for publicists, and the championship of Segovia – who called him "one of the most brilliant guitarists in the world" – certainly didn't hurt.

Yet, there was a lot missing. In concert, his performances were flawed, and on recordings, they were tasteful and competent, but flat and rather faceless. Eventually, Parkening decided that the touring life wasn't for him, and in his late twenties, he retired to a large estate in Montana, where he devoted his energies to raising horses. Now and then, in the mid-1970s, he emerged to give a concert or a master class, and he even published a method book. But for all practical purposes, he had retired from the concert and recording circuit. Then, in 1982, he resurfaced – this time as a born-again Christian, whose stated aim was "to share in music the joy and hope of the Christian life." And after several years away from the recording studio, he released an LP devoted to his new passion, "Sacred Music for the Guitar."

Meanwhile, yet another generation of guitarists was coming of age in the 1960s. These players, who are now in their late twenties, came to the guitar at an extraordinary time. On the one hand, if they were attracted to the instrument's classical voice, they had an abundance of role models, and they could scout out the literature through hundreds of

Christopher Parkening

recordings by players of all sorts of temperaments and interpretive approaches. On the other hand, the guitar itself – albeit in a considerably different form – was riding the crest of a wave of popularity, thanks to rock'n'roll. If studying the violin or the piano seemed a little strange to one's peers, there was nothing at all unusual about mastering the fretboard. In fact, several of today's budding virtuoso guitarists confess to having played in high school rock bands, or later, in college avant-garde jazz ensembles; and they retain interests not only in the classical music they play in concert, but in popular forms too – as is only natural. This generation is now taking its place in the concert world, and it is already shaping up as quite a formidable – and large – group.

Leo Brouwer

Leo Brouwer is a figure of considerable interest in the classical guitar world, although his concert performances in the United States have been rare. He is, of course, better known as a composer than as a player, and he has produced a number of contemporary masterpieces. The colorful, swirling *La Es-*

Eliot Fisk

piral Eterna, composed in 1971, is already a standard work that most young guitarists have in their repertoires, and it has been recorded by several of them. Nearly as popular, but in an entirely different style, is the lively, folksy *Elogio de la Danza*, a work based on traditional Cuban dance rhythms. His set of *Etudes Simples* and *Pièce sans titre* are useful student scores – fairly easy, but in a contemporary idiom. Brouwer has also written a *Guitar Concerto* that mixes aleatoric (chance) elements with carefully and specifically notated sections. On a more whimsical note, Brouwer has composed duet arrangements of two Lennon-McCartney tunes, "The Fool on the Hill" and "Penny Lane" – arrangements that are sometimes clever, sometimes Muzak-like, and representative of neither Brouwer nor the

Beatles, but a change of pace from what is usually considered as the norm.

Eliot Fisk

Two of the most promising young American guitarists are Eliot Fisk and Sharon Isbin, both of whom are exceptional Baroque interpreters. Fisk is a particularly enigmatic player whose work can be a paradoxical blend of fire and ice. He has developed a brand of technical wizardry that can be astounding, particularly in terms of velocity and in bringing a keyboard-like clarity to individual notes and to contrapuntal lines within larger textures. His performances are not always note-perfect; and at times, the feeling of compulsion driving them gives an impression of cold, sharp-edged steeliness. Yet, at his best, Fisk is able to push the limits of sheer finger-power.

Allied to Fisk's techincal facility is a fascination with the intellectual side of the art. If you ask him about the works on a program, he'll launch into structural analyses and explorations of motivic or intervallic relationships that most of his audience won't recognize as such, but which inform his own interpretive preparations – and which, he firmly believes, are inevitably communicated and understood, if only on a intuitive level. The paradox is that behind his high-gloss, state-of-the-art technique and his penchant for analysis, there lurks a thoroughly old-fashioned kind of Romantic fire – stylistically quite different from Bonell's, and as strongly individualistic. When playing familiar works – particularly from the Spanish and Latin-American literature – he seems driven to seek new ways of phrasing and recasting works so that they are entirely his own. He is, to the guitar, very much akin to what Glenn Gould was to the piano – not so eccentric, perhaps, but certainly as provocative and original. In Baroque music, Fisk's personality is entirely different: having studied with harpsichordist and Scarlatti scholar Ralph Kirkpatrick, he has a keen sense of style, and his ornamentation, which is sometimes quite lavish, always bears an almost compositional structural logic.

Women Guitarists

Sharon Isbin, like Fisk, studied with a harpsichordist, Rosalyn Tureck, and has been collaborating with Tureck on a series of annotated editions of the Bach lute suites. At this end of the literature, there are several similarities between these two guitarists – primarily, their insistence on crispness and linear independence. Also notable is their approach to ornamentation: in both cases, trills and turns are played across two strings, to give the same effect as a keyboard trill, rather than the soft slur of the easier and more standard single string trill. This is not entirely a new approach – Ida Presti and Alexandre Lagoya pioneered it, and many players of the younger generation have adopted it.

Isbin's other strong suit is her contemporary music performance, and she has commissioned several works, including an interesting concerto by Ivanna Themmen. Something of a radical feminist, Isbin is one of a growing number of female players making their way in the classical guitar world, and she is one of the best. Among her colleagues are Alice Artzt, a player whose concert performances can be uneven, but who has made several nicely polished and inventively programmed recordings. Liona Boyd, a British-born Canadian player, has garnered a good deal of attention that is due more to her long blond tresses and her soft-focus album covers than to her playing, which may be generously described as substandard in these times of technical exellence and interpretive ingenuity.

David Leisner

In recent years, several more young players have distinguished themselves either in specialized fields of guitar literature, or as general players. David Leisner, for one, has not really specialized, but has nevertheless developed a unique repertoire in several areas: he has convinced several of the more prominent American composers either to write works for him, or to allow him to transcribe pieces himself, and he has composed several intriguing works of his own. Leisner was also the first to record music by Johann Kaspar Mertz, and he has published editions of several of that lately rediscovered composer's works.

The Avant-Garde

David Starobin, like Leisner, Fisk, Isbin, and Barrueco, is based in New York. His established specialty is contemporary music of the more avant-garde variety, and aside from a healthy number of solo works, his repertoire includes virtually every contemporary chamber score requiring a guitar, since it is to Starobin that New York's many new music ensembles almost invariably turn when they need a player who can negotiate difficult modern writing. Other cities around the world have guitarists in equivalent positions: in London, for instance, David Russell and Timothy Walker do a lot of the avant-garde playing.

The field has grown so quickly, in fact, that it would be impossible, in this space, to even briefly survey the careers of all the interpreters whose work can be said to have an impact, and whose work deserves recognition. Indeed, each musical season brings with it a new crop of younger players, many of whom show strong musical characters and seem to be on their way to careers that will bear watching. However, most of the better players who have not been covered in the main section of this chapter are represented in the discography that follows.

PROSPECTS

In its five-century history, the guitar has had its share of fallow periods and its times of expansion; but as we approach the mid-1980s, its prospects seem healthier than ever. Now there are four generations of guitarists before the public, each with something unique to offer in its approach to music-making. Recitals of short vignettes have been replaced by programs built of substantial works – complete Baroque suites, multimovement 19th-century sonatas, or contemporary works – and guitarists' approaches to style have been updated.

Part of the key to the guitar's coming of age may be that today's young players are becoming less parochial about the guitar itself; that is, they are thinking of the instrument as a means rather than as an end, and concentrating on the sound of the music rather than on the sound of the guitar. In any case, as the number of world-class guitarists has increased, so has the size of the guitar's audience – a fact not lost on record companies, which are producing a steady flow of guitar LPs, including reissues of historical performances that had either gone out of print, or were only available on 78 rpm discs. Added to this are festivals devoted to the guitar and its literature (one of the most important being Toronto Guitar, held every three years) and prestigious international contests, in which young players can vie for the recognition they need to launch their careers.

History being what it is, it is entirely possible that the guitar will again fade into the musical woodwork – that it will again have to undergo structural modifications, and that several generations of performers will have to crusade on its behalf before its true capabilities are known. But in one form or another, this ancient instrument will always be with us. And for the moment, the guitar as we know it is firmly entrenched.

DISCOGRAPHY: CLASSICAL GUITAR

Compiling a selected discography in a field as broad and quickly expanding as the guitar inevitably presents a number of problems in both the actual selection of discs, and in the organization of the choices. Hundreds of classical guitar LPs are currently in print, and each month sees the release of perhaps a dozen more (including those issued on major labels, small labels, and by foreign companies). Some guitarists – Segovia, Bream, Williams, and Pepe Romero, for instance – have each issued more than twenty or thirty discs, covering an extraordinary amount of literature in performances that are, for the most part, beautifully played and highly recommendable. Choosing from the output of these prolific players alone proves a difficult task, and considering their many worthy, if less frequently recorded, colleagues compounds that difficulty.

There were two paths open in the organization of the discography. The first would have been to follow the historical narrative of the text, presenting the discs by period, composer, and work, giving alternate performances of frequently recorded works where possible. The selections were made keeping those aims in mind; however, it was finally decided that the discography should be arranged not by period or composer, but by performer. As such, the discography might serve as a kind of illustrated survey of today's guitar performance world.

ALICE ARTZT
20th Century Guitar Music
Hyperion A66002

Guitar Music by Francisco Tárrega
Meridian E77026

Guitar Music by Manuel Maria Ponce
Meridian E77041

Alice Artzt is an American player whose recordings present nicely rounded surveys of particular composers or styles, in performances that are thoughtful and well turned, if not quite as fiery as those of some of her colleagues. This is particularly so on the Ponce disc, which includes an introspective view of the *Folias* variations, and gentle renditions of the "Weiss" Suite and the Sonatina Meridional. On the 20th Century disc, she mixes the familiar – Tansman's *Cavatina*, Falla's *Homenaje* – with delightful but less well-known music by John Duarte, Tom Eastwood, and Owen Middleton. The Tárrega disc is an exercise in stylistic excess, with one side devoted to several Tárrega favorites (*Capricho Arabe, Recuerdos, Danza Mora*) and the other to the composer's odd transcriptions of Handel, Haydn, Schubert and Men-

delssohn. The performances are full of *portamento* and old-fashioned phrasing, an approach augmented by the use of "La Leona" – a guitar claimed to be a Torres (although this is disputed by some), but certainly a mid-19th-century instrument, in any case, with a rich, deep tone.

CARLOS BARBOSA – LIMA
Scarlatti Sonatas
Westminister WGS 8209

The Music of Antonio Carlos Jobim and George Gershwin
Concord Concerto CC 2005

A Brazilian player who should have made many more recordings than he has, Carlos Barbosa-Lima made his disc debut in 1973 with the delightful recital of nine Scarlatti sonatas, in his own transcriptions, making them sound as appropriate to the guitar as they are to the harpsichord. The second disc straddles several worlds – Brazil and the United States, jazz, and classical approaches – and does so skillfully. The Gershwin selections (including two of the *Preludes*, "Summertime," "Swanee," and other favorites) work surprisingly well, again in the guitarist's own transcriptions.

AGUSTIN BARRIOS
Agustin Barrios Vol. 1&2
El Maestro EM 8002

Vol.3
El Maestro EM 8002V3

These three discs are of extraordinary historical value – and what's more, even though their digitally cleaned-up sound still sounds somewhat primitive – they make great listening. Drawn from Barrios's 78 rpm recordings, these LPs include Barrios's own works in his inimitable renditions, as well as a few unusual transcriptions. The first two volumes (packaged together) include an informative illustrated booklet. Those who prefer to hear Barrios's music played by today's virtuoso guitarists and recorded in more up-to-date sound should investigate the Barrios discs of John Williams (CBS M 35145) and Guy Lukowski (Angel S 37844).

MANUEL BARRUECO
Albeniz and Granados
Turnabout TV 34738

An extremely promising player, the Cuban-born Barrueco has also recorded discs of South American music (TV 34676), Scarlatti, Giuliani, and Paganini (TV 34770), and Bach (Vox VCL 9023); but far away his finest to date has been this collection of arrangements (his own) from Albeniz's *First Suite Española* and Granados's *Spanish Dances*. In most cases, these are faithful to the piano originals (here and there treble and bass are transposed without ruining the effect of the original), and several of the more frequently played movements are omitted here in favor of hitherto unplayed ones. Barrueco's playing is bright and brilliant, and he dispatches technical and interpretive difficulties with ease.

BALTAZAR BENITEZ
Latin-American Music for the Guitar
Nonesuch H-71349

This young Uraguayan shows great sympathy for this music, making a strong case for Abel Carlevaro's *Preludios Americanos* and Ponce's beautiful set of variations on a theme of Cabezón. The highlight, though, is a selection of three Barrios works, including the gorgeous tremolo study, *El último canto*.

CARLOS BONELL
Guitar Music of Spain
Nonesuch H-71390

Rodrigo: Concierto de Aranjuez/Fantasia para un Gentilhombre
London LDR 71027

A British player of Spanish descent, Carlos Bonell brings a great deal of romantic lyricism to his performances. The Spanish recital includes a pair of spirited dances by Emilio Pujol, along with lively renditions of short works by Tárrega, Rodrigo, Torroba, and Sanz, and a touching version of Sor's *Fantasia Elegiaca*. Bonell's performances of the Rodrigo concertos are among the finest, sensitively played and warmly recorded.

JULIAN BREAM
20th Century Guitar
RCA LSC 2964

70's
RCA ARL1-0049

Dedication
RCA RL25419
(SO FAR ONLY AS IMPORT)

Villa Lobos: Concerto and Preludes
RCA LSC 3231

Villa Lobos: Etudes, Suite Poplaire
RCA ARL1-2499

Julian Bream has, as mentioned above, recorded more than thirty LPs, about half of which are played on the lute. Of the guitar discs, there are many outstanding collections, including the surveys of Baroque Guitar (RCA LSC-2878), Romantic Guitar (LSC-3156), and Classic Guitar (LSC-3070), plus his current series tracing the history of Spanish music (which, at the time of writing, was set to include his first recordings on the *vihuela* and Baroque guitar). Yet, despite his strengths throughout the repertoire, I have chosen several of his recordings of 20th-century guitar music, a part of the literature he puts across with exceptional flair and conviction. Little need be said about the Villa-Lobos discs; but for one short movement of the *Suite Popolaire*, these cover all of that composer's guitar works, in performances as vibrant as you'll find anywhere. The 20th Century Guitar disc contains several pivotal scores – Martin's *Quatre Pieces*, Brindle's *Polifemo de Oro*, and the Britten *Nocturnal* among them. *Dedication* contains works written for Bream by Walton, Henze, Maxwell Davies, and Richard Rodney Bennett, some of them thorny works, the others less so; while *70's* is devoted exclusively to contemporary British works, with Richard Rodney Bennett's Concerto for Guitar and Chamber Ensemble as the centerpiece.

OSCAR CÁCERES/ LEO BROUWER
Oscar Cáceres Interprets Leo Brouwer
MHS 3777 (Musical Heritage Society)

This disc contains virtually all the solo guitar works Brouwer composed before 1973, as well as the Danzas *Concertes*, with string orchestra, and the *Micropiezas* for two guitars (with Brouwer himself as the second). The music itself is intriguing, and has lately been taken up by many a guitarist. For those interested in Brouwer as an interpreter of music other than his own, he has recorded an interesting and aggressively embellished Scarlatti disc, also available on MHS (3735) (both discs originally recorded by Erato, France).

ALIRIO DIAZ
The Classic Spanish Guitar
Vanguard SRV 357/8 SD

This two-disc set contains twenty-seven works, mostly from the Spanish literature, with a bit of Scarlatti and traditional Venezuelan music mixed in. It is all very familiar fare – some Milán, Mudarra, and Narváez *viheula* pieces, Sor Studies, Albeniz *Asturias* and other works, Falla's *Homenaje*, a Segovia-penned study, "Remembranza" – but in Diaz's hands, these chestnuts seem fresh and alive.

ELIOT FISK
The Latin American Guitar
MusicMasters MM 20008

American Virtuoso
MusicMasters MM 20032

These two discs show quite different sides of Eliot Fisk, a young American guitarist with an unbeatable technique and impeccable musicality. The Latin-American disc contains a dozen short works on one side – including samplings of Barrios, Lauro, Sojo, and Sagreras – and Ponce's *Folias* variations on the other. Both sides are a tour de force and are bound to keep you on the edge of your seat. *American Virtuoso* is a Baroque disc, with a recording of the Bach *First Lute Suite* that will please those who like their Bach ornately embellished. Works of Scarlatti and Froberger are also included.

SHARON ISBIN
Classical Guitar Vol. II
Sound Environments TR 1013

Like Fisk, Sharon Isbin presents her Bach with a good deal of embellishment; and although she plays the same suite, her approach is quite different. Also a brilliant player with an incisive technique, Isbin pairs her Bach suite with two modern works, the Britten *Nocturnal* and Brouwer's *Espiral Eterna*, both played magnificently. Baroque and modern music are her strengths; she seems less comfortable in her performances of Spanish works.

MIGUEL LLOBET
Miguel Llobet
El Maestro EM 8003

Like the Barrios set, this is a compilation of recordings originally issued on 78rpm discs, including both solo performances, and duets with his student Maria Luisa Anido. According to Pujol, who knew Llobet well, the latter hated his recordings; for today's player, they serve as a glimpse into the style of a bygone age.

IDA PRESTI/ ALEXANDRE LAGOYA
Music for 2 Guitars
Philips 6768 657

Many have attempted the difficult art of guitar duet playing, and some have done quite well; but no guitar duo has ever achieved the perfection of ensemble combined with interpretive warmth that marks these Presti and Lagoya performances. The music is diverse – Scarlatti, Bach, Soler, Sor, Debussy, Albeniz, Granados, Falla, and several others, including a work of Presti's – and the playing, even fifteen years after Presti's death, is electrifyingly fresh.

DAVID LEISNER
The Viennese Guitar
Titanic Ti-46

This is Leisner's debut recording, and contains an impressive sampling of music by Johan Kaspar Mertz, as well as a pair of Giuliani's better concert works, all conveyed with an appropriately Romantic spirit and a fine sense of nuance and phrasing.

MICHAEL NEWMAN
Italian Pleasures
Sheffield Lab 16

Michael Newman, another extremely talented young American, has thus far released only "direct-to-disc" LPs – discs recorded "live" onto a lathe, rather than onto tape. His first outing, which contained the Bach *Chaconne* and some firey Spanish works (Sheffield Lab 10) was an eye-opener, but flaws in the Bach made it wear thin over time. The Italian disc, however, is close to perfection, containing Giuliani's *Introduction, Theme, Variations and Polonaise*, for guitar and string quartet; a fairly lightweight but charming Carulli duet, with Laura Oltman; and a flashy solo work by Legnani, all conveyed with both technical strength and interpretive sensitivity.

NIGEL NORTH
Robert de Visée
L'Oiseau Lyre DSLO 542

DAVID RHODES
Baroque Guitar and Lute
Titanic Ti-5

Both these discs contain examples of Baroque guitar music played on reproductions of period instruments, which of course sound entirely different from their modern descendants. Both players are steeped in the conventions of the style, and their performances will sound quite alien to those used to Visée and his contemporaries in modern guise. These performances may, however, be closer to Visée's own, and merit investigation by anyone curious about the way guitar style has changed over the centuries.

ANGEL ROMERO
The Divine Giuliani
Angel SZ 37326

One of the Romero quartet who has established a solo career, Angel Romero's affinities are for Spanish and Romantic music. On this disc, he essays two of Giuliani's *Rossiniane* (tributes to Rossini) and a pair of variation sets, with sparkling clarity of purpose.

PEPE ROMERO
Giuliani: Concertos Op.36/Op.70
Philips 9500 320

Giuliani: Concerto, Op.30 Rodrigo: Concierto Madrigal
Philips 6500 918

Giuliani: Solo works
Philips: 9500 513

Sor: Sonatas
Philips 9500 586

Boccherini Quintets (complete on 3 discs)
Philips 9500 621, 9500 789, 9500 985

Pepe Romero is a less impetuous, more mature, and technically more finely polished player than Angel, and has developed quite a few specialties – plus a penchant for thoroughness. Besides all the Giuliani concertos and quite a few solo works, he has recorded all the Rodrigo *Concertos* and most of *his* solo works as well. His concerto discs, backed by Neville Marriner and the Academy of St. Martin-in-the-Fields, are particularly impressive ensemble efforts, and his solo playing embodies a winning, propulsive quality, particularly in the 19th-century literature.

ANDRÉS SEGOVIA
The EMI Recordings 1927-39
Angel ZB 3896

Segovia Plays Bach
Saga 5248

Castelnuovo Tedesco: Concerto (plus various solo pieces by other composers)
EMI/HMV HLM 7134 (import)

Golden Jubilee
MCA 3-19000

Mexicana
MCA 2532

Presumably, any serious guitar collector will want *all* of Segovia's recordings. For starters, though I'd recommend his earliest discs, recently collected and reissued on the first three volumes listed above. Transferred from 78rpms made between 1927 and the late 1940s, these capture Segovia at the height of his form, and at his most eager to make an impression. They cover a good deal of literature, concentrating, naturally, on works either transcribed by or composed for Segovia. The *Golden Jubilee* set, marking the fiftieth anniversary of his concert debut, also contains many a gem, particularly Segovia's recording of Rodrigo's *Fantasia para un Gentilhombre*. On *Mexicana*, the highlights are two of Ponce's four-movement Sonatas, *Mexicana* and *Clasica*, excellent works hard to find elsewhere.

GORAN SOLLSCHER
Guitar Music of Bach and Sor
DG 2535 011

Greensleeves
DG 2532 054

A young Swedish player who won first prize at the Paris Guitar Competition a few years ago, Sollscher plays Baroque music on an eleven-string guitar, and later music on a standard instrument. His Bach is a picture of structural logic and purity of sound, underpinned by the rich basses his expanded guitar provides. The centerpiece of the second disc is not really *Greensleeves*, but the Bach *Chaconne*, flanked by other Renaissance and Baroque works and a set of Sor variations (*Marlborough*).

DAVID STAROBIN
New Music With Guitar, Vol. 1
Bridge DG 2001

David Starobin has built a strong reputation as an adventurous player open to the most demanding new works and techniques. This sampling includes both chamber and solo works by Henze, Wuorinen, Kolb, and Bland, presenting music not to be found elsewhere, brilliantly performed.

JOHN WILLIAMS
Virtuoso Variations
CBS MS 7195

Spanish Music
CBS M 30057

Duo (with Itzhak Perlman)
CBS M 34508

Arnold & Brouwer Concertos
CBS M 36680

Again, a tough choice. *Virtuoso Variations*, an early disc, is just what the title says, containing several essays in variation form (among them the Bach *Chaconne*, Giuliani's *Handel variations*, Batchelar's *Monsiers Almaine*, and the *24th Paganini Caprice*), all played with astonishing finesse. That quality marks all of Williams's recordings, of course, and the *Spanish Music* disc (containing all the standards, from Sanz's *Canarios*, to Albeniz's *Asturias*) is positively fire-breathing. *Duo* is more relaxed, containing Paganini and Giuliani violin and guitar duets. The Arnold Concerto (composed for Bream, who has also recorded it) is an atmospheric, jazzy piece that suits Williams well, as does the more adventurously modern Brouwer concerto. The adventurous will also want to investigate Williams's recordings of the concertos written for him by Andre Previn (CBS M31963) and Patrick Gowers (CBS

M35866), the latter also rather jazzy and unusual.

KAZUHITO YAMASHITA
Mussorgsky: Pictures at an Exhibition
RCA ARC1-4203

As a performance of the Mussorgsky piano work, familiar to most through Ravel's orchestration, this is sometimes a bit pale; but as a display of guitaristic virtuosity and editorial ingenuity, this performance of the complete *Pictures* is dazzling.

NARCISO YEPES
500 Years of Spanish Guitar Music
Vol.1: DG 139 365; Vol.2 139 366

Music of Brouwer, Carulli, Conge, Kuhnel, Robinson, Sor
DG 2531 113

Rodrigo: Concierto de Aranjuez — Concerto Madrigal
DG 2531 208

A crusader for the ten-string guitar, Yepes plays in a highly individualized, often clipped manner that appeals to some listeners. Among the finest of his many recordings are his two-disc survey of Spanish music, from vihuelists to contemporary works, and a recent disc of music composed either for the lute or specifically for the ten-string guitar, including Brouwer's *Tarantos*, composed for Yepes. The first to record Rodrigo's popular *Aranjuez* concerto, Yepes has returned to the work several times on disc. His latest version, listed above, is one of the more unusual in the catalogue, a performance in which Yepes allows his individuality to shine brightly. Also of interest are several discs of vocal music on which Yepes accompanies Teresa Berganza, among them one containing songs of Manuel de Falla and Federico Garcia Lorca (DG 2530 875).

The Birth of the Blues

by Pete Welding

Despite the widely held belief that the blues has always been there, it is actually one of the more recent forms of black American folksong, having originated in the lower South in the period immediately following Emancipation. There are, for example, no references to blues or any similar lyric-song forms in any of the earliest published works dealing with black folk music, in the numerous slave narratives published as part of the Abolitionist movement, or in any of the nineteenth century travelers' accounts of the life and folkways of the southern United States. The earliest published accounts of the blues all date from the early twentieth century: Charles Peabody's reports from Coahoma County, Mississippi, published in the *Journal of American Folklore* in 1903; Howard W. Odum's similar reports from Lafayette County, Mississippi, and Newton County, Georgia, published in the same journal in 1911; composer W.C. Handy's accounts of his having heard the incipient blues in the Mississippi Delta in 1903; veteran blues singer Gertrude "Ma" Rainey's assertion that she first heard the music in 1902 while touring Missouri, and so on.

THE BIRTH OF THE BLUES

These and numerous other accounts, including the recollections of early blues recording artists and recording directors, buttress the current assumption that the blues, while drawing on a number of expressive techniques associated with earlier black folksong forms, only took shape as a distinct new species of lyric song in the turbulent period following the Civil War, its birthplace the later plantation culture of the Deep South – the cotton crop states of Mississippi, Alabama, Arkansas, Louisiana, Missouri, and

B.B. King

51

Poster advertising minstrel show

Tennessee. The music undoubtedly developed in response to the radically altered cultural conditions of the post-Emancipation South, which found many newly-freed blacks suddenly cut off from the familiar, comforting moorings of traditional Southern life and folkways. The blues came into being as a means of defining a new black cultural identity and helping the individual to integrate himself into this new perception.

It is for these reasons that the lyrics of blues differ radically from those of earlier black folksong – the worksongs, spirituals, play-party songs, dance, and other social music of the pre-Civil War period – all of which were communal rather than solo musics, designed to provide for the maintenance of the larger community of interests represented by black culture in general. The blues, on the other hand, was almost exclusively a solo music, one that permitted, if it did not encourage, the individual singer-performer to express the singularity of his own experiences, perceptions, values, and aspirations. It is this, along with the characteristic blues song form, that set the blues apart from other traditional black folksong, for many of the expressive techniques it employed in vocal phrasing and in accompaniment had been used in earlier black folksong practice: tonal ambiguity (the so-called "blue notes"); a high degree of interaction between vocal and accompaniment; a supple, syncopated handling of rhythm; a frequent use of mixed meters, most generally an alternation between duple and treble meters; a similar frequency in the use of modal and scalar patterns in place of conventional harmony, and the like.

Forms

The most general form of the blues consists of a three-line verse set to twelve bars of music, each line consisting of four bars, organized by the following harmonic scheme: the first four bars are based on the tonic (I) chord; the second four are divided into two two-bar segments, the first on the subdominant (IV) chord, the second returning to the tonic; the final four bars are again divided, the first two bars on the dominant-seventh (V) chord, the third on the subdominant, returning to the tonic on the final bar of the verse. The most usual rhyme scheme, AAB, has the first line repeated with no or with very slight variation, while the third line offers either a complementary or contrasting thought that sets off the initial one. The sung portion generally takes up a little bit more than half of each four-bar line, the remainder completed by instrumental commentary in call-and-response fashion (possibly of African origin).

Simple, succinct, flexible, the blues form has been capable of supporting a wide variety and complexity of thought, and has been varied in any number of ways to accommodate whatever could not be conveniently expressed in the basic twelve-bar, I-IV-V format. It has served, with perfect utility and adaptability, for well more than a century and shows no sign of having outlived its usefulness.

There is every indication that a lively tradition of accompanied and unaccompanied lyric song and instrumental music very different from those of the older plantation culture of the Eastern Seaboard flourished over broad areas of the Deep South by the early years of the present century. From both the advanced level of its development and its wide geographic distribution there may be inferred an indeterminate period during which the blues was formed, developed, and disseminated. The mobility of large numbers of itinerant blacks, pursuing a variety of occupations (including that of performing music) in the rural South, as well as broad population shifts that took place among blacks in the post-Emancipation years, may possibly account for the distribution of the new musical genre over large areas of the South and into the North in a relatively short period of time.

The Guitar Emerges

With the genre went the guitar as well, the favored instrument of the blues. Until this period the guitar had been used largely as a parlor instrument for the accompaniment of sentimental and popular songs, but with the appearance of the blues it assumed a far more active and important role in black American folksong practice, eventually completely supplanting the banjo and, to a lesser degree, the fiddle, the two instruments that had dominated black folk mu-

sic until the blues emerged. (The fiddle in time was almost completely eclipsed by the smaller and less expensive harmonica, which took over many of the instrumental functions formerly assigned the fiddle in string bands and other small blues ensembles.)

Commercialization

The commercialization of the blues began in 1912 with W.C. Handy's publication of "Memphis Blues," an adaptation of a piece he had composed earlier for a Memphis mayoral campaign. It received further impetus through his publication of, among other works, "St. Louis Blues" and "Yellow Dog Rag" in 1914, "Joe Turner Blues" and "Hesitating Blues" in 1915, and "Beale Street Blues" in 1917. When the new genre was allied with the newly emergent instrumental jazz idiom – the vogue for which was initiated in 1917 with the first recordings of this music by the Original Dixieland Jazz Band – coupled with the phenomenal success of singer Mamie Smith's 1920 recording of "Crazy Blues" and the subsequent launching of what might be described as a blues recording industry, the genre's dominance was virtually assured. By the 1940s the blues had almost completely eradicated the older forms of black folksong in all but the most isolated of black communities.

Picking and Singing

The dominance of the genre inevitably led to the dominance of the guitar as well. The practice of using guitar for blues accompaniment seems to have been carried forward with the dissemination of the blues itself, and this pattern was picked up and given additional impetus by the recording of large numbers of country blues performers beginning in the mid-1920s. The impact of this development undoubtedly had the effect of intensifying an already strong tendency toward the use of the guitar and away from the older banjo and fiddle and the musical idioms they traditionally had been associated with, which were shouldered aside by the brash arrival of the blues and its running mate, the guitar.

While it is true that the focus of this survey centers on the role of the guitar in blues, it cannot be emphasized too strongly that the blues is first and foremost a vocal music. For the blues listener, songs and their interpretation by emotionally persuasive vocalists are far more important than the instrumental settings accompanying them. This has held true for the music's entire history. Then too, its themes invariably have dealt with the subject of greatest concern to its listeners: the pleasures and

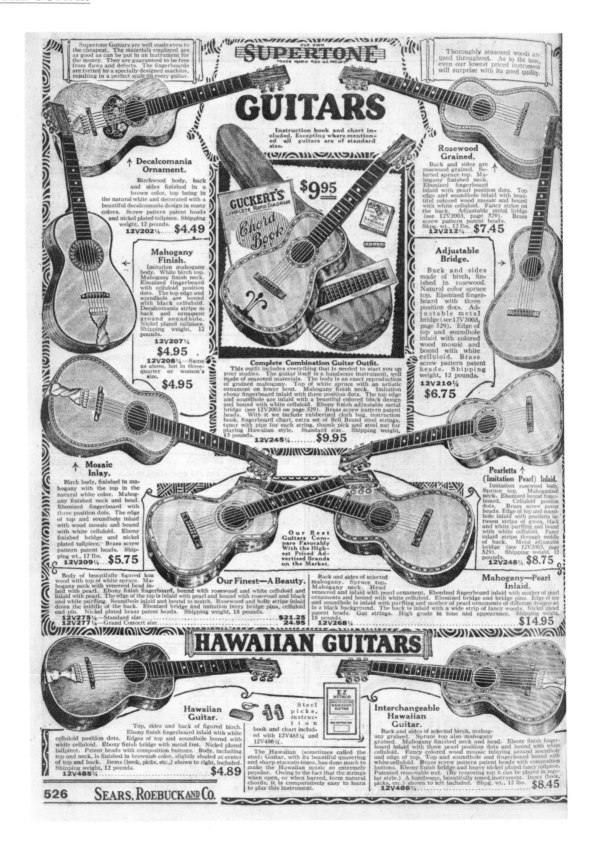

54

pains of physical love, the topic of virtually all popular song. Where the blues has differed from most popular love songs, however, is in the refreshing candor and directness with which it comments on the subject – realistically, honestly, frequently cynically – with little of the artificiality or sentimental attitudinizing so characteristic of traditional Anglo-American folksong, country music, or popular song. On the contrary, the blues has always sought to tell it like it is and, more than any other single influence, its hard-edged, gritty realism has had an incalculable, ongoing influence on all American music since its time. So, too, have the guitar styles developed for and by the blues.

Blues Musicianship

Like any folk artist, the blues performer is generally a self-taught musician who most often approaches the playing of a formal instrument – be it guitar, violin, mandolin, or piano – informally, with little or no awareness of the traditionally "correct" or accepted modes of playing it. Since he brings to his handling of the instrument no preconceptions of its supposed limitations, he often devises thoroughly new playing techniques, employs the instrument in ways it had not previously been used – in short, he treats it in unorthodox fashion. In a sense, each new blues musician learns the instrument anew and evolves his own pragmatic, highly personal approach, generally, however, he usually bases his musical style on those of such musicians in the vicinity who serve as his models and from whose more practiced handling of the instrument he comes to understand its capabilities and use within the local musical idiom.

Styles and Developments

While this has led, naturally, to a rich profusion of playing approaches, there are three main and distinct stylistic areas of blues and blues guitar playing. They may roughly be classified along regional lines as Mississippi-Deep South; Texas; and East Coast (ranging along the eastern seaboard from Florida to Maryland).

In the country blues, it must be remembered, the guitar is much more than a mere accompanying instrument that provides a rhythmic-harmonic foundation to support the voice. A blues performance is a complex, subtle totality in which the interaction of sung and played lines is complete, the guitar usually acting as responsive chorus to the voice, providing commentary on the sung text, taking over from the voice at the end of each sung phase, extending the thought and expression of the words, and often car-

Race records advertisement

rying much more meaning and emotional intensity than do the word themselves.

Since the guitar interacts so totally with the voice – is used as a second voice, in fact – the differences in the three areas of blues style are due not so much to the manner in which the guitar is used (primarily, at any rate) as to the way the voice is conceived and used in each of the three, with the instrument taking its lead from the vocal conception that is the convention in each of the three regions.

MISSISSIPPI – DEEP SOUTH BLUES STYLES

The blues style long associated with the later plantation culture of the lower South is not surprisingly – given the fact that the music undoubtedly developed there in the post-Emancipation years – the most archaic and "primitive" sounding of the three. Certainly the blues style of the area, as revealed in representative recordings from the late 1920s and early 1930s, is a rough, spontaneous, clamorous, of-

Son House

The singing is heavily rhythmic and generally confined to a relatively narrow melodic range that reflects its grounding in the older declamatory field cries. The oldest blues from this region offer the most rudimentary vocal expression, many of the songs qualifying as such in only the most limited sense: in that they are only slightly removed from speech patterns. The tone in which they are sung is, in writer Sam Charters's words, "forced through the clenched throat, as though the singer were forcing himself to speak. A phase becomes a choked growl; a deeply felt verse becomes a tightened falsetto."

Guitar Styles

In this music the guitar participates intimately in the emotional development and ranges from the intricate, pulsant rhythms of House and Patton, with the voice rushing over a reiterated rhythmic pattern and in which treble interjections "speak" at the end of sung phrases (House's "Preachin' The Blues" and any number of Patton's performances); through the only slightly expanded harmonic palette and varied rhythms of Brown ("Future Blues," "M&O Blues"), with the guitar developing moving bass lines against acid-etched figures in the treble; to the insistent thrumming cross-rhythms of Harris ("Bullfrog Blues") and Tommy Johnson (his anthemic "Big Road Blues," for one); the sad, wild, lonely sound of Skip James ("Hard Time Killin' Floor"), and on to the strange, free-associated cante-fables of Bukka White in which the guitar moves from unison figures below the voice to a repeated rhythmic motif at the end of the sung portion.

Charley Patton

The earliest blues from the Deep South of which we are aware are those of singer-guitarist Charley Patton, born in the central Mississippi town of Edwards circa 1887–1890 and hence at least a generation older than most of the early bluesmen to have recorded in the 1920s. As a teenager he moved to the huge Dockery Plantation in Sunflower County where he remained until 1929, when he started recording, influencing the next generation of Mississippi blues performers, House and Brown among them. Patton's guitar playing was strongly rhythmic in character, speech-inflected in fact, making extensive use of syncopations and interacting greatly with his vocal lines whose rhythms served as the basis for his accompaniments. On occasion his vocal instrumental lines were rhythmically independent of one another, producing complex cross-rhythms, as on his 1929 "Screamin' And Hollerin' The Blues,"

ten crude and unfinished one in which stark, unrelieved emotion takes precedence over coherently developed story lines. As performed by singers from this area, the songs are often fragmentary, their individual verses sometimes bound together by only the most tenuous of narrative ties and existing almost solely for the expression of strong, uncontrollable feelings that may be only vaguely hinted at in the actual words of a song. Often monosyllabic cries, humming, moaning, and other wordless ejaculations carry far greater "meaning" in this music than do the songs' words. The songs seem only a step from the wordless field-cries and hollers of an older generation.

Vocal Styles

In the region's preferred style – as exemplified in the work of such tradition-bearers as Charley Patton, Son House, Willie Brown, William Harris, and others – the voice is dark, heavy, often thick and congested, with a peculiar crying quality – the singer often sounds on the verge of tears as, for example, House on "Sun Goin' Down" – and suffused throughout with an emotional intensity that is all but overpowering, the words seemingly torn from the singer's throat.

among others. Most of his music was scalar rather than harmonic in character, using a gapped or broken scale similar to the pentatonic on almost two-thirds of his recordings, the diatonic scale on the remainder. In addition to standard tuning (E-A-D-G-B-E), which he played primarily in the keys of E and C, Patton also performed in several open-chord guitar tunings – most often open-G (D-G-D-G-B-D) for such pieces as "Screamin' And Hollerin' The Blues," "Banty Rooster Blues," "It Won't Be Long," "High Water Everywhere," and "Tom Rushen Blues," among a number of others, while open-E (E-B-E-A♭-B-E) was used on only a few of his recordings, most notably "Mississippi Boll Weavil Blues" and "A Spoonful Blues." He died in April, 1934, of mitral heart disease, the first great Mississippi bluesman.

His influence has been considerable. It was first and most vividly felt in the work of his chief students, Willie Brown (probably born in Tennessee circa 1890) and Eddie "Son" House (born Lyon, Mississippi, in 1902), both of whom offered contrasting, somewhat simplified versions of his approach. House actually had learned to play some four years before meeting Patton in 1930 but soon fell under the sway of his music, as did Brown in the early years of the century. House's recordings possess a grave, sober majesty that results from the steady, powerfully rhythmic manner with which his guitar underlines and punctuates his taut, gripping singing in a bottleneck style of perfect economy. Brown's and Patton's music provided Tommy Johnson (born Terry, Mississippi, around 1896, and raised in nearby Crystal Springs) much of the inspiration for his own much-imitated style which, like most Mississippi blues, was primarily rhythmic in character.

The Blues Recorded

Beginning in the mid-1920s and continuing almost uninterruptedly through the early 1940s, large numbers of country blues performers were recorded either in the permanent recording studios of large record firms in Chicago and New York City or in the mobile facilities they sent to such urban centers in the South as Memphis, Alanta, New Orleans, and the like. Through the latter, blues styles of specifically local origin and appeal were recorded and the resulting phonograph records shipped back to the localities that had produced them for sale there. This practice accounts for the wide diversity of country blues styles documented from 1924 on; recording directors of the period were indiscriminately receptive to anything and everything – the music, after all,

Charley Patton

was of relatively recent origin at the time and few if any guidelines had been established. The result was that a great deal of music was recorded, some of it inconsequential, much of it possessing the solid, enduring virtues of traditional expression, and a smaller portion exceptional for the strength, power, and originality of its handling of traditional forms and motifs. Virtually every performer of talent was given at least an initial opportunity to have his music recorded; if his records sold moderately well, he was invited to undertake additional recording. Thus large numbers of performers recorded but a handful of selections each, while a much smaller number of more popular or talented blues artists were recorded more extensively, producing in some cases dozens of recordings, and on occasion many more than that.

As a result of this activity, most of the important local blues traditions of the early folk blues were documented through the work of their representative practitioners, major and minor alike. In addition to the music and musicians of Mississippi – the so-called "cradle of the blues" – those of Alabama, Tennessee, Arkansas, Louisiana, Missouri, and western Georgia were sampled as well, with the result

From left to right:
Son House, Skip James, Mississippi John Hurt

that we have a fairly comprehensive cross-section of rural blues styles as they were practiced during the early decades of this century. Despite the presence of numerous local schools or traditions throughout the breadth of the lower South, there was a great similiarity to the blues of this large area, their common or shared elements far outweighing the differences resulting from local habit or preference. As has been noted earlier, the folk blues were primarily rhythmic in character, accompaniment patterns deriving chiefly from the sung cadences they supported. Much of the music was scalar or modal rather than harmonically ordered, and frequently the music was asymmetric in terms of structure, as the blues performer extended or abbreviated accompaniment patterns at will in the heat of performance, with the result that verses varied considerably from the twelve-bar norm.

Guitar as Accompaniment

Summarizing the characteristics of country blues accompaniment practices from this large area, folklorist David Evans has noted: "Blues instrumental accompaniments display many of the same characteristics as the vocal melodies, such as syncopation, blue notes, improvisational variations from one stanza to another, and the use of several strains or 'parts' in the same piece.... Blues instrumentalists use a variety of special effects and techniques not often employed in playing classical music. They may, for example, modify their instruments.... Guitarists may add extra strings or tap on the body or 'hammer' on the strings with their fingers. In general, playing tends to be percussive, and a 'dirty' tone is heard along with a clear one. Guitarists often use unorthodox or open tunings, and with the latter they may slide a knife or a bottleneck or piece of metal tubing worn over a finger of the left hand on the strings to create a whining effect. This slide technique makes it easy to play blue notes. They can also be played by 'choking' or bending the strings, and, on the harmonica, by 'bending' notes.

"Often a blues accompaniment does not consist of full chords played behind the singing but only the suggestion of the chords. The subdominant harmony in the fifth and sixth measures of a twelve-bar blues might be suggested by the inclusion of the fourth or sixth degree in a chord that is otherwise based on the tonic, and similarly for the dominant harmony. Sometimes there is no suggestion of chord changes and the harmony remains in the tonic chord throughout, or in some tunes a drone or ostinato is set up over which a single line is played. Many blues accompaniments, particularly those produced by only a single instrument, are not really 'harmonic' at all. Instead, only one note may be played at a time, and the harmonic feeling is created by arpeggios and other sequences or by occasional chords."

The Decline of Local Styles

These descriptive remarks apply to most of the country or folk blues from the lower South, including most such local blues styles. The latter tended to decline in influence as blues performers traveled widely and, as a result, were exposed to other regional styles, elements of which were then incorporated into their individual approaches. Then too, as performers started playing together in small ensembles – in string bands, jug bands, or small combos for dance, club, or outdoor playing engagements – local or idiosyncratic approaches necessarily had to give way to standarized formats, metrical and harmonic regularity, and agreed-upon structures. Furthermore, when rural-based blues performers clustered in cities, as they did in Memphis, Atlanta, Chicago, and elsewhere, individual regional styles eventually blurred into a more or less undifferentiated stylistic mass, the sum total or common denominator of all such local styles. There are, in fact, no specific local styles associated with these urban centers simply because there were so many blues performers, hailing from so many other localities, active in them at any given time.

It may be because regional differences were eradicated in the blues' tendency toward a much greater incidence of, and reliance upon structural uniformity and regularized performance practices in these cities that we view them as comprising local traditions of their own. Aside from the fact that there

Blind Willie McTell

were a fair number of twelve-string guitar players based in the Atlanta area during the 1920s and 1930s (Bob and Charlie Hicks, Blind Willie McTell, George Carter, and others), there would appear to be no real Atlanta style. Likewise, Memphis boasts no single overall approach to the music that might be described as a peculiarly Memphian school of blues beyond the fact that large numbers of musicians from the lower South, including many extremely talented local guitarists, made their way there in the hope of establishing their reputations and making more money from their music in the wider employment opportunities such cities boasted. Most of the important musicians one identifies with Memphis – Furry Lewis, Gus Cannon, Frank Stokes, Memphis Minnie Douglas, Joe and Charley McCoy, Robert Wilkins, Dan Sane, and many others – all hailed from Mississippi and arrived in the city with their playing styles already fully formed.

Leadbelly

Mance Lipscomb

TEXAS BLUES STYLES

It might well be, as some have claimed, that the Texas blues style is considerably older than that of the Mississippi-Deep South area. Such Texas blues performers as Blind Lemon Jefferson and Texas Alexander began to make recordings about the same time as did the earliest Mississippi singers, yet the work of the Texas singers had by this time already been refined considerably. Though the Texas blues style was powerful and direct, it was not crude or unfinished in the same manner as was the Mississippi style. On the contrary, it was highly sophisticated in comparison with the far rougher approach favored by Delta performers.

Characteristics

Even such singers as Henry "Ragtime" Thomas and Huddie Ledbetter, who performed in the older Texas country styles, worked in a manner that was considerably more deliberate and sophisticated than that of the country bluesmen of the lower South. The melodic line was more supple and was sung in a higher, clearer voice, employing an appropriately lighter, more sinuous accompaniment than the harsher styles of the Mississippi Delta and surrounding environs. The Texas blues performers who succeeded them – Jefferson, Alexander, and others – sang in a high, arching voice in a style that was

pared to the bone, stripping away all trace of the nonessential, leaving only the bare emotional skeleton. In David Evans's characterization, it has "a good bit of the 'moaning and droning'" of the Mississippi-Deep South blues approaches, "but it is less percussive and has a lighter emphasis on individual notes. The melodies and sometimes the instrumental parts are more embellished than they are in the stark Delta style."

In this approach the guitar took over in a series of melodic extensions and variations, often of great brilliance and inventiveness, at the completion of the sung phrases, while it generated relatively simple, free rhythmic patterns behind the singing. An instance of the intrinsic musicality and relative sophistication of the Texas musical traditions is currently afforded in the beautifully detailed singing and playing of Navasota songster Mance Lipscomb, whose stunning work in the older Texas folksong traditions has been documented in a number of recordings made following his discovery two decades ago. In his strong, vigorous music Lipscomb has brought to life the broad range of black folk music traditions that flourished in Texas in the early years of this century (Lipscomb was born in 1895), of which the blues is merely one part, and which largely had gone by the board as a result of the one-sided

Lightnin' Hopkins

emphasis on the blues after recordings created a vogue for the genre in the 1920s. (Singer-guitarist Elizabeth Cotten also represents an aspect of this broad "songster" tradition – encompassing a wide spectrum of pre-blues black folksong forms and practices – as do the Georgia-born one-man band Jesse Fuller, Maryland singer-twelve-string guitarist Bill Jackson, and Virginia's John Jackson, all of whom have been recorded during the course of the last quarter-century.)

Recent Performers

In recent times the natural heir of the Texas blues style has been Houston's Sam "Lightnin' " Hopkins, in whose strikingly individual playing and singing can be heard the same lean, open, long-lined sound that coursed through the older recordings of his cousin Texas Alexander, with their sensitive Lonnie Johnson accompaniments. Born in Centreville, Texas, on March 15, 1912, Hopkins recorded so extensively, though rarely at the expense of genuine emotional depth, that he, for all practical purposes, has represented the blues style of his native state for many current listeners. An extraordinary gifted singer and guitarist with a personal style whose work is throughly rooted in tradition, Hopkins was

singularly successful in bridging the demands of popular recording and the folk music audience he addressed in the latter decades of his life, unmatched perhaps by any other blues artist of recent times.

Other contemporary Texas blues performers have included singer-guitarist Lowell Fulson, who most often works as a latter day urban rhythm-and-blues performer, as do Clarence "Gatemouth" Brown, equally proficient on guitar and violin, and Albert Collins; singer-guitarist Melvin "Lil' Son" Jackson; and singer-pianist Robert Shaw. The Texas blues traditions, which also include those of nearby Oklahoma, still remain the least-investigated of all regional blues styles, although Paul Oliver and Houston playwright-folklorist Mack McCormick have been engaged in the arduous work of formulating an approach to the state's black music traditions.

EAST COAST BLUES STYLES

Through the 1930s and the early years of World War II, the characteristic sound of the blues was the bright, brassy exuberance of the city blues that were ground out by the hundreds, if not thousands, primarily in Chicago, which early had been established

Columbia *New Process* Records

"PEG LEG" HOWELL

WHEN "Peg Leg" Howell lost his leg, the world gained a great singer of blues. The loss of a leg never bothered "Peg Leg" as far as chasing around after blues is concerned. He sure catches them and then stomps all over them.

Nobody ever knows just what will happen next when "Peg Leg" Howell is let loose with a guitar, but it always is sure to be good.

"Peg Leg" Howell is an Exclusive Columbia Artist

NEW JELLY ROLL BLUES—*Accompanied by His Gang*	14210-D	75c
BEAVER SLIDE RAG—*Accompanied by His Gang*		
TISHAMINGO BLUES	14194-D	75c
COAL MAN BLUES		
NEW PRISON BLUES	14177-D	75c
FO' DAY BLUES		

Peg Leg Howell

as *the* important center of blues recording activity. The sound was an outgrowth of the third major style of blues, that associated with the East Coast. "In the East Coast and Piedmont area of Georgia and the Carolinas the blues are better documented," Evans has noted, "but in Florida, Virginia, and Maryland recording activity and research have been less extensive. The East Coast blues style is the lightest of all in emphasis. It shows a slight influence from white folk music and a heavy one from ragtime. The blues scene in this region seems to have been dominated by an elite group of blind and otherwise handicapped professional musicians, who have emphasized great instrumental virtuosity at the expense of some of the intensity found in Delta and Texas styles."

Characteristics

The music from this broad geographic area is essentially quite melodic, with a sweet, consonant sound, the overall feeling one of smoothness and richness. The style drew together a number of strains in black music. At the roots were the minstrel tradition (basically a white burlesque of black musical style that had, in turn, gone back into, and nourished black tradition itself) and ragtime, with not a little influence from Anglo-American folksong and coun-

try music. These were brought to bear on the blues forms that were developing around the period of Emancipation and, as a result of their more extensive grounding in European music, attained to a higher degree of musical sophistication – in the areas of melody and harmony, at any rate, the rhythmic element lagging behind – than did the more "African" or primitive styles to the west, in the Mississippi Delta and the Texas-Oklahoma territories.

If the East Coast way of guitar playing was characterized by a high degree of organization and structural uniformity, occasionally attaining to a simple contrapuntal style in the pitting of bass figures against melodic statements in the treble, for example, it often achieved this complexity at the expense of spontaneity and emotional intensity. Of necessity, the playing style had to be much more strictly regularized to facilitate the broadened melodic and harmonic refinements so typical of the region's approach to blues and other black folksong.

Outstanding Performers

Naturally, the term "East Coast Blues" is, as are the other two designations used here, an oversimplification of what was a bewildering complex of widely varying styles. The term can indicate only a few of the qualities that bind together – in theory, if nowhere else – such oddly disparate stylists as Tampa Red, Blind Blake, Peg Leg Howell, Blind Boy Fuller, Bill Jackson, Blind Willie McTell, Pink Anderson, Brownie McGhee, and a host of other performers. Within the East Coast blues category the stylistic range is particularly broad, extending from the roughest country styles (Georgia's Peg Leg Howell or Charlie Jackson) through the beautifully balanced playing of Blake and Tampa Red, and on to the most fully ordered and finely wrought, almost architectonic of approaches that borrow greatly from white country music disciplines. "East Coast Blues" can indicate only the broadest outlines of a discipline; seeking a common denominator it discounts all the nuances of expression, the idiosyncracies of technique, the very qualities in fact that distinguish the work of one blues performer from that of another and make the blues the highly personal, exciting music it so manifestly is and has been.

Nor do such terms and distinctions take into account the stylistic mavericks – like Mississippi John Hurt whose gentle singing and intricate guitar playing sound nothing like those of the typical Mississippi Delta bluesman, whose music is in fact so far removed from ideas of "influence," tradition, or regional style as to seem the product of a totally different world. And there are any number of musicians, like Hurt, who can be instanced as constituting exceptions to these generalizations. As Evans points out, "Peg Leg Howell, Barbecue Bob [Robert Hicks], and Charlie Lincoln [i.e., Charlie Hicks] are a good deal rougher than most other East Coast performers; and musicians as varied as Henry Thomas, Blind Lemon Jefferson, J.T. Smith, and Smokey Hogg hardly give a very firm basis for positing a homogeneous Texas style. Perhaps the rambling life-style of many blues singers explains some of these exceptions. Traveling blues singers pick up and leave songs and musical ideas wherever they go. Other blues singers are highly individualistic performers for reasons of their own."

Then, too, one must bear in mind that distinctions between regional approaches were blurred considerably when the mass media began to poke into every nook and cranny of the land. Records, radio, films, and later television – all have exerted a tremendous and far-reaching effect on our nation's folk musics, and the oral traditions that once shaped a region's peculiar musical style have now given way to "aural" traditions and a cultural homogeneity. Acculturation proceeds at an alarmingly swift pace, and the folk performer of modern times, thanks to recordings, radio, and so forth, can select his source models from anywhere and everywhere, like B.B. King has, and will not be bound by such considerations as the prevailing musical style of his immediate environment.

THE BLUES ORIGINALS
Then there are the originals, those greatly talented, individualistic performers whose innovations stretch the music's traditions, lead it in new directions and otherwise initiate new growth and development. These are the performers who leave their mark on the music, keep it vital and relevant, and influence other players. The blues has had its share of them, and has been by far the richer for their presence: Blind Lemon Jefferson, Lonnie Johnson, Big Bill Broonzy, Robert Johnson, T-Bone Walker, Muddy Waters, B.B. King, and a handful of others.

Blind Lemon Jefferson
One of the very earliest country-based performers to be recorded, Blind Lemon Jefferson, along with guitar virtuoso Lonnie Johnson, was probably the most widely influential blues artist of the late 1920s.

Sonny Boy Williamson performed on the King Biscuit Time *radio show*

Through the example of his stunning musicianship and deeply affecting singing, he undoubtedly paved the way for Leroy Carr and Scrapper Blackwell, Big Bill Broonzy, the urbane city blues of the 1930s – the so-called "Bluebird beat," T-Bone Walker and, by extension, the modern electric blues of B.B. King and his emulators. Jefferson saturated, as well, the blues traditions of his native state, as is readily apparent in the work of Texas Alexander, Smokey Hogg, Lil' Son Jackson, Lightnin' Hopkins, and scores of others.

Born in 1897 near Couchman, Texas, youngest of seven children born to farmer Alec Jefferson and his wife Classie, he was blind from birth. Music being one of the few livelihoods then available to a sightless black, Lemon began singing and playing guitar as an adolescent, undoubtedly following the customary practice of learning from older performers in the area, and thus acquiring its local song traditions as well. In the years before World War I, perhaps as early as 1911 or 1912, he was reported performing for rough-and-tumble dances and all-night parties in nearby Wortham, Texas. By the age of twenty, after some years of making music for the various social functions that punctuated the Texas farm year, Jefferson moved to Dallas, where music jobs were more plentiful. During ten years in Dallas, it

Blind Lemon Jefferson

rhythms. Direct exposure to a wide sampling of regional blues styles probably accounts for much of the distinctiveness of Jefferson's music, which is totally unlike that of any other Texas bluesman of the period. Beginning to record in 1926, he was also the first to achieve any kind of broad commercial success with this strong, unadulterated country-derived style, which ran counter to the prevailing theatrical sound of the female jazz-blues singers so popular at the time. Several of his Paramount recordings reportedly were among the most widely sold blues discs of the late 1920s.

The finely detailed self-accompaniments to which his high, arching vocals were so perfectly set bespeak an astonishing musical sophistication and sensitivity for a self-taught player. The conceptual richness of the vocal-instrumental interaction, the great fluency with which intricate instrumental passages were executed, the strongly improvisatory character of many of the accompaniments – all demonstrate a thoroughgoing mastery of the guitar that had to be the hard-won result of endless hours of practice. Jefferson's accompaniments are marvels of invention, light in touch and brilliant in conception and execution. And incredibly varied, too. They are not so much responses to the vocal phrases – the more or less standard blues guitar role – as interdependent lines with a complementary motion of their own, quite like the harpsichord or lute continuos to which much baroque vocal music was set.

A further great strength of Jefferson's music lies in the powerful imagery of his lyrics. Sometimes he makes use of some of the great body of "floating" verses and lyric motifs drawn upon by virtually all traditional blues singers, but on the whole there is a vast amount of superior, moving folk poetry, ranging from almost wholly traditional to highly individualized expression, in the lyrics to his songs. Such of them as "Rabbit Foot Blues," "See That My Grave Is Kept Clean" and "Match Box Blues" have been associated with him ever since he recorded them. Others, like the prison songs – "Hangman's Blues," "Blind Lemon's Penitentiary Blues," "Prison Cell Blues," and so on – are broadly based in traditional expression yet bear Jefferson's unmistakeable touches throughout. This is true even of pieces such as "That Black Snake Moan" or "Rising High Water Blues," which were modeled on the successful recordings of others.

Jefferson's finely-wrought, intricate and, above all, highly original way with traditional blues exert-

was much the same – a tough, harsh, uncertain life, but the only one he knew. He drew a reasonable living from his music: he married, started a family, even bought a car and hired a driver to take him around to his engagements. It must have been during these years of performing – often from sundown to sunrise, at back-country dances and parties, in lumber and levee camp barrelhouses, in the rough Dallas brothels, where Leadbelly has said they worked as a team – that he acquired his incredibly broad range of song materials, from simple chantlike songs not much removed from field hollers and worksongs, through ballads and prison songs, to the richly detailed, introspective blues for which he is most noted.

Then too, Jefferson traveled widely, which may help explain the diversity of his music. Several Memphis blues performers, Robert Wilkins among them, have reported hearing him there in the 1920s, and Jefferson also has been reported as having been in Alabama, Georgia, parts of the Eastern Seaboard and, more important to his musical development, the Mississippi Delta region. The impress of the music of this region is quite clear in Lemon's guitar work, particularly in his use of mixed-meter ed a strong impact on black musicians of the time. One has only to listen to the recordings of other, more representative bluesmen of his day to come to a speedy recognition of Blind Lemon's undisputed mastery of blues form and his all but astonishing musical sensibility. They must have staggered listeners accustomed to the more modest ways of local bluesmen. Bristling with ideas of great originality and intricacy, densely packed with newly minted phrases, lines and figures, Jefferson's recordings became objects for the closest study. There is scarcely a blues veteran alive, major or minor, who has not acknowledged his debt to Jefferson, remarking either on the striking character of his instrumental work or on the high quality of his songs, many of which have become staples of the blues repertoire since he first recorded them.

From the start Blind Lemon Jefferson was his own man, and he remained recognizably so throughout his recording career, 1926-1930 (he died in Chicago, possibly of heart failure or overexertion, the latter year). Once having heard his music, you'll always recognize it. And that can be said of too few blues performers. On the evidence of the more than eighty recordings he left as his legacy, the Texas singer-guitarist must be considered one of the preeminent artists of black American music, a spellbindingly original interpreter of traditional country blues, and one of the most influential shapers of its traditions. His music endures.

Lonnie Johnson

Along with Jefferson, Broonzy, and Blind Blake, Lonnie Johnson was one of the first blues guitarists to achieve commercial success, and it was their success that greatly contributed to, if it did not create, the commercial demand for country blues. Born in New Orleans, probably on February 8, 1894, and raised in a musical household, Johnson had mastered violin before taking up the guitar in 1917, and in fact had had a successful career as a jazz and blues violinist both in New Orleans and St. Louis, where he performed in cornetist Charlie Creath's band on the riverboats that plied the Mississippi River. Winning a talent contest at the Booker T. Washington Theater in 1925 led to Johnson's being awarded a recording contract with OKeh Records, and throughout the following year he produced an average of two selections a month.

"His activities and achievements over the next fifteen years or so were staggering," observed blues commentator Larry Cohn. "He recorded as a blues artist, becoming one of the most successful and prolific of all time, was active on the black vaudeville circuit (T.O.B.A.), the Keith circuit (accompanying comedians), married Mary Johnson (nee Smith), a fine blues singer and composer in her own right, was recording accompanist to artists such as Martha Raye, Texas Alexander, Victoria Spivey, Clara Smith, and many, many more. He recorded with Louis Armstrong, Duke Ellington, and The Chocolate Dandies, recorded monumental blues duets with Eddie Lang, unequalled in excellence to this day, toured with Bessie Smith in her show 'The Midnight Steppers,' had his own radio show in New York City, worked with jazz figures such as Putney Dandridge, Johnny and Baby Dodds, and seemed to virtually live in recording studios. Obviously a tireless artist and performer, it was a rare situation indeed where his presence did not enhance what was being undertaken. His own recording activities were prolific and he recorded hundreds of sides as a blues artist, being without doubt one of the most commercially successful blues artists to have ever attacked the idiom."

Unlike Jefferson or Broonzy, however, Johnson had no background in the country blues, or in ragtime either, although he certainly had been exposed to both. Raised in New Orleans, he grew up hearing (and later performing) that city's rich fund of music and it is as a result of this that his blues playing was as melodically fertile and harmonically knowing as it was. The deep resources of imagination and creativity that marked his playing – whether linear, chorded, chord-supported linear, or any combination of the three – were solely the product of his genius and had not been anticipated in the work of any other blues or jazz guitarists of the time. "His instrumental duets with the white jazzman Eddie Lang," observed blues historian Don Kent, "set a standard of musicianship that remains unsurpassed by blues guitarists. In Johnson's single-string vibrato style lie the basic precedents of such jazz greats as Django Reinhardt and Charlie Christian, while B.B. King readily acknowledges Johnson's influence on his style. Thus Johnson enjoys the double distinction of having influenced musicians who themselves became enormously influential in the field of guitar-playing."

"In retrospect," Kent concluded, "Johnson had an unusual recording career; he had no real signature songs and recorded only a few standard or traditional tunes (like "Careless Love"). Instead, he had a

Lonnie Johnson

fund of basic arrangements that he was able to adapt to several keys; for this reason it is often difficult to determine the keys of his non-chordal performances. On some he may be playing in the key of D and capoing to E^b, or playing in the key of E (his favorite) and tuning half a step lower. Even within a single key or arrangement, he manages to attain so many variations in tone and accenting that his riffs are rarely predictable. He was doubly fortunate in possessing – as Broonzy and most other blues guitarists did not – a superb concert guitar that was responsive to all his tonal nuances; on some sessions he probably used a Bay State model. Historically, Johnson is noted for his flat-picking approach. It is possible that before he began recording most bluesmen only used a flatpick to play backing bass guitar. In the realm of popular entertainment, the only flatpicking guitar soloist to precede him was Nick Lucas. Yet it is said that Johnson originally fingerpicked many of his accompaniments, and was able to produce the same results."

Although his career was a long and productive one, with Johnson partipating in literally hundreds of recording sessions on his own or backing other performers, extending from 1925 up until the time of his death in Toronto, Canada, on June 6, 1970, the guitarist's most important activities, contributions,

and influences were exerted in the period 1925-41. In his brilliantly original work from this period he completely altered blues guitar, helped to initiate jazz guitar, influenced countless musicians in both idioms, and set in motion a number of strains that were to have far-reaching consequences in American music. He has been characterized as "the first jazz guitarist who could solo in an articulate manner, comparable to performers on other instruments of jazz," an accomplishment that stems from "early musical training on the violin" which, "combined with his special natural music talents made him aware of the single-note capabilities of the guitar as a solo voice."

Big Bill Broonzy

Big Bill Broonzy was born William Lee Conley Broonzy in 1898 (or 1893) in the Mississippi Delta town of Scott, one of seventeen children born to his former slave parents. Raised there and in Arkansas, where his parents worked as sharecroppers (and he with them), Broonzy was drawn to music early, inspired by a musician-uncle who taught him to play fiddle, mandolin, and guitar, and taught him many songs as well. By fourteen he was already performing at "two-way" – i.e., segregated black and white – picnics and other rural entertainments. Following army service during World War I, he settled in Chicago which then supported a huge, bustling music scene. There he fell under the influence of popular blues guitarist Papa Charlie Jackson who added considerably to Broonzy's arsenal of guitar technique.

Following several years of activity there, his reputation steadily growing, Broonzy first entered the recording studios in 1927 to cut a quartet of guitar-accompanied country blues. These were never issued, but the singer returned in November of that year and February of the following to redo two of them as well as two additional sides for Paramount Records, all of which were released. Beginning in 1930, however, his recording career stepped up markedly with a batch of performances for the Perfect, Gennett, and Champion labels, many of which were issued, for reasons best known to the record companies, under various pseudonymns.

While the bulk of these early to mid-1930s Broonzy efforts are in his highly personalized extensions of rural-based ragtime and blues styles, a number of them reflect the then-current vogue for the double-entendre blues popularized by such as Georgia Tom and Tampa Red, Bo Carter, Ethel Waters, and a host of others. These early solo pieces

Big Bill Broonzy

and two-guitar or guitar-and-piano duets established Broonzy's preeminence as a blues instrumentalist and eventually led to his position as one of the leading studio musicians of the late 1930s and 1940s blues recording scene.

Broonzy's mastery of country blues is evidenced in any number of his recordings. His 1928 "Starvation Blues," for example, is a stark catalogue of the misfortunes of the disenfranchised black in the postwar economic depression. Over a somber and relatively simple country-styled guitar accompaniment Broonzy chants the grim lyrics with deep feeling and power, producing a mood of overwhelming desperation. If this telling performance is very much within the contours of typical rural blues of the period, the solo performance "Long Tall Mama," recorded a scant four years later, demonstrates the great strides he had made in evolving a personal, virtuosic guitar style. Broonzy's refinement and extension of basic country blues accompaniment style, as demonstrated by this and other performances, was one of great subtlety and imaginativeness, harmonically and rhythmically suggestive, and of a surpassing musicality. In its complexity and richness of detail the approach can be compared only to that of Blind Lemon Jefferson, the only other blues stylist of the period to have developed a musical approach of such commanding, but never obtrusive, virtuosity.

This essentially orchestral approach is set forth in other Broonzy recordings of the 1930s: the two eight-bar blues "Banker's Blues" and "Mississippi River Blues;" the brilliant "Saturday Night Rub," which conjures up images of Chicago house-rent parties; "Stove Pipe Stomp," and several performances on which he uses plectrum, notably "I Can't Be Satisfied" and "How You Want It Done?," astonishing displays of instrumental virtuosity in which the fullness and harmonic implications of Broonzy's rapidly articulated linear playing suggest that of a keyboard continuo.

This uncommon instrumental fluency undoubtedly was the result of Broonzy's mastery of the conventions of ragtime playing, which placed a premium on musical complexity, and this facet of his skills is laid out in fine order on such pieces as the 1930 solo "Skoodle Do Do" and the duets from the same year, the astonishing "Pig Meat Strut" (with Frank Brasswell) and "Brownskin Shuffle" (with Steele Smith), and other recordings on which he appears as accompanist, two fine examples being Tampa Red's 1929 "Eagle Ridin' Papa" and singer Jane Lucas's 1930 "Hokum Stomp," which also boasts Georgia Tom Dorsey's rock-ribbed piano in addition to the guitarist's insinuating, inventive lead playing.

In the early 1930s Broonzy recorded a number of the most intricate and well-executed guitar duets ever recorded in a ragtime vein, some compelling examples of country blues guitar as well, and also large numbers of the then popular double-entendre hokum songs. "The primary difference between the hokum and ragtime sides," noted blues researcher Kip Lornell, "is that on the ragtime sides the emphasis is on the musicianship and not the verbal antics. Admittedly, the instrumentation is quite the same and, overall, the tone is similar."

"During the 1930s, Bill's influence was felt by virtually all who came into contact with him," Larry Cohn has written. "He was the major participant in hundreds of recording sessions. In many sessions he was the major performer, and at other times he was the organizing force behind the session of another individual and took part as assisting artist. Nevertheless, whatever his status was each time, his overwhelming influence was always felt, and his most individual stamp and qualities are obvious on recordings much too numerous to mention. Respected as an outstanding guitarist, his talent for writing songs was no less imposing. A prolific composer, he was responsible for perhaps more than 300 compositions during his lifetime, including the blues standard "Key To The Highway," generally credited to mouth-harp player and singer Jazz Gillum.... In addition, his human warmth, charisma and general gregariousness made a distinct and lasting impression upon all who came into contact with him."

Broonzy continued to record through the 1930s, 1940s, and on into the 1950s, but by the latter years had remolded himself into a "folksinger," the main thrust of blues during the period having moved to the electrically amplied small ensemble approach of the post-World War II period, to which he was unable to accomodate himself. In 1957 he became extremely ill and had to undergo a serious operation for cancer, one of the more unfortunate results of which was that he was no longer able to sing. Following the operation he continued to play guitar for as long as he was physically able to do so, but his health rapidly deteriorated. His death came on August 14, 1958.

Other Guitarists

Other respected and influential guitarists of the late

1920s and early 1930s include Francis "Scrapper" Blackwell, born is Syracuse, North Carolina, in 1903, but a longtime resident of Indianapolis, whose brilliant, long-lined, primarily linear inventions in support of popular singer-pianist-composer Leroy Carr, with whom he performed until the latter's death in 1935, were widely admired for their harmonic sophistication, melodic daring, and perfectly controlled articulation; Memphis-based guitarist-singers Frank Stokes and Dan Sane, who recorded a number of poised, beautifully balanced country blues duets that were notable for the stunning interaction of their complementary parts no less than their deliberate, understated emotional power; similarly, Mississippi-born Memphis Minnie Douglas's solo performances and duets with Joe McCoy and, later, Ernest Lawler revealed an original, modestly inventive handling of the conventions of country blues that was not only popular with record buyers but which prefigured later developments; other admired players include Josh White, Tampa Red (Hudson Whittaker, of whom more anon), Carl Martin, Billy Byrd, William Moore, and a host of others.

RAGTIME

As noted earlier, the East Coast blues styles evolved under the heavy influence of ragtime, and featured a highly musical approach that placed a premium on musicianship. Unlike most Delta or Texas blues, it was harmonically oriented (even to the extensive use of passing chords), and was marked by an easy, infectiously lilting swing. The two chief and, hence, most influential representatives of this school of blues guitarists were both blind musicians, Blind Blake and Blind Boy Fuller, both of whom recorded fairly extensively.

Described by one knowledgeable enthusiast as the best ragtime guitarist to have recorded, Arthur Blake possibly hailed from Jacksonville, Florida, but, in any event, apparently traveled widely before settling in Chicago in 1926 and recording for Paramount Records until 1932, when he dropped from sight. With Blind Lemon Jefferson and Ma Rainey, Blake was one of the label's most successful blues artists, his records reportedly selling well right up until the onset of the Depression. Most of the performances from his early recording days were either fast ragtime instrumentals, generally played in the key of C ("West Coast Blues" and "Seaboard Stomp," for example), medium-tempoed ragtime songs, like "Too Tight," played in the key of G, or slow blues in

these two keys ("Early Morning Blues," "Stonewall Street Blues," and "No Dough Blues," in C, and "Panther Squall" and "Hard Road Blues" in G). Over the next few years he began to vary his music somewhat, primarily in the area of rhythmic accenting, playing in additional keys, and on occasion demonstrating great fluency in rapidly-articulated single-string playing, as, for example, his stunning linear work on the mid-1929 duets with pianist Alex Robinson, "Hookworm Blues" and "Slippery Rag."

Blind Boy Fuller

Blakes's music figured prominently in that of Blind Boy Fuller, born Fulton Allen in Milledgeville, North Carolina, in 1903. He took up guitar after his family had moved to Rockingham, North Carolina, demonstrating phenomenal instrumental prowess at an early age and performing at country suppers, dances and other rude affairs in the tobacco country, "busting" music on the streets of such cities as Charlotte and Durham, where he eventually settled. There he acquired a "lead boy," George Washington, who was known as Bull City Red, whom he taught to play guitar and who also played washboard. Others of his musical associates included singer-guitarist Blind Gary Davis and sightless harmonica player Sanders Terrell (Sonny Terry). Fuller began recording in 1935 and over the next half-dozen years recorded some 135 titles on his steel-bodied resonator guitar before an infected bladder put an end to his musical career, and death claimed him on February 13, 1941.

"Fuller's outstanding playing and his capacity for attracting superior musicians to his side ...and the great success of his records ensured him continual employment in the last half dozen years of his life," Paul Oliver has observed. "He played in Burlington, Raleigh, Greensboro, and way over in Memphis, attracting crowds wherever he appeared. Fuller's combination of country dances, rags and blues appealed to the hill-dwelling Negroes of the Carolinas and Tennessee, and his earthy vitality made him immensely popular. He could be both poetic and tough in his blues, as "Pistol Slapper" exemplifies, and he had a deep respect for tradition, as such blues as "Careless Love" and "Red River Blues" evidence. Some of his blues were unashamedly sexual in their content but he was never a salacious party singer; there was no need for a singer and musician of his caliber to attempt to win over audiences by shallow suggestiveness: "Rattlesnakin' Daddy" is a proud statement of his prowess."

If there has been a Carolina blues style, it is simply Fuller's ragtime-based blues approach, which has been carried forward in the music of his associates and disciples: Gary Davis, Brownie MsGhee, Floyd Council, Welly Trice, Ed Harris, Sonny Jones, Ralph Willis, and to an extent Buddy Moss, Curley Weaver, Fred McMullen, and Dan Pickett, among others.

SLIDE GUITAR

One of the more interesting new guitar techniques the blues performer has developed has been described as slide or bottleneck guitar. In this technique a knife, bottleneck, or length of metal tubing is moved along the strings of the guitar which, when struck, produce a whining sound similar to that of Hawaiian guitar or the steel guitar of modern country music. A striking example of the blues musician's unconventional handling of a conventional instrument, slide, or bottleneck playing has been a feature of country blues for as long as the music has been documented. It was so widely used in the blues of Mississippi and Georgia, for example, that the technique has taken any number of forms, from purely percussive to melodically decorative, often being used in conjunction with the voice, which it can imitate with uncanny accuracy and which it underscores, replies to, or both. At one time or another it has been used by virtually every guitarist of the Deep South, and some have developed a phenomenal aptitude with it – Son House, for example, Tampa Red, Rambling Thomas, Bukka White, Kokomo Arnold, Fred McDowell, Oscar Woods, Bo Weavil Jackson, Casey Bill Weldon, Robert Johnson, and many others. Such a listing of performers also suggests another interesting feature of slide guitar: that there is, in Stephen Calt's words, "no definitive bottleneck style or sound, or even a regional bottleneck style, only expert guitarists who exploit its possibilities in their own ways."

Tampa Red

The two most influential of these have been Tampa Red and Robert Johnson, each of whom has had a staggering impact on the course of bottleneck guitar. Tampa Red represents what might be described as the major urban approach to the idiom for, following his late 1920s recordings of hokum and other novelty blues material with pianist-composer Georgia Tom (Dorsey), the guitarist became one of the most successful commercial blues performers of the next two decades, performing in the urbane,

Tampa Red

regularized blues style associated with the recording studios of Chicago and influencing large numbers of performers who followed in his wake.

Born Hudson Woodbridge in Smithville, Georgia, on December 25 or January 8, 1900, 1903, 1904, or 1908 (at various times he cited all four dates as his birthdate), he was raised in Tampa, Florida by his grandparents, whose surname Whittaker he has used ever since. He learned guitar early, initially taught by his older brother Eddie and a local player named Piccolo Pete, but the development of the slide guitar style for which he is best known was his own brilliant adaptation to blues of the Hawaiian steel guitar music that was in vogue when he was a young musician. It is the influence of this music that probably accounts for the smooth, melodic, relatively sophisticated character of Tampa's handling of slide, which is quite different in most important respects from the conventional bottleneck approaches used in the country blues of the Deep South.

He traveled widely through the lower South in the 1920s and 1930s, meeting and performing with many other blues artists, but had already settled in Chicago as a teenager. In 1925 he met Tom Dorsey and within a few years they had become one of the best-known black recording teams of the late 1920s. Initially they backed such performers as Ma Rainey, but in 1928 scored a huge success with their recording of Dorsey's mildly salacious "Tight Like That," which became one of the most phenomenally popular recordings of the time, triggered a vogue for double-entendre blues, and made them into race record stars. Even after Dorsey's religious conversion a few years later and his subsequent involvement in the then-new Gospel song movement, Tampa's star shone brightly, and his recording and live performing continued unabated for more than two decades during which he remained one of the music's foremost figures – a fine singer, a versatile and prolific songwriter, and the most accomplished player of slide guitar the music ever has seen.

Despite his preference for the open-E tuning favored by many country blues guitarists, Tampa's handling of slide guitar was notable for the uncommon fluency and accuracy – even at the fastest of tempos – of his use of the slide, in his case a small glass bottleneck worn on the little finger of his left (or fretting) hand, as well as the great imaginative fertility of the single-string melodic phrases, riffs, and solos he created with such apparent ease over the standard harmonic blues base. Closely allied with his clean, fluent execution was a tone of warm liquidity, though somewhat nasal in character, produced as it was by a steel-bodied instrument employing an acoustic resonator, as well as a dextrous, interesting uses of bass notes that he inserted into the melodic flow at appropriate, though not always predictable or regular intervals. Elegant, supple, with a subdued legacy from ragtime, Tampa Red's was the first bottleneck guitar style of broad popular appeal, and it was widely imitated in succeeding years, most successfully by Robert Nighthawk and Earl Hooker, among many others. Tampa easily outstripped in popularity and influence such accomplished players as James "Kokomo" Arnold (born in Lovejoys Station, Georgia, in 1901) or "Casey Bill" Weldon (born in Pine Bluff, Arkansas, in 1909), both of whom demonstrated great fluency with the slide, although each of their approaches was much too unconventional or idiosyncratic (Arnold fast, loud, raucous, and rhythmically erratic, Weldon perhaps too sophisticated, too influenced by Hawaiian steel guitarists) to exert much in the way of influence on

other players as Tampa did. Arnold is best remembered for his songs "Old Original Kokomo Blues" and "Milk Cow Blues," a double-sided 1934 hit recording, and Weldon for his 1936 "We Gonna Move To the Outskirts of Town," among others of their compositions.

The Bluebird Beat

Along with other, much-recorded blues artists of the late 1920s and early 1930s, Tampa Red, Arnold, and Weldon were instrumental in making the blues into a music of wide popularity with black audiences of the time and, through the influence of their recordings, regularizing the music to such a degree that in a relatively brief time most regional differences tended to blur. For the blues the 1930s were a time of consolidation and retrenchment; the lessons of the earlier decade had been learned, local styles of limited sales potential discarded, the idiom's "stars" discovered and extensively recorded, and a blues recording apparatus established in Chicago from which proceeded, in almost assembly-line fashion, most of the blues dispensed by the commercial record industry. Using a cadre of dependable, versatile composers and instrumentalists, the Chicago studio-produced blues of the period were notable for their consistency and competence. The professional standards of such productions were uniformly high, and many of the records so produced were excellent by any criteria, as were the songs themselves, a large number of which subsequently entered into tradition. The instrumental work on such records was of an exceptionally high caliber, produced by the idiom's top players, and this had the result of raising the overall instrumental standards of the blues, as younger performers learned from and absorbed the work of the idiom's foremost, pace-setting players involved in the records.

Such a movement inevitably drew attention away from the country blues, particularly when location recording was curtailed during the middle 1930s. Still, while the focus of blues recording centered upon the studio-produced blues of Chicago – the so-called "Bluebird beat" – the country blues were continuing to flourish, grow, and change. This is no more clearly seen than in the work of singer-guitarist Robert Johnson whose mid- to late 1930s recordings brought the blues of his native Mississippi Delta to the absolute pinnacle of their artistry and set the stage for the next step in their development, the electrically amplified blues of the immediate post-World War II period. There can be little doubt that

Dancing at a juke joint

in Johnson's music one hears the most stunning, deeply expressive, and perfectly controlled slide playing in all the country blues.

Robert Johnson

Born in the Yazoo River basin of Mississippi around 1912, Johnson took up harmonica first, which he mastered quickly, then turned his attention to guitar. Son House met Johnson in 1930 when both were living near Robinsonville, Mississippi, and the youngster would steal away from his strepfather's to attend the Saturday night dances at which House and Willie Brown performed. Seventeen or eighteen at the time, Johnson was just beginning to study guitar. Some time later, House recalled, Johnson ran away from home to escape farmwork; when he returned six or seven months later, he not only had a guitar of his own, to which he had added a seventh string, but he had utterly mastered it, performing with the same astonishing technical adroitness and imaginative resourcefulness that marked his recordings of 1936 and 1937. House believed the younger

man had sold his soul to the devil in order to gain such fluency and control of the instrument.

A performer of fantastic expressive strength, Johnson was undeniably the most gifted natural poet the form produced; the imagery of his best work is unrivaled and unique in all of the blues – for examples, his "If I Had Possession Over Judgement Day," "Stones In My Passway," "Me And The Devil Blues," and the powerful "Hellhound On My Trail." His work is a veritable catalog of the very best and most expressive instrumental devices of the Mississippi Delta blues. On some pieces – "Preaching Blues" is a good example – his guitar work was so overwhelmingly powerful as to overshadow completely the words it ostensibly supported; it carried considerably more force and intensity than the already powerful lyrics. At times he punctuated his singing with instrumental phrases that beautifully underlined the mood of stark tragedy the words were conveying, as the treble punctuations on "When You Got A Good Friend."

In all of Johnson's singing and playing, however, there is an air of desolation and unrelieved anguish that is one of the most affecting experiences in all the blues. And as a summing up of the very best the Delta blues produced, Johnson's work is unsurpassed in its artistry and emotional power. (Moreover, the seeds of such influential postwar styles as those of Muddy Waters and Elmore James are contained in Johnson's singing and playing.) Based on the instrumental practices House and Brown employed, Johnson's brilliant extensions and elaborations took the blues style of the area to their fullest, most deeply expressive levels. They were the most complex, intricate, and advanced country blues ever heard. In his music the guitar does not support or respond to his voice so much as it simultaneously articulates the same thoughts with equal intensity, amplifying and coloring them, and on occasion contrasting with them. He needs, it seems, both voice and guitar to express the total complexity and subtlety of his thoughts, and in fact the two are so perfectly fused in his mind as a single utterance that the words of his songs come fully alive only in his performances, as the guitar fleshes out the bones of the words.

He was one of the most gifted slide guitar players ever, his control of the slide well nigh perfect. In his occasional playing partner Johnny Shines's estimation, Johnson "could find a way to make a song sound good with a slide, regardless of its contents or nature. His guitar seemed to talk, repeat and say words with him like no one else in the world could. This sound affected women in a way that I could never understand. One time in St. Louis we were playing…"Come On In My Kitchen." He was playing very slow and passionately, and when we had quit, I noticed no one was saying anything. Then I realized they were crying, both women and men." In the opinion of many who heard and performed with him—and this is more than adequately supported by the twenty-nine recordings he left as his legacy and the final testimony of the Delta blues – Johnson was easily the most sensitive user of the bottleneck the country blues has ever produced. Son House, on whose playing Johnson modeled his, is perhaps the only one who might challenge Johnson's mastery of slide playing.

ELECTRIC BLUES

Electrical amplification came to the blues, as it did to all popular and folk-based musics, in the late 1930s, and by the early years of the following decade

Record advertisement from The Billboard

had claimed sizable numbers of the music's guitarists, who eagerly embraced the increased sound volume its use afforded them. Initially of course amplification resulted in no change in, or response to, the stardard approaches most such guitarists followed; it simply allowed them to play what they had been playing with much greater volume and less picking force.

T-Bone Walker

One of the first blues performers to recognize and respond to the special characteristics of amplification through the development of an instrumental approach in which the amplified sound of the guitar figured prominently was Texas-born Aaron "T-Bone" Walker. Rightly considered the true father of modern blues, his pioneering instrumental work of the late 1930s and early 1940s almost single-handedly reshaped blues guitar into the agile, horn-like, harmonically-enriched form that has become so familiar through the work of every blues guitarist who's put pick to string since. Walker's career as a blues performer was far more broadly comprehensive than just this, however, encompassing every major development in black folk-based popular music of the twentieth century.

Born May 28, 1910, in Linden, Texas, and raised there and in Dallas, to which relatively cosmopolitan city his musical family moved when he was still a youngster, Walker took up the guitar at thirteen and over the next several years gained proficiency on it and on banjo, mandolin, violin, and piano. He soon was participating in family musical activities, playing at house parties and picnics, and learning from musician-friends of the family as well as from recordings. When Lonnie Johnson performed in Dallas, Walker always sought to attend his performances, invariably learning something from his keen observation of Johnson's technique. He also learned much from Blind Lemon Jefferson, for whom he served as "lead boy" for a time. Walker in addition greatly admired the music of the popular team of Leroy Carr and Scrapper Blackwell, and studied their recordings diligently. All four of his models— Johnson, Jefferson, Carr, and Blackwell—were among the most accomplished, forward-looking and sophisticated musicians of the 1920s blues performing scene, whose music evidenced a greater interest in, and awareness of, broader harmonic bases for blues than was usual for the time. Walker was to retain and gradually to extend this interest over the next decade or so, ultimately culminating in the brilliant, individualistic electric guitar playing with which he galvanized blues audiences in the late 1930s.

From the age of sixteen he was a professional musician, performing for all manner of parties, dances, picnics, shows, and social affairs in the Dallas area, with touring carnivals and medicine shows through the twenties and into the thirties. In 1929 he made his first recording, two selections recorded at a mobile unit set up in Dallas by Columbia Records, which were issued as by "Oak Cliff T-Bone." Apparently it sold poorly, as he was not invited to undertake further recording. In 1933 he met and performed with guitarist Charlie Christian, with whom he formed a playing and dancing partnership, performing for handouts at clubs and on the sidewalks of the city, while Walker at the same time was a member of the sixteen-piece Lawson-Brooks orchestra that played for dances in the Dallas-Abilene-Amarillo-Waco territory, and occasionally as far afield as Oklahoma City. When Walker left Dallas in 1934, he passed this job to Christian.

It was shortly after settling on the West Coast that Walker acquired an electric guitar, which he claimed to have played some four or five years before first recording with one in 1939. Prior to his joining the Les Hite Orchestra in that year the guitarist had led a number of small groups in Los Angeles nightspots through the late 1930s, during which time he had begun to develop the long-lined hornlike guitar style for which he was shortly to become noted. With Hite he began to draw attention to his strong, virile singing, his growing abilities as a composer, and his ever-increasing fluency and confidence on electric guitar. "T-Bone Blues," recorded with the Hite band, became a nationally successful record, the first of many Walker was to have, and over the next decade or so he became one of the most popular of black recording artists, often having several of his recordings listed simultaneously in the charts of best-selling rhythm and blues records. Among the most notable of these were "Mean Old World," made in 1942 with the band of pianist Freddie Slack, and the song for which he is best known, the enduring classic "Call It Stormy Monday," which was an immediate, huge hit for Walker in 1947 and went on to become one of the most widely recorded standards of the modern blues.

During the 1940s Walker toured with his own musicians and entertainers, maintaining a grueling schedule of cross-country travels until declining health necessitated his disbanding of the group in 1955. Back in Los Angeles, his health restored, he soon was performing as before, though he only rarely ventured beyond the Southern California area. During the late 1950s and early 1960s record sales for blues declined, as black audiences turned increasingly to other musical forms, and as a result from this period on jazz and folksong listeners comprised the major portion of Walker's audience. Recurring ulcer troubles forced an ever-increasing curtailment of the guitarist's activities as the 1970s advanced. He found it difficult to stand for any length of time, and often chose to feature another guitarist with his group while he played and sang from the piano. Late in 1974 he underwent hospitalization for pneumonia, to which he ultimately succumbed on March 17, 1975. He was sixty four, and with him died what his foremost disciple, singer-guitarist B.B. King, described as "the prettiest sound I think I ever heard in all my life."

Urban Blues

At much the same time as Walker was achieving

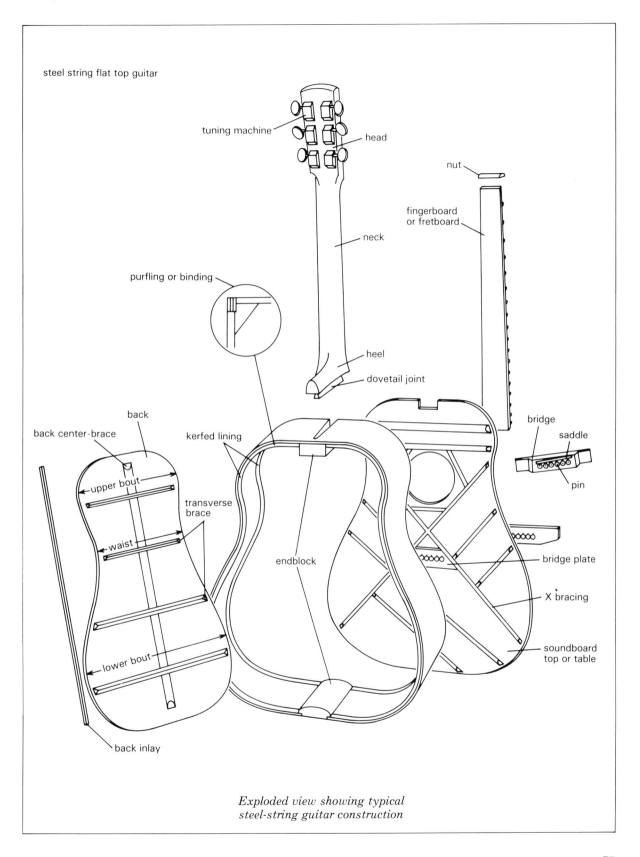

steel string flat top guitar

tuning machine

head

nut

fingerboard
or fretboard

neck

purfling or binding

heel

dovetail joint

back

back center-brace

kerfed lining

bridge

saddle

pin

upper bout

transverse
brace

waist

endblock

bridge plate

X bracing

lower bout

soundboard
top or table

back inlay

Exploded view showing typical
steel-string guitar construction

Muddy Waters

success in the post-World War II period with the sophisticated, jazz-based linear guitar style he had perfected over the previous decade, electric amplification was reshaping the traditional blues of the Lower South into a vital new music in Chicago, Memphis, Detroit, and elsewhere. The performers who claimed the attention of the restless postwar black audiences in these cities were men like Muddy Waters, John Lee Hooker, Howlin' Wolf, Elmore James, and others, and their blues were hard and mean, loud and clamorous, insistent in their heavy, driving rhythms. The postwar blues of these performers represented a return to the rough, vigorous music of their Mississippi origins, though somewhat updated to accommodate a band style that employed heavily amplified instruments.

Muddy Waters

The development of the modern blues style associated with Chicago – primarily a rhythmically forceful ensemble approach utilizing amplified guitar, bass guitar and harmonica, drums and frequently piano as well – owes much to the pioneering work of Muddy Waters. Born McKinley Morganfield in Rolling Fork, Mississippi, in 1915, Waters grew up in the shadow of Son House, Willie Brown, and Robert Johnson, the premier blues performers of the region. Taking up guitar as a teenager, he absorbed the local style through emulating them, and by the time the Library of Congress visited the area and recorded him in 1942 and 1943, he had become one of the finest representatives of the region's musical style: a strong, persuasive singer and a forceful, sensitive bottleneck guitarist. Moving to Chicago shortly afterwards and acquiring an amplified instrument, he gradually made his way on the local club scene and by the late 1940s had built a solid local following, which his recordings for the independent Aristocrat (later Chess) Records operation soon spread nationwide.

Waters's earliest recordings were in pure Mississippi Delta style, his heavily amplified slide guitar supported only by Big Crawford's percussive bass, and they created a sensation. They soon added drums, then a second guitar, Little Walter's urgent, inventive harmonica, and by the early fifties the Waters band comprised two guitars, piano, harmonica, and drums, with bass added for recording. Its records were loud, mean, and magnificent, and while some accommodations had to be made for ensemble cohesiveness, much of the raw force and earthy vigor of the Mississippi country blues was retained in its music. Waters himself was a stunning performer whose dark, heavy singing and slashing bottleneck playing, both derived from House and Johnson, were strong and distinctive, and for more than a decade he was fortunate enough to enjoy considerable recording success with his own adaptations of traditional song materials or with the songs bassist-composer Willie Dixon created for him. He continued performing and recording right up until 1983, when death finally stilled that magnificent voice.

Other Slide Guitarists

Waters was not the only modern blues performer to base his approach on that of Robert Johnson. Elmore James, Hound Dog Taylor, and Homesick James Williamson, among a few others, built successful careers on their simplifications of Johnson's slide technique, and although none of them possessed the subtlety or versatility of their mentor, Elmore James came closest to approximating it. Johnny Shines and Robert Lockwood Jr., both of whom had learned from and performed with Johnson in the 1930s, continued the Johnson line into the postwar period with great fidelity to the original, although neither man achieved much in the way of commercial success with his Johnson recreations. Lockwood, for example, fared much better as a recording sideman with Little Walter and other performers where his fluency and imaginativeness found a much more fulfilling outlet than they did when he recorded on his own. In the late 1970s the two men formed a performing and recording partnership that has produced some enjoyable music.

Howlin' Wolf

Waters's only serious rival during the 1950s was Howlin' Wolf, born Chester Burnett in Aberdeen, Mississippi, on June 10, 1910, whose music was firmly rooted in that of Charlie Patton from whom Wolf had learned in the late 1920s, and whose guitar style was almost exclusively rhythmic and frequently modal in character. Likewise, John Lee Hooker's popular boogie music owes much to Patton as well as such Mississippi performers as Arthur Petties, Tommy McClennan, and Robert Petway. His playing and singing go back to the oldest Mississippi blues traditions; crude and often aharmonic, his mu-

Howlin' Wolf

sic is strong and hypnotically insistent, with a powerful rhythmic impetus that more than makes up for its limited melodic-harmonic compass. During the 1950s and early sixties singer-guitarist Jimmy Reed (born Leland, Mississippi, 1926) enjoyed popularity with a style of great simplicity, his laconic singing underscored with an easy, relaxed guitar style based almost wholly on bass patterns derived from boogie-woogie and blues piano, the whole spiced by his modest harmonica playing.

In sum, what these postwar blues performers did was, in effect, simplify the styles of their musical forebears. The music of Waters and Wolf is not nearly so complex or stunningly detailed as is that of their models – Robert Johnson and Charlie Patton, respectively. But what they did do – and well too – was to work out band approaches that were strong and powerful and that were regular enough to permit five or six men to perform in concert without unduly compromising the force and passion of the older, less regular country blues. And that's no little accomplishment.

THE NEW BLUES

These early postwar blues approaches found favor with various, largely localized blues audiences – in particular those of Chicago, which satisfied large numbers of newly urbanized Southern blacks who shared common backgrounds with blues performers from the same region – but most such musical styles enjoyed relatively brief and limited degrees of success. The tempo of modern life was much too quick, its experiences too complex, and its rate of change much too rapid to be mirrored, for very long, by approaches so firmly rooted in the black past. For these reasons the blues of Waters, Wolf, Hooker, and other postwar performers from the lower South, for all their strength and beauty of expression, failed to sustain beyond their initial years of popular acceptance. They were much too rigidly anchored to the country blues of the agrarian South to reflect more than a transitory, early stage of the modern black experience.

B.B. King

The approach developed by B.B. King, which synthesized black Gospel music, traditional blues, jump band music, jazz and, to a degree, mainstream popular music, has proven much more widely and enduringly expressive of postwar black culture, and for these reasons has had a more universal appeal and longer-lasting impact. Like Waters and many other postwar blues performers, King was a native Mississippian, born Riley B. King on September 16, 1925, on a plantation near Indianola, about 125 miles south of Memphis, and spent much of his early life in farm labor. At fourteen he took up guitar, first performing religious music and singing with a quartet of his school chums, then turning to blues, which he learned primarily from local and touring performers such as Robert Lockwood Jr. and Sonny Boy Williamson, and also from recordings. Blind Lemon Jefferson, Lonnie Johnson, Robert Johnson, and Louis Jordan were particular favorites. While serving in the Army during World War II King had his first exposure to the recordings of Count Basie and his singer Jimmy Rushing, jazz guitarists Charlie Christian, Django Reinhardt, and Oscar Moore, and T-Bone Walker (whose recording of "Call It Stormy Monday" greatly impressed him), performers whose styles were to exert strong influences on the shaping of his own approach to blues guitar.

Following his mustering out, King began to perform publicly, traveling to towns in the Mississippi countryside where he sang and played on street-corners for tips, often making as much in a day of "busting music" as he did in a week of farm work. In 1947 he moved to Memphis where he sought out his cousin, Mississippi country blues singer and guitarist Bukka White, who taught him a great deal, and began to perform at local clubs and on radio station WDIA, which helped extend his reputation. At this time he formed his first group, a trio with pianist Johnny Ace and drummer Earl Forrest, for playing engagements in Memphis and the surrounding country. In 1949 he made his first recordings, four selections for the Bullet label which, while not terribly distinctive when compared with his more mature work of a few years later, did indicate that a number of interesting developments were taking place in his music. The use of horns in section, deriving from his love of orchestral jazz, was one of these. Gospel music, one of his earliest musical experiences, was of course another, and this influence is most evident in his freely expressive approach to singing, generally more melodic in character and rich in the use of melisma, falsetto, and other techniques associated with Gospel singing and, in consequence, remarkably free of the cadential, more narrow compass of country blues.

However, what most markedly differentiated King's music from that of his contemporaries was the brilliant guitar style he had fashioned from all of his influences – traditional blues and religious song, the blues and jazz guitarists he so admired, but chiefly T-Bone Walker. King often has acknowledged the great impact Walker's music made on him, and credits him with having developed the modern blues guitar style. In assimilating Walker's style into his own, King gradually smoothed out the older man's aggressively staccato attack into one of greater subtlety, emphasizing a more relaxed legato handling of line that much more closely approximated that of his singing, using the guitar in fact as a responsive extension of his voice. (One of the techniques he perfected, flawlessly controlled note-bending achieved by stretching the guitar strings with the fingers of his left hand, duplicates the vocal melisma of Gospel singing.) This was a process that took several years to bring about, and on his earliest RPM recordings, dating from 1949 and 1950, may be heard a guitar style still in its formative stages, King performing with a harder, more aggressive attack and a harsher tonal quality than has characterized his more familiar mature approach.

After a number of attractive, well-conceived and

ably-performed records for RPM, most of which sold respectably, King scored his first major hit in 1951 with "Three O'Clock Blues," which remained on the R&B sales charts for more than four months. It immediately established him with the national blues audience, led to lucrative bookings at the leading clubs and concert halls of the R&B circuit, and enabled King to assemble and keep together a first-rate orchestra of seasoned professionals. With this fixed, he was free to concentrate on perfecting the fleet, long-lined, jazz-inflected guitar style toward which he had been working so determinedly, and from the early 1950s on his playing increasingly took on the original, distinctive character so long identified with him and which has become universally known, admired, and emulated as the foremost guitar style of the modern blues.

"Three O'Clock Blues" was succeeded by a large number of top-selling records during the fifties and sixties, and in 1970 King made a breakthrough into the wider arena of pop music with his groundbreaking "The Thrill Is Gone," the first of his records to appeal simultaneously to large numbers of blues and popular music listeners, selling hugely to both audiences. Since then his appeal has been enormous and universal, and in the nearly four decades of his professional life the guitarist has seen the blues style he developed in the late 1940s and early 1950s become the dominating sound of the modern blues and he, as its architect and single finest representative, one of the most important figures in all of blues history.

Lowell Fulson

The only performer of modern times who does not appear to have been influenced by King, who in fact developed from many of the same sources an alternative approach of originality and power, is Lowell Fulson. Born in Tulsa, Oklahoma, in 1921, Fulson was raised in a musical household, gravitated toward music an an early age, and quickly absorbed the local musical traditions. By the time he was sixteen he had been playing professionally for some years, had accompanied church singers for six of them, and had learned to play mandolin as well. He too fell under the sway of Blind Lemon Jefferson and Lonnie Johnson, among other important blues performers of the twenties and thirties and like King, he greatly admired Charlie Christian and Louis Jordan, diligently studying both performers' recordings during the early and middle 1940s when he was concentrating strongly on the refinement of a personal mode of expression.

Fulson's early musical experiences included the usual performing at dances, houseparties, juke joints and the like, working with a large country-and-western string band led by banjoist Dan Wright, and accompanying noted blues singer Texas Alexander. He continued to polish his playing while in the Army during World War II, first in Oakland, where he spent most of his tour of duty, and later in Guam where he entertained at a rest camp operated for submarine personnel. After the war he returned to Oklahoma, but by mid-1946 was back in Oakland where he made the first of his numerous recordings, achieving conspicuous success with those he made for Swing Time, of which "Everyday I Have The Blues," "Blue Shadow," "Lonesome Christmas," and "Low Society Blues" are particularly outstanding. Signing with Checker Records in 1953, he continued his chart success with "Reconsider Baby," "Hung Down Head," and "Tollin' Bells." After settling in Los Angeles, Fulson switched to the Kent Records label and again experienced considerable success with such recordings as "Black Nights," "Tramp," "Make A Little Love," and "I'm A Drifter," among others, some of the strongest and most attractive recordings in his fully matured style.

Because of their common influences there are strong parallels in King's and Fulson's approaches to music, but the differences that set them off are appreciable. Kinetically, King's is the more regular approach, smoother, more fluidly legato of line than is Fulson's choppier, more staccato and aggressively rhythmic attack (which recalls that of Walker). Undoubtedly this is a result of the more pronounced influence from jazz on King's musical conception, which can be characterized as the "cooler" of the two approaches, King in effect playing Lester Young to Fulson's Chu Berry, if an analogy from jazz can be used to suggest their differences. Jazz is less important an influence on Fulson's music than it is on King's music. In this case, the mix of influences is differently constituted – the liking for Louis Jordan's exuberant jump music, which both men shared, plays a much more emphatic role in Fulson's music.

THE NEXT GENERATION

So powerful and all-pervasive has been the influence of King (and to a lesser extent Walker and Fulson) that it has to one degree or another colored the work of every blues guitarist to have appeared since his time. The first generation of King-influenced performers includes Albert King, Freddie King (none of them related), Buddy Guy, Otis Rush, and Magic Sam, all of whom have developed individual-lized playing styles rooted in King's suave linear ap-proach.

Albert King

Oldest of these by a decade, Albert King (born Indi-anola, Mississippi, April 25, 1924) began performing on the instrument in 1939, when he acquired his first guitar, learning from local players in the Mississippi-Arkansas region in which he grew up, notably El-more James, Howlin' Wolf, Willie Johnson, Robert Nighthawk, and others. He had his first taste of per-forming in 1953 when he joined a small group, the In-The-Groove Band, for local engagements in the Oceania, Arkansas, area. Later that year King, af-ter having worked briefly with Jimmy reed, record-ed a few sides for Chess Records that remained un-issued for more than two decades. Over the next half-dozen years he worked on perfecting his music while he supported himself with nonmusic jobs in the St. Louis area, where in 1959 he recorded for the local Bobbin Records label in a more fully developed style. This led to his signing with the much larger King Records operation with which he had his first hit, 1962's "Don't Throw Your Love On Me So Strong." Four years began the most productive phase of his still-continuing career when he joined the Stax Records roster and, with Booker T. and the M.G.'s and the Mar-Keys horn section in support, enjoyed pheonomenal success with "Laundromat Blues" and "Born Under A Bad Sign," among the most rivetingly powerful and distinctive blues of the late 1960s, establishing his reputation and exerting a tremendous influence on young guitarists of the time – among them, Eric Clapton, Peter Green, and Michael Bloomfield.

Possessed of a deeper, more nasal singing voice than B.B.'s, Albert's approach on guitar emphasizes a more pronounced rhythmic attack that stems from his shouting vocal style, and his instrumental tone is much broader, biting, and metallic-sounding than his mentor's. His lines have tended to be spare, though he is not without his excesses in this area, particularly in live performance, and he achieves great effectiveness through such simple devices as repetition, wringing all manner of vibrations from a single note, phrasing against the beat and, in Robert Palmer's characterization, "juxtaposing predictable runs and sudden, surprising turnarounds to create tension, building from low register to high, from

lines based on thirds to jumps up to elevenths ...[in-flecting] every note he plays on guitar with atten-tion to its individuality, making the instrument 'talk'."

Freddie King

Freddie King (born Gilmer, Texas, September 30, 1934) and George "Buddy" Guy (born Lettsworth, Louisiana, July 30, 1936) share a number of stylistic similarities in that each has perfected a permutation of B.B. King's style that emphasizes speed and flu-ency of execution that, taken with a similar pen-chant for high levels of amplification, have resulted in highly exciting, energetic playing approaches. Although he was a fine, expressive singer, King achieved his reputation through a series of fleet, driving instrumentals – of which the anthemic "Hideaway," "Sen-Sa-Shun," "San-Ho-Zay," and "Driving Sideways" are some of the more fami-liar – notable for the ingeniousness of their con-struction and the telling use they made of their creator's dazzling technical command and inventive resourcefulness. These are much better known than his many fine vocal performances, of which his 1960 hit "Have You Ever Loved A Woman" is a particu-larly stunning example.

Buddy Guy

Guy, too, is an extraordinarily gifted player whose best work is gripping, imaginative and, above all, exciting as any in the long-lined, harmonically-extended modern vein. While initially shaped by the country-based music of John Lee Hooker and Light-nin' Hopkins, among others, Guy's mature style is al-most wholly B.B. King-derived, and in his early (and still best) recordings he managed to strke a keen balance between the controlled lucidity of King's approach and a straining, near-manic urgency that, coupled with his strident, edgy tonality, stinging attack, and taut, constricted vocal delivery, resulted in an approach of great force, and excitement, qualities strongly evident in his classic early recordings, "First Time I Met The Blues," "My Time After A While," "Ten Years Ago," and "Stone Crazy," his only charted R&B single. The major weakness of Guy's playing, which he shares with Freddie King, has been an over-reliance on technique for its own sake, a tendency that reveals itself in blistering fusillades of notes spit out at breakneck speed, creating a good deal of superficial excitement but rarely possessing much in the way of sustained thematic development or real organic coherence. Unfortunately, Guy's in-person and recorded performances of the recent past have all too clearly indicated that his tendency to substitute manner for matter has come to dominate his playing, which now runs the risk of trivializing, if not parodying the more controlled handling of technique that made his groundbreaking early work so satisfyingly distinctive.

Otis Rush

A similar situation obtains in respect to Otis Rush (born Philadelphia, Miss., April 29, 1934), along with Guy and Magic Sam one of the more noteworthy of the second generation (that is, post-Muddy Waters) of modern Chicago blues performers. A largely self-taught guitarist who initially modeled his playing approach on those of Waters, Hooker, and Hopkins, among others he heard after moving to Chicago in 1948, Rush over the next several years gradually moved from this base into a more polished, thoroughly modern approach to the blues. He took B.B. King as his chief – some would say only – stylistic model, and has well mastered its conventions. Beginning to record for the Chicago-based Cobra label in 1956, Rush scored immediate success with his first release, *I Can't Quit You Baby,* which placed well in the national R&B sales charts, His succeeding records for the firm maintained this high standard – "Three Times A Fool," "All Your Love." "Jump Sister Bessie," and "Checking On My Baby" (magnificent!) are marvelous and secured his reputation with blues aficionados without, however, duplicating the success of that first record. On the dissolution of Cobra in 1959, Rush undertook a few sides for Chess Records, of which *So Many Roads* is a particularly stunning example of his approach at its best and most impassioned, his intense, anguished vocal underscored with fluent, tasteful guitar lines of real power and individuality. Following this he signed with Duke Records, where the pattern continued. The recordings were, in general, excellent modern blues, with Rush performing at close to peak abilities, although the band settings he was furnished were not terribly distinguished or very helpful in attracting new listeners weaned on B.B. King, as was presumably their intention. They too failed to translate to sales. Since that time Rush has continued to record, primarily album efforts aimed at the white blues fan who since the 1960s has comprised by far the major audience for blues performers, and to perform here and abroad, often appearing on concert and festival stages. But the power of his early recordings has yet to be equaled, let

alone surpassed, and the promise they represent largely remains unfulfilled. In recent years he has performed little, even in his hometown of Chicago, where he leads an almost reclusive existence.

Magic Sam

As a result of his untimely death in 1969, at age 32, Magic Sam's (born Samuel Maghett on February 14, 1937, in Granada, Miss.) music has been held in much higher regard than was the case when he was alive and performing regularly. Still, of all the Chicago blues musicians of his generation, it was he who had evolved the most potentially original handling of post-B.B. King blues guitar. Despite his use of thumb and fingers in lieu of plectrum, Sam's attack was considerably more biting and percussive than those of Rush or Guy, and his overall approach to the instrument emphasized a driving, energetic, almost frenzied rhythmic intensity. Much of this stemmed from his performing experiences in the clubs and taverns of the city's West Side ghetto where, working most often in a trio format of guitar, bass, and drums, he was forced to develop an approach of seizing power to compensate for the lack of a supporting, chord-feeding instrument such as piano or second guitar. His was the earliest of blues guitar approaches to emphasize to any great degree the expressive potentials of high amplification (though he came nowhere near the techniques employed by rock guitarists), and his accomplishments in hammering out such an approach served as models for the younger blues guitarists who have followed in his wake in Chicago and elsewhere. Few, however, have performed with the tasteful, finely focused power that marked Magic Sam's best work, exemplified in such of his recordings as "All Your Love" (his best known), "Easy Baby," "Love Me With a Feeling," or "All Night Long."

The Next Generation

Additional modern blues performers who have perfected various redactions of the all-pervasive B.B. King approach have included Little Milton Campbell, who has achieved primary success as a smooth and convincing vocalist equally at home with traditional-styled blues and popular soul music idioms. The West Coast offers Johnny Heartsman and Arthur Wright, whose limber and tasteful linear musings have enlivened any number of records by other performers over the last several decades (Wright, for example, has been featured on many of the finest and most successful recordings by the popular vocalist Little Johnny Taylor). There is an

Albert King

Buddy Guy

Albert Collins

outstanding trio of Texans, singer-guitarist-violinist Clarence "Gatemouth" Brown, who has made many excellent recordings over a performing and recording career that now spans three-and-a-half decades; the younger Albert Collins who, like Freddie King, scored his greatest success with a series of adroit, blistering guitar instrumentals, like "Frosty," "The Freeze," "Sno-Cone," and "Deep Freeze," among others – although he is also a capable, if somewhat limited vocalist, it is his stinging, immensely exciting guitar work that makes him one of the blues' current heroes with white audiences; and most recently Johnny Copeland, another competent singer whose forceful, imaginative way with the guitar has found favor with many young listeners. In the Chicago area have been several players who have displayed their solid mastery of the idiom without, however, achieving much in the way of wide recognition – Luther Tucker, Louis and David Myers, Luther Johnson, Sam Lawhorn, Phil Upchurch and others, most of whom have performed as sidemen in the bands of better-known performer-singers. The list of such performers could be extended to many times this length without citing any guitarist who has brought to perfection an approach of such power and individuality to challenge King's supremacy. After more than thirty years, B.B. continues to dominate the field of modern blues.

In more recent years the modern Chicago blues traditions have been perpetuated, if not exactly carried forward, by a number of younger performers who continue to pursue the music in the city's neighborhood blues bars and taverns, as well as the clubs, concert and festival stages of the U.S., Europe and Japan where interest in the blues still runs high. Representative of this latter-day movement have been such singer-guitarists as Lonnie Brooks (who earlier performed as Guitar Junior), Son Seals, Jimmy Dawkins, Jimmy Johnson, and a number of others. It should be pointed out, however, that few if any of this generation of players have developed approaches of any true originality or distinctiveness when contrasted with those of the earlier performers from which so much of this recently-produced music derives. With rare exceptions these younger performers – most of whom are in their late thirties and early forties – simply have appropriated the techniques, repertoires, and mannerisms of their models and, with only the slightest of variations and realignments, sought to develop performing careers of their own with these borrowings.

THE FUTURE

The process is no different than that which any blues performer of the music's past has gone through in learning and mastering the conventions of the discipline. In the past, though, this took place in the context of a living, constantly expanding continuum, with a solid base in a sizable black listenership with which the performer felt kinship and a real cultural affinity, to which and for which he addressed his music, and which supported and nourished his efforts through record sales and attendance at his in-person performances. Such a broad-based support no longer exists for the blues, and probably has not since the mid-1960s. To maintain growth and continued development in the blues, like any music, requires a steady influx of both new listeners and new performers – neither can exist without the other – and since the 1950s the blues has witnessed a steady decline in the black constituency that until that time had constituted its primary audience. The emergence from this time on of a number of competing musical forms – soul music, funk and other modern dance musics, and the accelerating assimilation of black music into the larger, homogeneous world of mass-taste popular music – has accounted for the gradual erosion of the black blues audience, as well as the defection of younger black musicians and performers to the potentially more lucrative pop music field. While in years past many of the brightest and most promising of young black performers might have fueled the blues with new blood and new ideas, leading to its continued growth and expansion, this, unfortunately, has not been the case for the last two decades or more.

Over the century and more that it has been with us, the blues has enriched American and all world music with some of the most vital, potent and emotionally persuasive music we've been blessed with. The deep, fundamental human values of its themes, the directness, unaffected naturalness and fervent honesty with which they have been expressed and, not least, the thrilling, richly satisfying vocalized sound of the blues have touched listeners everywhere and made it into a music of truly universal, enduring appeal. Because of these qualities the blues, as one of its more popular compositions proclaims, will never die but will continue to renew and extend itself, as it has done so often in decades past. And when the next important step in its long, continuing process of evolution occurs, as it surely will, odds are that it's a guitarist who will be behind it.

DISCOGRAPHY: BLUES GUITAR

BLIND BLAKE
Biograph Records

All of the Paramount recordings, made between 1926 and 1931, by the facile singer-guitarist whose polished, ragtime-based blues were to exert a significant influence upon popular blues recording artists such as Big Bill Broonzy, Scrapper Blackwell, and others have been reissued on five LPs on the Biograph label, no one of which is better or more essential than any of the others. Sample one and if you like his good-natured music, there are four more Blake sets to satisfy you. In addition to the sets by Fuller and Blake, there are several fine anthologies of blues and other black folksong from the East Coast, of which Origin Jazz Library's *Let's Go Riding* and Yazoo's *East Coast Blues* are particularly noteworthy.

BILL BROONZY
The Young Big Bill Broonzy
Yazoo 1011

Broonzy's amalgam of country blues and ragtime guitar approaches, which led to the development of one of the most technically adroit instrumental approaches in all the blues, is well delineated in the 14 selections in this album, spanning the years 1928–35. His expertise as a soloist of sensitivity and versatility led to his secondary career as accompanist and studio musician who performed on hundreds of blues recordings from the late 1920s to the immediate postwar years. Other worthwhile sets include Yazoo's *Do That Guitar Rag*, which complements the above album, and Epic's *Big Bill Blues* (still available as a British import), which surveys the later, more commercial stage of his career in the Chicago studios.

BLIND BOY FULLER
Blues Classics 11

Easily the foremost musician of the Piedmont/Carolina area, blind singer-guitarist Fulton Allen, better known as Blind Boy Fuller, under which name he made a good number of commercial recordings from 1935 until his death in 1940, is well served in this 14-selection album, which contains some of his best, most representative work and is further enlivened by the presence of blind harmonica player Sonny Terry and washboard player Bull City Red, with whom Fuller often worked on the streets of the region's tobacco towns.

LOWELL FULSON
Tramp
Kent 520

The definitive Fulson retrospective album remains to be done, the one that illustrates his development from a traditional country-based performer to one of the finest and most original modern electric bluesmen with a style representing one of the few successful alternatives to that of B.B. King. This set reprising his admirable mid- to late-1960s recordings for the Los Angeles-based Kent Records operation, including the stunning *Black Nights* and *Tramp*, among others, and as an illustration of his mature stylistic strengths it cannot be beat. The best of his earliest postwar recordings have been well surveyed in Arhoolie's *Lowell Fulson*. Sadly, none of his striking 1950s Chess recordings is currently available domestically, although there are several European compilations of this material available through import shops.

BUDDY GUY
British Chess 2010
A Man and the Blues
Vanguard 79272

OTIS RUSH
Groaning the Blues
Flyright 560

MAGIC SAM
West Side Soul
Delmark 615

The best of Guy's early recordings for Chess Records, such as the powerful *I Was Walking Through The Woods*, which established his reputation, are contained in the first listed album, a British import. More readily available is the slightly later Vanguard set, a bit more restrained in character, but boasting fine, expressive singing and playing from Guy and crisp, unerring ensemble work led by pianist Otis Spann. All of Otis Rush's classic Cobra Records sides are offered in the Flyright compilation, again a British import, but these are so marvelous and so far superior to anything he has done since, it remains the only Rush set worth seeking out. Magic Sam's Delmark album is a classic, seamless work, gripping and powerful, in which everything comes off beautifully, a wonderful testimony to his distinctive singing and playing. All of these sets are definitive statements by the second wave of postwar Chicago bluesmen whose achievements have yet to be bested.

JOHN LEE HOOKER
Dark Muddy Bottom
Specialty 2149

Hooker Alone
Specialty 2125

Hauntingly powerful, harrowingly dark in character, unrelenting in their rhythmic ferocity, Hooker's existential boogies and stream-of-consciousness sung ramblings are without parallel in the modern blues, and some of the finest are offered without parallel in the modern blues, and some of the finest are offered in these two sets. While out of print, *Moanin' And Stompin' The Blues* (King 1085) is well worth looking for, as it contains some of the most gripping music Hooker's ever recorded, almost frightening in its intensity.

SON HOUSE
The Legendary 1941–1942 Recordings
Folk Lyric 9002

After House's half-dozen commercial recordings of the late 1920s (collected in various OJL anthologies), the recordings he undertook for the Library of Congress in Robinsonville, Miss., more than a decade later, the best of which are brought together here, were the first to document at all extensively the stately majesty of his singing and bottleneck guitar playing, among the most expressive in all the blues. The balance of House's L of C recordings, including several with a small band, along with additional performances by Willie Brown, Fiddlin' Joe Martin, harmonica player Leroy Williams, and David "Honeyboy" Edwards, may be found on *Walking Blues*, on the British-produced Flyright label, available in shops specializing in imports.

BLIND LEMON JEFFERSON
Milestone, two-record set, 47022

Another essential album for any blues collection, this 32-selection sampling of Jefferson's original 1926–29 recordings for the Paramount label offers many of the singer-guitarist's best-known and widely influential pieces, songs that following his introduction of them have since gone into oral circulation, becoming part of the very fabric of the blues and being employed by countless performances since his time. The intricate, finely wrought guitar settings Jefferson devised for his singing were among the most influential, widely imitated of their time, and this album contains most of the best of them. Additional recordings of the Texas blues and folksong traditions include RBF's *Blind Willie Johnson*, Yazoo's Johnson survey

Praise God I'm Satisfied, and Yazoo's two admirable compilations, *Tex-Arkana-Louisiana Country* and *Blues From The Western States*.

LONNIE JOHNSON
Woke Up This Morning, Blues In My Fingers
Origin Jazz Library OJL-23

Perhaps the best single-LP introduction to the hugely influential music of Johnson in a strict blues context, this admirably selected compilation of 16 of his recordings from 1927–32 well illustrates the brilliance and originality of the guitarist's fresh, audacious approach to blues playing, notably his venturesome, freely improvised linear work and advanced harmonic sense. Along with Broonzy, Johnson was greatly instrumental in shaping the urban blues approach that dominated the music over the next several decades. A fine supplementary album, which also surveys this same period is Mamlish's 14-selection *Mr. Johnson's Blues* which, in addition to solo pieces, offers a generous sampling of the guitarist's work as accompanist to such performers as Texas Alexander, Victoria Spivey, Mooch Richardson, and others.

ROBERT JOHNSON
King Of The Delta Blues Singers
Columbia 1654

Sixteen of the most gripping of Johnson's 1936 and 1937 recordings are reprised in this essential album, clearly showing the expressive heights to which he brought the Mississippi Delta blues. Textually, Johnson's are among the most harrowingly expressive in all the blues, shot through with moving folk poetry of the highest order, and underscored with guitar playing of singular power, sensitivity and interactivity with his taut, anguished singing. As a major influence on such performers as Muddy Waters, Elmore James, and others, Johnson's striking music exerted a pow-

erful influence on the early postwar blues. A second volume (same title) offers the balance of Johnson's recorded output, including his original recordings of two of his best known and widely recorded pieces, *I Believe I'll Dust My Broom* and *Sweet Home Chicago*. Postwar performers who have followed in his wake include Waters, James, Johnny Shines, Robert Lockwood, Hound Dog Taylor, Homesick James Williamson, J.B. Hutto, and others.

ALBERT KING
Masterworks
Atlantic, two-record set 2-4002

This recent 18-selection compilation brings together seven selections from King's seminal 1967 Stax album *Born Under A Bad Sign*, the most thrilling, completely satisfying recording he's ever made, along with 11 more recent examples of his driving, metallic-sounding guitar work and convincingly gritty vocals from his Utopia and Tomato recordings, offering a good retrospective of this fine artist's distinctive way with the electric blues.

B.B. KING
Live at the Regal
MCA 27006

This stunning set of "live" performances, recorded at the popular Chicago theater, remains one of the single finest distillations of King's ever recorded, as well as being the finest "live" blues recording ever. Not only does it capture the performer at the top of his game, singing with perfect conviction and playing up a storm, but also documents King's performing charisma and the interaction between him and his hugely appreciative black constituency that charge his performances with such electricity. An essential album, to be sure. There are many additional King albums available on the MCA and Cadet/United labels, as he has recorded extensively over the last 35 years.

FREDDIE KING
17 Original Greatest Hits
King/Gusto 5012

Living up to its title, this 17-selection album brings together all of the singer-guitarist's important 1960s singles for the Federal label, including the instrumentals "Hide Away," "Side Tracked," and "San-Ho-Zay," and the finest vocals he has recorded, among them "You've Got To Love Her With A Feeling," "I'm Tore Down," "Have You Ever Loved A Woman," and "Lonesome Whistle Blues." Easily his best and most important work, although in later years he made a number of enjoyable, highly listenable albums for both Shelter and Atlantic Records.

BLIND WILLIE McTELL
The Early Years
Yazoo 1005

In this absolutely stunning album are reprised most of the classic blues recordings on which McTell's great reputation so securely rests. The Atlanta street singer, a singular 12-string guitarist and a most compelling vocalist, had few equals in the Georgia blues, and other of his recordings may be found on the Yazoo and Melodeon labels, of which the latter's *Blind Willie McTell: 1940* offers a far-ranging program of blues, spirituals, dance pieces, traditional ballads and popular songs originally recorded for the Library of Congress. Additional recordings from the region include Yazoo's *The Georgia Blues*, RBF's *The Atlanta Blues*, Origin Jazz Library's *Peg Leg Howell & His Gang*, the John Edward Memorial Foundation's *Atlanta Blues, 1933*, and British Flyright's reissue of Piedmont's exemplary compilation *Kings Of The 12-String*.

CHARLEY PATTON
Founder of the Delta Blues
Yazoo, two-record set 1020

This 28-selection compilation admir-ably surveys the full range of this seminal Mississippi blues performer's magnificent, gripping music, including a number of religious pieces and blues-ballads along with his justly celebrated blues. In addition to superior sound quality, the set boasts comprehensive musicological annotations and lyric transcriptions, making this an absolutely essential album for anyone investigating the country blues, of which Patton is the first authentic figure of genius.

TAMPA RED
Bottleneck Guitar, 1928–1937
Yazoo 1039

KOKOMO ARNOLD-CASEY BILL WELDON
Bottleneck Guitar Trendsetters of the 1930s
Yazoo 1049

The Voice of the Blues
Yazoo 1046

Country Blues Bottleneck Guitar Classics, 1926–37
Yazoo 1026

Slide or bottleneck guitar styles, from pure country to polished urban, are surveyed in these four fine sets in which may be found virtually the full range of the technique's use in the blues in the prewar period. The most influential and accomplished of the performers represented in these sets, Tampa Red, recorded widely both as a solo artist, half of the successful team of Tampa Red and Georgia Tom (Dorsey), and as an accompanist to others, and Yazoo's survey of his accomplishments is as entertaining as it is intelligent. Only slightly less influential were Arnold and Weldon, particularly the former, both of whom recorded widely during the 1930s, and whose contrasting approaches are nicely sampled in the Yazoo set given over to their work. The remaining two albums, well chosen anthologies both, fill in the gaps and suggest something of the phenomenal stylistic diversity the technique has supported from those of strong, almost solely percussive power to the subtlest, most finely wrought of decorative linearity, from the rawest of country approaches to the relative sophistication of polished urban ones and everything in between.

FRANK STOKES
Memphis Blues: Frank Stokes Dream
Yazoo 1008

As an introduction to the incredible Memphis blues scene of the late 1920s and early 1930s, this set would be hard to beat, containing as it does stunning performances by Frank Stokes, Furry Lewis, Memphis Minnie (and Kansas Joe), Cannon's Jug Stompers, Noah Lewis, and others, although Origin Jazz Library's *The Blues in Memphis* and Yazoo's *Memphis Jamboree* run it very strong seconds. Additional recordings from this important blues crossroads of the Lower South include Yazoo's *10 Years in Memphis, Frank Stokes: Creator of the Memphis Blues, Furry Lewis: In His Prime*, and the 2-LP set *The Memphis Jug Band*; Herwin's *Robert Wilkins: The Original Rolling Stone* and the 2-LP *Cannon's Jug Stompers*; RBF's *Sleepy John Estes, 1929–40*, and Blues Classics' *Memphis Minnie, Vols. 1 and 2*.

HENRY THOMAS
"Ragtime Texas"
Herwin, two-record set 209

A model of its type, this set reissues the complete recordings of this early Texas singer, guitarist, and reed-pipes player whose repertoire, which included blues, ragtime pieces, narrative ballads, and some autobiographical songs, provides important indications of the diverse elements shaping black American folksong. The recorded sound is exemplary and the set offers as well as extensive essay on Thomas' life and times by folklorist Mack McCormick. And the music's immensely enjoyable.

T-BONE WALKER
Classics of Modern Blues
Liberty, two-record set LWB-533

This compilation of 28 of his marvelous Imperial Records singles from the 1950s indicates the strength of Walker's modern electric blues approach, forged in the two previous decades from the traditional blues of his native Texas, the jazz-based Swing of the region, as well as other borrowings from jump music, jazz and, to an extent, popular music styles. At the core of his approach is his distinctive, staccato electric guitar style, long-lined and harmonically sophisticated, which had a tremendous effect on the development of the modern blues of the postwar period, particularly B.B. King, who drew upon and extended Walker's greatly influential approach. Walker's seminal Capitol and Black & White recordings of the 1940s are available as a British import and, because of their importance, are well worth seeking out.

MUDDY WATERS
Down on Stovall's Plantation
Testament 2210

Rolling Stone
Chess 8202

Waters' 1941–42 recordings for the Library of Congress, in pure Robert Johnson style provide a pivotal link between the music of the Mississippi Delta and the postwar Chicago blues. Most of the 13 selections in the Testament set are solo performances, several have second-guitar accompaniment, and four feature a marvelously rough country string band of which Waters was a member. An essential set for any serious blues collector. *Rolling Stone*, the only currently available domestic sampling (and the original label) of Waters' powerful, pacesetting postwar recordings for the Aristocrat, later Chess, Records operation in Chicago, brings together 14 selections spanning the singer-guitarist's entire career and gives a

fairly satisfying representation of his tough, powerful music. There are any number of excellent European reissues of Waters' groundbreaking Chess recordings, and just about any one of them provides a finer sampling of his music than this one. In addition, there are two budget-priced reissues of Waters' Chess performances on the Stack-O-Hits label, *The Original Hoochie Coochie Man* and *Mississippi Rolling Stone*.

Collections:
Really! The Country Blues
Origin Jazz Library OJL-2

A pivotally important early LP survey of country blues recordings from the late 1920s and early 1930s, this album was the first to point to the seminal work of such fountainheads of the music as Charlie Patton, Tommy Johnson, Son House, Skip James, and others, and spurred research into them and their music, leading to the proliferation of data about the early rural blues that has accrued over the last two decades. In the intelligent iconoclasm of its selections, the set remains unequaled in surveying the stylistic breadth of the music. Other valuable anthologies include Origin Jazz Library's *Country Blues Encores* and *The Country Girls*; and RBF's *The Country Blues, Vols. 1 and 2* and the 2-LP set *The Rural Blues*.

The Mississippi Blues, Vols. I-III
Origin Jazz Library OJL-5, -11, and -17

Among the earliest reissues of vintage country blues recordings organized along regional lines, OJL's three LP collections of Mississippi Delta blues remain among the very best samplings of this vital, hugely influential music. The first volume is easily the finest, containing as it does marvelous performances by House, James, Willie Brown, Robert Wilkins, Bukka White, William Harris, Kid Bailey, and Mississippi John Hurt,

among others. The second and third volumes continue mining this rich vein, and are only slightly less essential than the first, which offers many of the acknowledged gems of the music. Following OJL's lead, many other albums from this source area have been compiled, among which those from Yazoo Records are particularly noteworthy.

Chicago Blues: The Early '50s
Blues Classics 8

Memphis and the Delta
Blues Classics 15

Detroit Blues
Blues Classics 12

Three admirable anthologies documenting the emergence of the electric blues ensemble of the post-World War II era, and indicating that the traditional blues of the rural South formed the basis for early postwar blues developments. The sets also underscore the fact that this was a broad geographic movement, occurring simultaneously both in the North and the South among younger blues performers. All three sets offer similar-styled musical approaches in that basic instrumentation, save drums and, where used, piano, is electrically amplified, generally heavily so, with ensembles ranging from duo and trio to sextet. The Chicago set excludes Muddy Waters and Howlin' Wolf, but offers excellent early sides by Homesick James, J.B. Butto, Johnny Shines, Little and Big Walter, among others. The Memphis-based set is, not unexpectedly, quite rural in its emphasis, with representative performances by Elmore James, Boyd Gilmore, Sunnyland Slim, and others, while the Detroit album boasts fine performances by John Lee Hooker, Baby Boy Warren, Bobo Jenkins, Big Maceo Meriweather and Eddie Kirkland. Valuable supplementary sets include Maskadine's *On the Road Again*, Nighthawk's *Chicago Slickers* and *Detroit Ghetto Blues, 1948-54*.

Jazz: Guitar like a Horn
by Pete Welding

The guitar constituted an integral part of blues and country music from their earliest beginnings, but it was something of a late bloomer in jazz. Nowadays, of course, it is such a popular, widely used instrument, with a rich, varied history that has supported a staggering array of playing styles, that it is difficult to conceive of a time when this was not the case. But this development, it must be remembered, has been crowded into a relatively brief time span. While the guitar formed part of early jazz practice to some degree at least, alternating with the banjo in the rhythm sections of some of the earliest jazz ensembles, it only really came into its own as a jazz instrument during the late 1930s and early 1940s, when a number of fundamental soloistic approaches followed on the perfection of electrical amplification. It was primarily this development that freed the guitar from its traditional accompaniment role and permitted it to take wing as a solo instrument on equal footing with horns or piano. Realistically speaking, the great bulk of jazz guitar history has been written only from the late 1940s on, when a new generation of players weaned on both Charlie Christian and the innovations of bebop put the instrument on the sustained course of development that has since characterized its use in jazz. Few instruments, in fact, have witnessed such a quantum-leap process of evolution as the guitar has gone through over the last thirty-odd years.

THE BEGINNINGS
In the period from 1917-26, when jazz was first being documented on record, most jazz ensembles used the banjo in their rhythm sections. Its more strident, percussive sound was ideally suited to

George Benson

the brassy heterophonic music produced by the New Orleans-derived bands of the period, in which the gentler sonority of the acoustic guitar would have been all but lost in the busy welter of ensemble sound. Then too, the acoustical recording process in use at the time favored the more penetrating sound of the banjo. However, when electrical recording was introduced during the middle of the decade, the more sensitive microphone replacing the large funnel-shaped recording horns of the acoustical process, it became possible to make recordings of much greater clarity and subtlety. This move inevitably benefited the guitar, which began to be heard more and more on recordings from then on. The increasing use of the string-bass in lieu of the heavier-sounding, more cumbersome tuba of the earliest jazz groups also assisted in this switch from banjo to guitar, for the latter blended easily and more naturally with the lighter-toned, more flexible contrabass. Many of the early jazz banjoists were guitarists as well (doubling was almost mandatory at the time) – Johnny St. Cyr, Ceele Burke, Bill Perins, Eddie Lang, Mike McKendrick, Eddie Condon, and many others performed on both instruments. But the period's almost exclusive emphasis on banjo precluded any dramatic developments in the guitar's use as a solo instrument until two daring, forward-looking players appeared and changed all this.

The two – Eddie Lang and Lonnie Johnson – could not have been more different in background, yet their careers intertwined in a fruitful collaboration that was to have far-reaching effects on the history of their instrument. They were the first true jazz guitarists, and the importance of their pioneering efforts, separately and together, in shaping the first significant solo approaches for the instrument in a strict jazz context cannot be overemphasized. By the time they emerged in the mid- to late 1920s, each had distilled a characteristic way of handling the instrument that was, simply, head-and-shoulders above those of their contemporaries, each the product of their differing musical experiences no less than their innate abilities. Yet, as their several recorded collaborations attest so eloquently, they complemented each other stunningly, each benefiting from the encounters.

Eddie Lang

Eddie Lang was born Salvatore Massaro on October 25, 1902, in Philadelphia, youngest of ten children of Carmela and Dominic Massaro, a guitarist and maker of stringed instruments who had emigrated

Eddie Lang

to America from Naples some years earlier. The elder Massaro had an abiding interest in music and taught all his children to play mandolin and guitar. The young Salvatore began violin studies at seven years of age, persevering with them for the ensuing eleven years and performing in school orchestras in Philadelphia, where he met fellow violinist Giuseppe "Joe" Venuti with whom he formed a close friendship and musical collaboration, lasting until Lang's death in 1933. (The name by which Massaro was known all his professional life came from a local professional basketball player he had admired in boyhood.) In addition to violin, Lang studied guitar, performing at first on a scaled-down instrument his father had made for him. According to an older brother, Thomas Massaro, Eddie devoted much time to mastering the guitar, which, aside from the rudimentary instruction he received from his father, he taught himself to play. And he progressed rapidly. From all reports, Lang was an exceptionally talented natural musician who possessed a phenomenal ear – he had only to hear a piece once before knowing it perfectly – an ability that gave rise to the erroneous notion that he was a musical illiterate. On the contrary, his years of violin studies with respected local teachers had given him a solid grounding in the fundamentals of music, including sight reading, which stood him in good stead in his subsequent orchestral playing experiences.

Lang-Venuti Duets

As Lang grew proficient on guitar, he and Venuti got into the habit of performing violin-guitar duets for their own amusement. "We used to play a lot of mazurkas and polkas," the violinist recalled. "Just for fun we started playing them in four-four... Then we started to slip in some improvised passages. We'd just sit there and knock each other out." This soon led to professional engagements in the Philadelphia area with drummer Chick Granese (with whose trio the fifteen-year-old Venuti was then performing at Shott's Cafe), and over the next several years their musical collaboration flowered. By the early 1920s the Lang-Venuti duo had developed a technical adroitness and musical sophistication far in advance of those of their contemporaries on the burgeoning East Coast jazz scene. Their repertoire embraced popular songs, classical and light-classical fare, and traditional Italian dance music in addition to the jazz that so fired their imaginations.

Lang's first major professional activity began in 1920 when he joined Charles Kerr, leader of Philadelphia's foremost dance orchestra, as six-stringed banjo-guitarist. He remained with Kerr for the next several years, gaining in experience and electrifying fellow musicians with the increasing freshness and audacity of his playing. These qualities were spotlighted in the frequent "stop" choruses, mixing single-string lines with chorded punctuations, assigned him by the leader. In the winter of 1923 Lang joined the Scranton Sirens, playing both banjo and guitar, remaining until the following summer when he was asked to join The Mound City Blue Blowers, a novelty trio then riding high on the strength of a hit record, *Arkansaw Blues*. Led by singer Red McKenzie, who also performed on a tissue paper-wrapped comb, the MCBB consisted of kazoo player Dick Slevin and banjoist Jack Bland. Lang's guitar fleshed out the trio's rather thin sound, and he was prominently featured in its numerous playing engagements as well as on the six recordings, Lang's first, made with the group in late 1924 and 1925.

A Growing Reputation

By this time Lang's reputation as an inventive, richly musical guitarist was gathering momentum, with the result that his services as an accompanist were eagerly sought by recording directors of the period, who used him in a variety of settings, accompanying many popular and blues vocalists, from Sophie Tucker and Al Jolson to Texas Alexander and the magisterial Bessie Smith, and in the rhythm sections of both small jazz ensembles and large orchestras. Lang was the compleat guitarist, in fact, and by the middle of the decade had become, in jazz historian Richard Hadlock's words, "more in demand than perhaps any other jazz musician in the country...especially on recordings, where microphone balance could easily compensate for the guitar's lack of carrying power."

In addition to this extensive recording activity, Lang also had his pick of lucrative theater, show, and broadcasting jobs, including work with some of the era's foremost dance bands, among them those of Jean Goldkette, Roger Wolfe Kahn, and Paul Whiteman. Most of these leaders favored elaborate, quasi-symphonic orchestrations as a means of legitimizing, or at least popularizing, jazz-based orchestral music and, while generally an indifferent sight reader, Lang played them with ease. "No matter how intricate the arrangement," Whiteman observed, "Eddie played it flawlessly the first time without ever having heard it before or looking at a sheet of music."

Small-Group Sessions

If this sort of work secured his reputation with the era's music establishment, it was his small-group playing that demonstrated the true breadth of Lang's mastery of the instrument as well as his gifts as a sturdy, resourceful improviser. Then, as now, jazz players have found themselves ideally equipped to undertake commercial studio recording which, while financially rewarding and technically often quite challenging, rarely draws on the players' deeper resources of creative expression. This comes to the fore in their work with their peers. For Lang these impulses were most satisfyingly released in the numerous small-group sessions he made throughout the 1920s with his close friend Venuti – the Blue Fours and Blue Fives the violinist led – and such topflight jazz instrumentalists of the day as Benny Goodman, Jack Teagarden, Tommy and Jimmy Dorsey, Adrian Rollini, Frankie Trumbauer, Red Nichols, and a host of others, as well as in the fifteen solo performances, most with piano accompaniment, he recorded from April, 1927, to February, 1932. It is with these performances that the history of jazz guitar properly begins, for as Venuti noted, "Who else was there? Eddie started it all."

Virtuoso Technique

Perhaps more than anything else, it was Lang's

Two Gibson L-5s, the jazzmaster's choice

near-virtuosic command of the instrument that, coupled with his versatility, set him apart from his string-playing contemporaries. From a strict jazz perspective, his most enduringly satisfying recordings were the small-ensemble ones made with Venuti and others, where the slight rhythmic stiffness that marked Lang's playing was subsumed in the groups' collective pulsation, imparting to his work an easy, resilient swing rarely to be heard in his solo recordings of the period. But it is in these solo and duet performances that the full measure of Lang's achievement is best taken. Such recordings as the unaccompanied "A Little Love, A Little Kiss" and "Prelude" (the guitarist's adaptation of a well-known Rachmaninoff work), the piano-accompanied "Rainbow Dreams," "Eddie's Twister," "April Kisses," "I'll Never Be The Same," and "Church Street Sobbin' Blues," and the two 1932 duets with fellow guitarist Carl Kress, "Pickin' My Way" and "Feeling My Way," well illustrate Lang's great strengths and special abilities. These include his poised, perfectly controlled single-string and chorded work; the unconventional (for the time) harmonic devices – substitute chords and unusual modulations, ascending or descending chromatic chord passages, out-of-key introductions, and the like – and rhythmic effects with which he leavened his music; his audacious combination of finger-picking and plectrum as a means of introducing tonal contrast into his performances; his effective use of harmonics, as well as the utter mastery of the left-hand pizzicato technique. No other player of the time could come close to Lang's total command of his instrument.

Mention must be made of the warm, rounded guitar tone he produced. Lang favored an arched-top instrument, one with F-holes in the top like a violin or cello rather than the more usual single round sound hole; he set its action high as a means of increasing volume and, in lieu of the thin strings preferred by most other guitarists of the time, used extremely heavy steel strings. The higher the strings are raised above the fingerboard, and the heavier the strings, the greater the pressure required to finger them properly, which may account in part for the rhythmic stiffness one hears in his playing, especially in the solo recordings. But Lang's tone was lovely, rich, and resonant, and immediately recognizable as his and his alone.

Death

After departing the cumbersome twenty-nine-piece Whiteman Orchestra in 1930, Lang continued his busy schedule of studio and radio work and in the fall of the following year became his friend Bing Crosby's featured accompanist, performing on the singer's nightly CBS broadcasts and in theatrical engagements, and appearing as well in Crosby's popular 1932 film *The Big Broadcast*. Plagued by chronic tonsillitis, Lang was persuaded by the singer to visit a doctor. "Many times afterwards I wished I hadn't," Crosby reported in his autobiography. "The doctor advised a tonsillectomy. And Eddie never came out from under the general anesthetic they gave him. Eddie developed an embolism and died without regaining consciousness."

Thirty-one years old at the time of his death (on March 26, 1933), Lang appeared on more recordings than any other guitarist of the 1920s and, through the influence of his compelling, individualistic approach to the instrument, almost singlehandedly created jazz guitar, rendering the banjo obsolete as a jazz instrument and setting his instrument on the course it has since followed. In one way or another, every jazz guitarist since has been in his debt.

LONNIE JOHNSON

Lang's only serious rival as the era's foremost jazz plectrist would have been Lonnie Johnson, had Johnson elected to pursue this musical direction. While he participated in a number of recording sessions with such leading jazz performers as Louis Armstsrong, Duke Ellington, Charlie Creath, and McKinney's Cotton Pickers, Johnson worked almost exclusively as a blues performer and achieved great success as one of the idiom's most popular and influential singer-guitarist-composers with a long and productive career that spanned more than five decades.

Born in New Orleans on February 8, 1894 (or 1899), one of thirteen children, Alonzo Johnson, like Lang, was raised in a household where music was greatly prized. His musician father led a popular local string band that Lonnie joined at an early age. Again like Lang, Johnson's first instrument was the violin but he soon had added to this a proficiency on guitar, mandolin, banjo, string bass, and even piano – "All the things you could make music on," noted blues guitarist and composer Big Bill Broonzy, who knew Johnson well in St. Louis during the 1920s. Up until 1917 when he traveled to London with a touring musical revue, remaining for two years, Johnson largely performed in the New Orleans area, in the sporting houses of the city's

Lonnie Johnson

entertainers on the black vaudeville circuit, where he appeared as a featured singer-guitarist as well as accompanying other entertainers. He toured with Bessie Smith's 1929 show *The Midnight Steppers*, had his own radio show in New York City, and worked with such jazz performers as Putney Dandridge in Cleveland and Johnny and Baby Dodds in Chicago, where he also performed with other blues artists, including pianist Roossevelt Sykes and singer-harmonica player John Lee "Sonny Boy" Williamson.

Scattered through Johnson's numerous recordings from the middle 1920s through the early 1930s are close to two dozen performances with the era's top jazz musicians, of which his 1927 guest appearances with trumpeter Louis Armstrong's Hot Five – "I'm Not Rough," "Hotter Than That," and "Savoy Blues" – and those with Duke Ellington and His Orchestra from the following year, particularly the stunning "The Mooche," are among the most important and satisfying. His marvelous two-bar exchanges with Armstrong were especially outstanding – in musicologist Gunther Schuller's opinion, "certainly one of the highlights of classic jazz." In these recordings Johnson demonstrated the uncommon technical agility and fluency of his improvisational gifts in company with some of the most accomplished, creative soloists the music ever has known. In such fast company the guitarist more than holds his own, for his ability to fashion meaningful variations on the thematic materials was without parallel among his blues guitarist contemporaries.

Duets with Lang

This is even more clearly evident in the few instrumental solos he recorded – the waltz "Nile of Genago" and "To Do This You Gotta Know How" from 1926, and "Playing With The Strings," "Stompin' 'Em Along Slow," "Away Down In The Alley Blues," and "Blues in G" of two years later – notable for the spacious, unhurried mastery of melodic variations they reveal no less than for Johnson's harmonic savvy and natural rhythmic resilience. These qualities inform his gripping lead playing on the ten instrumental duet recordings he made with Lang in 1928 and 1929. In those racially segregated days it was felt advisable to mask Lang's participation under the recording pseudonym "Blind Willie Dunn" (reportedly the name of a black newsboy from whom Lang purchased his daily newspaper), especially since the recordings were released as part of OKeh's

fabled Storyville district, often in company with trumpeter Punch Miller. Since most of his family perished during a wartime influenza epidemic, on his return from England he settled in St. Louis where he performed in local theaters with his violinist brother James and pianist DeLoise Searcy, and with the bands of Charlie Creath and Fate Marable on the excursion boats that plied the Mississippi River.

Early Recordings

Winning a blues contest sponsored by a St. Louis theater led in late 1925 to Johnson's first recordings, for OKeh Records, launching a recording career that, with occasional interruptions, was to continue over the next four decades and encompass a vast number of sides. Beyond the hundreds of recordings he made under his own name, Johnson accompanied many other performers, among them Texas Alexander, Chippie Hill, Clara Smith, Victoria Spivey, Johnnie Temple, Georgia White, and even Martha Raye, primarily on guitar, his main instrument, but occasionally on violin. In addition to his extensive recording, Johnson was one of the most popular

An early jazz combo onstage

"race record" series and thus were sold primarily to black listeners. Combining the two players on record was a brilliant, audacious idea which, happily, enriched jazz with some of the finest, enduringly important guitar recordings in the music's history. While Lang was the better known player, it is Johnson's incendiary, unremittingly creative playing that dominates their collaboration.

With the exceptions of a few choruses (two verses on "Midnight Call," the introduction and one verse apiece on "Blue Guitars" and "Blue Room," for example) Lang almost exclusively confines himself to providing simple, unobtrusive bass lines and occasional chorded punctuations to Johnson's fleet, coruscating, ever-resourceful linear inventions. Since they were on the common ground of the blues, Johnson's utter mastery of the idiom is patent in the confident, effortless way he charges through chorus after spontaneous chorus of bristling, unflaggingly imaginative playing, never at a loss for telling ideas, never descending to the banal but, on the contrary, always invigoratingly fresh and compellingly original. For his part in the recordings, Johnson performed on a twelve-string guitar, since the instrument's double courses of strings could reinforce the sweetly lyrical character of the guitarist's distinctive, urbane handling of the blues form, far more venturesome and sophisticated than most other blues players of the period.

Johnson, unfortunately, did not record extensively away from the blues, but among these recordings are some of the finest examples of acoustic jazz guitar ever recorded – those made with Lang constitute the first authentic masterpieces of the genre. They have had a major influence on each succeeding generation of guitar players.

THE INHERITORS

The legacy of Lang's approach to the instrument was carried forward by a number of guitarists who took him as model, chief of whom were Dick McDonough, Carl Kress, and George Barnes, while Johnson's blues-drenched linear style found its continuation in the playing of Teddy Bunn, Bernard Addison, Eddie Durham, and Al Casey, among others, eventually culminating in the revolutionary work of Charlie Christian a decade later.

Dick McDonough

Born in New York City July 30, 1904, Dick McDonough came to the guitar after having earlier mastered mandolin and banjo, playing the latter for four years in Georgetown University's college orchestra. Following graduation in 1925, McDonough joined Ross Gorman's Earl Carroll Orchestra, with which he made the first of his several hundred recordings. He soon had added guitar to his instrumental quiver, initially recording on this instrument behind popular vocalist Ukelele Ike (Cliff Edwards), and gaining all the while in skill and confidence as he persevered in its study. Attending classical guitarist Andrés Segovia's New York concert debut in 1928 inspired McDonough to delve more deeply into the instrument, which he did over the next several years, making such sustained progress that on Lang's death in 1933 he inherited Lang's mantle as the leading exponent of jazz guitar. For most of the decade McDonough and his close friend Carl Kress utterly dominated New York radio and recording activity involving guitar. "Both had great technique and super ears and fingers," noted bassist Sid Weiss, "and most important of all, they were great readers. This enabled them to fit in no matter what an assignment called for."

While the great bulk of McDonough's playing assignments involved commercial music-making, his mastery of jazz guitar is evident in his recordings with Red Nichols, Miff Mole, the Dorsey Brothers, Joe Venuti, Bunny Berigan, Frank Trumbauer, Adrian Rollini, Benny Goodman, and others, and perhaps most clearly of all in his duet recordings with Kress of which the most notable are 1934's "Stage Fright" and "Danzon," and 1937's "Chicken à la Swing" and "Heat Wave," and in the 1934 solo recordings "Chasing A Buck" and "Dick Bernstein Ramble," both fine examples of McDonough's deft melodic chording style.

McDonough's fondness for alcohol eventually got out of hand, and he began missing engagements so often he no longer was called for sessions. In May, 1938, he collapsed in an NBC radio studio of a ruptured ulcer; during the emergency operation that followed he succumbed.

Carl Kress

Carl Kress, who commemorated McDonough's passing in a lovely three-part solo work titled "Afterthoughts," was known as a consummate rhythm player who largely avoided the limelight, although he was easily the equal of any other guitarist active during the 1930s and 1940s. Born in Newark on October 20, 1907, Kress began piano studies at age twelve, but after two years lost interest and took up the tenor-banjo, which he largely taught himself to play. Inspired by Eddie Lang's earliest recorded efforts, Kress switched to guitar, at first performing on a four-string tenor guitar before moving on to the six-stringed instrument. Throughout his career Kress tuned his instruments to his own adaptation of standard tenor banjo tuning which, like the violin family, is tuned in fifths. Kress dropped the top A string a full octave and, on the six-string guitar, added two bass strings, again tuned in fifths. In Kress's tuning his guitar strings sounded, from lowest to highest, the notes B-flat, F, C, G, D, and A. For the guitarist used to conventional tuning (E, A, D, G, B, E) such a tuning would have proven almost impossible to play, yet Kress not only had no trouble with it but developed a distinctive approach notable for its speed and inventiveness, rapidly and clearly articulated chorded passages, an unusually effective use of the instrument's lower end, and even double-stopped melody playing on occasion.

From the late 1920s on, Kress's rich, resourceful rhythm playing enlivened any number of recordings and broadcast sessions, his initial assignments with Red Nichols and Paul Whiteman leading to extensive studio work over the next several decades. Most of this work was of a frankly commercial nature, but Kress was in demand as a jazz player as well, and in this context he contributed valuably to recordings by Nichols, Bix Beiderbecke and Frank Trumbauer, Jimmy and Tommy Dorsey, Miff Mole, Lee Morse, Adrian Rollini, The Cotton Pickers, and many others. In the context of jazz guitar, Kress's duets with Lang and McDonough are especially important, as are his solo performances of 1938 (the three-movement "Afterthoughts") and 1939 ("Peg Leg Shuffle," "Sutton Mutton," "Helena" and "Love Song"). Later duets included several with his protégé Tony Mottola (1945's "Jazz in G" is particularly stunning) and, beginning in 1961, with George Barnes with whom he formed a close partnership lasting until Kress's death of a heart attack in June of 1965. Barnes and Kress comprised the first guitar duo to perform in public instead of just on radio or recordings, and the first as well since Johnson and Lang to offer freely improvised rather than carefully orchestrated musical performances. Their collaboration, including their successful 1963 Town Hall concert, was memorialized in several LP collections that, while out of

George Barnes

George Van Eps

print, are well worth the trouble of seeking out in specialist shops.

George Barnes

Barnes, who generally played the linear lead to Kress's chordal accompaniment in their duo performances, was born in Chicago Heights on July 17, 1921. After studies with his father, he toured the Midwest with his own quartet from 1935 to 1939, making his recording debut in March of 1938 as accompanist to vocalist Louis Powell. Following the breakup of his group, the guitarist settled into radio work as a staff player at NBC in Chicago, and performed club dates with saxophonist Bud Freeman until drafted into the service. On his discharge, he resumed broadcast work, first at the ABC affiliate in Chicago, then moving in 1951 to New York City where he quickly became one of the most in-demand session guitarists, with a long string of commercial assignments to his credit. A versatile musician and respected craftsman on his instrument, he formed a well-received duo with guitarist Bucky Pizzarelli in the early 1970s, which lasted for several years, following which he joined forces with cornetist Ruby Braff in one of the most ingratiating small jazz groups of recent memory.

George Van Eps

While all of these performers are masters of chorded guitar, either melodically or rhythmically, the un-disputed champion of this approach is George Van Eps, generally considered by his peers to be un-equalled in the art of chord-style playing – in Carmen Mastren's estimation, "the guitar player's guitar player." He came to this mastery naturally, his father being the noted five-string banjo virtuoso Fred Van Eps whose more than half-century recording career commenced with Edison cylinders in 1897. Born in Plainfield, New Jersey, on August 7, 1913, Van Eps was a true prodigy, learning banjo by his tenth year, becoming a full-fledged professional musician by his eleventh, and a more than adept guitarist by his fifteenth. He made the switch to guitar after meeting Eddie Lang, then a member of Roger Wolfe Kahn's orchestra, and in fact he performed with Lang for more than six months when both were members of Smith Ballew's orchestra, with which Van Eps's older brother Bobby played piano. Most of Van Eps's work involved commercial playing assignments with sweet and dance bands of the 1930s, but he also recorded prolifically as a studio musician (it was not unusual for him to appear on more than 2,000 recordings a year) both in New York and from 1936, Los Angeles, backing large numbers of singers and instrumentalists, albeit anonymously.

In 1939, acting as consultant to Epiphone, he designed for their manufacture the first Van Eps mod-

Teddy Bunn

el seven-string guitar, with a low A string added to the standard six. This ultimately led to his highly regarded orchestral playing style in which he simultaneously performs bass, melody line, and harmonic underpinning, making for performances almost pianistic in their totality of expression. Only the young Canadian-born guitarist Lenny Breau has approached Van Eps's mastery of this approach, although any number of guitarists have attempted it since Van Eps first showed the way. As a theorist, he is best known for his pioneering *The George Van Eps Guitar Method*, published in 1939, and his *Harmonic Mechanisms* of 1980. Considering the extent of his influence on other guitarists, Van Eps has recorded relatively little on his own: a pair of singles in 1949, a single LP for Columbia Records in 1956, and three albums for Capitol Records in the 1960s, none of which, unfortunately, is currently in print.

Other primarily chordal/rhythm players include Carmen Mastren, Eddie Condon, Jack Bland, Frank Victor, Tony Gottuso, Allen Reuss, Freddie Greene,

Everett Barksdale, Dave Barbour, Remo Biondi, Ben Heller, Mike Bryan, John Trueheart, Gene Gifford, Ulysses Livingston, and Mike McKendrick.

Teddy Bunn

Of players in the pre-World War II period Teddy Bunn was probably the foremost exponent of the blues-inflected, single-string, acoustic guitar-style typified by Lonnie Johnson's pioneering work of the late 1920s. Unlike most guitarists of the 1930s, primarily rhythm players who might on occasion take either a brief chorded or a chord-supported solo, Bunn was first and foremost a guitar soloist who developed a swinging, percussive linear style that anticipated the electrically amplified hornlike approach introduced by Charlie Christian at the close of the 1930s. And unlike most other guitarists of the time, Bunn played without plectrum, using the thumb of his right hand to sound the strings, producing a warm, mellow tone but generating a powerful rhythmic attack through the force with which he struck the strings.

Totally self-taught and unable to read music, Bunn was born in 1909 into a musical family in Freeport, New York. By his twentieth year he was working professionally in music, accompanying a calypso singer, which eventually led to his backing up blues vocalists, a brief stint with Duke Ellington as a replacement for banjoist Fred Guy, and then work with the Washboard Serenaders/Stompers. It was through this group that Bunn met scat singer Leo Watson. He joined the singer in a string ensemble that became known as the Spirits of Rhythm and which, buoyed by Watson's ebullient singing and Bunn's bright, propulsive solos, caused a sensation when they were booked into New York's popular Kelly's Stables. With the Spirits he achieved his greatest prominence and recorded some of the finest examples of his solo work. Nor should his four 1940 unaccompanied solos for Blue Note be overlooked; "King Porter Stomp," "Bachelor Blues," "Blues Without Words," and "Guitar in High," well illustrate his punchy, driving style, his penchant for note-bending, and the tasteful, often poignant melodism with which he infused his playing. After a two-year stint with the popular John Kirby group, Bunn rejoined the Spirits in 1939 and for the next decade alternated between them and his own small groups. Save for a half-dozen titles, Bunn recorded little under his own name during this period, although he did back up such popular black performers as singer-alto saxophonist Louis Jordan and blues belter Joe

Turner. A stroke in 1971 was followed by a series of heart attacks, leaving Bunn partially paralyzed and blind. The latter, however, he considered no real handicap – "I never could read the notes anyway," he quipped, and while over the decade he sought to regain his playing skills he was ultimately unable to do so. He died in 1978.

Other Guitarists

Two other guitarists active in the pre-electric period developed interesting styles of their own. Al Casey was the guitarist with the sextet of hugely popular singer-pianist-composer Thomas "Fats" Waller, and his chorded solos were models of elegance, taste, and solid musical construction ("Buck Jumpin'," recorded in 1941 with Fats Waller and His Rhythm, is a particularly felicitous example of Casey's best work). Bernard Addison, a former big-band banjoist who made the switch to guitar in the late 1920s, developed an attractive chord-supported single-note style best described as a bluesier, more economical and rhythmically incisive version of Dick McDonough's. He was featured on recordings by Red Allen, Louis Armstrong, Sidney Bechet, Coleman Hawkins, Billie Holiday, Fletcher and Horace Henderson, Freddy Jenkins, Bubber Miley, and even Jelly Roll Morton, among many others.

DJANGO REINHARDT

During the middle 1930s jazz listeners suddenly became aware of a singular guitarist with a unique, lyrical yet driving style totally unlike that of any other player of the instrument. Taking Eddie Lang as his primary stylistic model but influenced by most of the major jazz soloists of the late 1920s and early 1930s, whose music he had heard only on record, Django Reinhardt had perfected a playing style of great melodic-harmonic freshness, natural swing, and bracing inventiveness in variations-playing. Reinhardt's was the first new voice on jazz guitar, to have appeared in a decade or more, with a striking, truly original approach to the instrument. He was, in fact, one of the most unflaggingly resourceful improvisers jazz guitar had seen until that time, fully on a par with Lonnie Johnson in his easy command of truly spontaneous music-making.

Early Days

What was most remarkable about his achievement was that Reinhardt had developed such an extraordinary mastery of the burgeoning art of jazz guitar wholly on his own and, as he was a resident of France, at a great remove, spiritual no less than

physical, from the centers of jazz development and activity in the United States. A musician almost from birth, he was born Jean Baptiste Reinhardt on January 23, 1910, in a gypsy caravan near Liverchies, Belgium, not far from the French border. Raised in typical wandering gypsy fashion, constantly on the move, particularly while World War I was raging, Reinhardt was drawn to music early; after his family had settled on the outskirts of Paris following Armistice, the twelve-year-old acquired a banjo-guitar which he set about teaching himself to play, practicing diligently until he had mastered the instrument.

He had only just embarked on a professional music career when, in 1928, he was seriously burned in a fire that devastated his caravan. His convalescence lasted more than a year-and-a-half and his left hand, which had suffered severe damage, was in bandages even longer. It was feared he would no longer be able to play but Reinhardt, undaunted, laboriously set about recovering the use of the hand. It took him well over a year to do so, and he was only partially successful – activity was restored only to the thumb, index, and middle fingers, the remaining two digits for all practical purposes remaining useless. Determined to resume playing, Reinhardt devised his own idiosyncratic fingering method to compensate for his diminished physical abilities. So are pearls produced by irritants.

The guitarist was back in action by 1930, playing in the streets and cafes of Paris's Montmartre district, traveling to other cities when the spirit moved him, and it often did. It was while performing in Toulon that the young guitarist reportedly heard his first American jazz recording, Louis Armstrong's "Dallas Blues," which instantly fired his imagination. Over the next several years he sought to master the revolutionary new idiom, seeking out and learning from American recordings, while supporting himself with a succession of orchestral jobs, accompanying popular vocalists, and occasional recording work.

Reinhardt and Grappelli

While performing in the orchestra of accordionist-bassist Louis Vola, Reinhardt got into the habit of jamming backstage with one of the group's violinists, Stephane Grappelli, in an attempt to approximate the violin-guitar duets of Joe Venuti and Eddie Lang they so admired. What started as an enjoyable way of passing the time between shows soon had developed into a full-fledged group. With the addition

Late 1950s (c. 1959) Gretsch 6120

Late 1930s (c. 1939) National style O resonator guitar

Epiphone Broadway (c. 1936)   *National style Duolian from the mid-1930s*

of Vola on bass, Roger Chaput, and, shortly afterwards, Reinhardt's brother Joseph on rhythm guitars, the Quintet of the Hot Club of France was born, taking its name from and making its official debut at a December, 1934, concert sponsored by the newly formed association of French jazz partisans, the Hot Club of France. The group's initial recordings were made before the month was out and, proving a sensation, the careers of Reinhardt and Grappelli were launched. The Quintet's all-string format was unique for the time, and in the guitarist and violinist it boasted a pair of formidably gifted improvising artists whose special yet differing abilities complemented each other stunningly.

Over the next five years the group recorded extensively, and on its dissolution Reinhardt continued to record with various small ensembles, leaving a rich, enduring legacy of works whose value increases as each passing year reconfirms the unusual character of the original quintet and the singularity of Reinhardt's gifts. The hallmarks of his style are a flowing melodism that is almost rhapsodic in nature, perhaps deriving from his Romany heritage; a supple handling of rhythm; an all but boundless melodic fertility that gives his improvisations a bristling, unclichéd vitality; a distinctive guitar sound; and, above all else, a musical conception so totally, unmistakably original in character that, once heard, it is never confused with any other. His touch and tonal projection were extraordinarily sensitive, yet he could bear down with great force when this was required. While he was a completely self-taught musician, he was not a naive or unsophisticated one – his use of diminished, augmented, minor-seventh and other passing chords was in advance of most of his contemporaries of the mid- to late 1930s. In his January, 1938, recording of "Sweet Georgia Brown," for example, Reinhardt ends his solo with a typical invention in octaves, prefiguring by more than twenty years Wes Montgomery's use and extension of this same device. Come to that, the impact of his playing on other guitarist has been staggering; he has influenced every jazz guitarist since his time, from Christian to Tal Farlow to Al DiMeola, and literally every one in between.

"The key to his artistry lay, I think, in his perceptive understanding of one of the first requisites of jazz: learn to express what you are," observed critic Martin Williams. "Django Reinhardt was a Belgian-born, French-raised, gypsy musician in love with American jazz, and he sounded like it. He was,

above all, a unique individual named Django Reinhardt. And he sounded like that too. He did not simply imitate. His playing was not merely derivative. And he certainly did not repeat some 'hot licks' in a jazzy style. He went to the heart of the matter, and he made a music."

Death

He continued making his music until his death, of a stroke, on May 15, 1953. "Django," his friend the esteemed orchestra leader and composer Duke Ellington once enthused, "is all artist, unable to play a note that's not pretty or in good taste. He's a great virtuoso." Despite the great appeal his music has had for several generations of players and listeners, Reinhardt has had few imitators; his music was much too vividly personal in character for that kind of slavish homage. It has only been in recent years that jazz guitar has witnessed the emergence of another performer who, coming from a similar background, has invited comparison with him: the young gypsy guitarist Bireli Lagrene, who has been electrifying European concert audiences with a self-taught style that draws on many of the same sources as did Reinhardt's a half-century earlier. It remains to be seen whether Lagrene, like Django before him, creates a music of his own.

Oscar Aleman

Reinhardt was not, however, the only non-American musician of the 1930s to earn accolades for the strength and originality of his playing. The Argentinian-born guitarist Oscar Aleman came to maturity at about the same time as Reinhardt, had a command of the instrument fully equal to his, possessed a knowledge of harmony far in advance of the Belgian gypsy's and, probably as a result of his early experiences as a professional dancer in Buenos Aires, evidenced in his playing a much greater sophistication in his handling of rhythm. "Aleman," noted critic Leonard Feather, "could outswing Reinhardt and was a far superior jazzman," an opinion that would be quickly seconded by anyone familiar with Aleman's relatively small recorded legacy. He was indeed a brilliant, audacious jazz soloist and a true variations player whose music was based on a much more interesting and advanced harmonic-rhythmic system than was the more rococo, decorative Reinhardt style.

But in comparison with Django's, Aleman's impact was negligible. It was Aleman's misfortune to attempt to establish himself in Paris during the very time Reinhardt was taking the French capital and, in fact, the entire continental jazz scene by storm, for, as Feather observed, "The French spotlight was not large enough to accommodate two guitarists." Aleman remained in France until after the German occupation ended – unable during his decade-long stay to dislodge Reinhardt or in any way challenge his hold on European audiences – recording a little and generally performing dance and orchestral music of a rather trivial nature.

In 1941 he returned to Argentina, resumed performing and recording with local players, toured South America and engaged in lucrative radio, television, and concert work as well as teaching, but for all practical purposes he languished in obscurity until death claimed him in November, 1980, his passing all but ignored by the international jazz press. The genius of his music is patent in such recordings as the unaccompanied solos "Whispering" and "Nobody's Sweetheart" (1938), the trio performances "Jeepers Creepers," "Russian Lullaby," "Just A Little Swing," and "Dear Old Southland" (1939), and in a number of the sides he made in his native land in the period 1941-45, including the all but astonishing version of "Sweet Georgia Brown," recorded in November, 1941, the finest example of his wholly distinctive artistry on record.

ELECTRIC JAZZ GUITAR

Aleman, among other guitarists of the period, often performed on an aluminum-bodied guitar that had a cone-shaped acoustic sound resonator built into the body of the instrument, one of a number of devices that were tried during the middle 1930s to give the guitar greater volume. While the resonator-guitar, as it was called, unquestionably produced a fuller sound, it did so at the expense of the tonality produced – thin, metallic, somewhat nasal-sounding, with little of the overtone characteristics associated with the acoustic instrument. And the volume increase the resonator provided was not all that significant. Further development of the jazz potential of the guitar would have to wait upon the perfection of a more efficient means of enlarging the instrument's sound, so that in terms of volume, it might perform on an equal footing with horns. Electrical amplification proved to be the answer, and it was not long in coming.

Eddie Durham

Eddie Durham, trombonist-guitarist-arranger with the Jimmie Lunceford Orchestra during the mid-1930s (after earlier playing experiences with a

Eddie Durham

number of the so-called Territory bands of the Southwest), generally is credited with being among the earliest to use the electrically amplified instrument on record. Durham has stated that the guitar heard on his 1935 recordings with the Lunceford band – notably "I'll Take The South," "Avalon," "Charmaine," and the celebrated "Hittin' The Bottle," which he composed, by the way, and probably his 1937 "Time Out," recorded while he was a member of the Count Basie Orchestra – was not an electric version of the instrument but, rather, an acoustic guitar with an aluminum resonator disc which amplified the sound somewhat. Durham further recalled that he did not record with a true electric instrument until his Kansas City Five recordings of March, 1938, at which four selections were recorded, one of which, "Good Mornin' Blues," contains the first solo choruses by an electric guitar ever recorded. Durham featured the instrument again on the performances recorded six months later by the Kansas City Six, of which the most memorable is "Countless Blues," offering as it does two of the finest choruses Durham ever recorded on the instrument, and boasting in addition superlative improvisations by Lester Young and Buck Clayton.

"At the time," Leonard Feather observed of Durham's introduction of the electric guitar on these recordings, "this was a total revelation: his clarity and fluency in delineating single-note passages was like nothing before in jazz annals. Because he soon became busy as a full-time arranger (for Glenn Miller, among others), and because of the tremendous and justified acclaim that greeted Charlie Christian when he descended on the Apple (jazz slang for New York City) in 1939, Durham's historic role in establishing the amplified guitar has too often been low/rated or ignored. An examination of this work on these two 1938 sessions should set the record straight."

It is Durham's contention, or at least his recollection, that it was not until a year or so after the Kansas City sessions that the electric guitar became at all widely available, and certainly the weight of recorded evidence is on his side. It is not until 1939 that one begins to hear what clearly can be discerned as electric guitar on record: Christian with Benny Goodman, Floyd Smith with Andy Kirk, Hurley Ramey with Earl Hines, Al Norris with Lunceford, T-Bone Walker with Les Hite, and so on.

T-Bone Walker

Better known as a blues performer, Walker asserted on numerous occasions that despite his not having recorded with electric guitar until 1939, he had been using one as early as 1935, acquiring it shortly before his move to the West Coast from his native Texas. "I was out there four or five years on my own before they all started playing amplified," he insisted. "I recorded my 'T-Bone Blues' with Les Hite's band in 1939, but I'd been playing amplified guitar a long time before that. The band didn't like the sound of it in the rhythm section, so I played ordinary guitar there. I had a banjo and guitar with me on the stand." He emphasized the point – "Oh, yes, I was before Charlie Christian on electric guitar. He was about the next one to have it."

CHARLIE CHRISTIAN

It is with Christian that jazz guitar truly came of age. His arrival was sudden, spectacular. One minute a total unknown, the next prominently featured with the most popular and influential musical organization of his time, the Benny Goodman Orchestra. Christian burst onto the national jazz scene like a comet, illuminated it with his fiery incandescence, and just as suddenly was gone, burned out at twenty-four, after only twenty-three months in the

Charlie Christian at a Kansas City jam session, 1941

jazz firmament. His talent was as prodigious as his imagination was boundless, and both were instantly recognized by his peers, who became his staunchest supporters. On a personal level, his generosity of spirit was legendary, his devotion to music total. It was an unusual night that didn't find the guitarist, his evening's stint with Goodman done, sitting in with musician friends at one jam session or another, often performing until daybreak or later. And it was at such afterhours sessions at Minton's Playhouse in Harlem that Christian, in company with Thelonious Monk, Dizzy Gillespie, Joe Guy, and other young turks, engaged in the musical experimentation that, as bebop, permanently altered the subsequent course of jazz.

Early Playing

Christian's great and enduring achievement, however, was the brilliantly original approach to playing jazz on the electric guitar he had fashioned in the decade prior to his joining Goodman in the summer of 1939. Born in Bonham, Texas, in 1916, he came of age in a musical environment. During his earliest years his trumpeter father and pianist mother performed in a Dallas movie theater; following their move to Oklahoma City when Charlie was five his father went blind and, to support his family, sang and played guitar on the streets. Eventually his three sons joined him in his sidewalk minstrelsy, Clarence playing violin and mandolin, Edward string bass, and Charlie guitar.

From the beginning the youngster displayed an uncommon aptitude for the instrument. Even his first homemade cigar-box guitar yielded what his childhood friend, novelist-essayist Ralph Ellison, later described as "his own riffs...based on sophisticated chords and progressions that Blind Lemon Jefferson never knew. No other cigar box ever made such sounds." To the instruction he received at home he added music lessons in the all-black school he attended. But most of what he knew he figured out for himself. Tenor saxophonist Lester Young, among the most distinctive and forward-looking musicians of the time, served as one of the young guitarist's chief models, and in the years after Christian had first heard him he sought to translate the saxophonist's long-lined, harmonically and rhythmically sophisticated mode of improvising to guitar.

While he was engaged in this attempt, he broadened his musical horizons by performing in local clubs with his brother Edward's band, following which he barnstormed for a time with Alphonso Trent's band, one of the better jazz ensembles of the Southwest. With Trent Christian played string bass, and those who heard him recall that he played in a manner that prefigured the exploratory, melodically resourceful approach of Jimmy Blanton and, later, Charlie Mingus. Returning in 1937 to Oklahoma City, where he formed a group of his own, Christian met Eddie Durham, who was then playing an early electric guitar with Count Basie. The amplified instrument fascinated the young guitarist who saw it, Durham recalled, as the means of achieving the hornlike sound and approach to phrasing toward which he had been working so determinedly since hearing Young.

His First Electric Guitar

Christian soon had an electric guitar of his own. With it, the last pieces fell into place and the Christian guitar style crystalized and took wing. Soon after, he rejoined Trent who, leading a sextet, embarked on a tour of the plains states. The young guitarist Mary Osborne heard the group in Bismarck, N.D., and mistook Christian's amplified guitar, the first she had heard, for a tenor saxophone being played through a P.A. system. Other musicians were quick to praise the mature artistry and originality of his conception. Early in 1939 Mary Lou Williams,

pianist with Andy Kirk's Clouds of Joy, heard Christian performing at the Ritz Cafe in Oklahoma City and told John Hammond of the young guitar wizard. When other musicians seconded her enthusiasm, Hammond went to Oklahoma City to hear for himself, was convinced, and promptly arranged for the guitarist to audition for Goodman.

The Goodman Audition

This took place on August 16, 1939, at a Los Angeles restaurant where the Goodman band was playing a brief engagement. During intermission Hammond unobstrusively set up an amplifier onstage, and when the clarinetist's sextet took the stand they were joined by the thin, bespectacled Christian. Miffed at not having been informed of Hammond's intentions, Goodman called a tune he felt the young guitarist would be unfamiliar with, "Rose Room." He had not reckoned with Christian's uncommon musical gifts, for as Hammond recalled, "Charlie had ears like antennae. All he had to do was hear the melody and chord structure once and he was ready to play twenty-five choruses, each more inventive than the last. Which is what happened. Before long the crowd was screaming with amazement. 'Rose Room' continued for more than three-quarters of an hour and Goodman received an ovation unlike any even he had had before."

By week's end the guitarist's prowess was widely known, for Goodman had featured him on his next national radio broadcast and permanently added him to his small group and big band. Returning with the band to New York, Christian was invited to take part in an all-star record date under Lionel Hampton's leadership, which included among its members Dizzy Gillespie, Coleman Hawkins, Benny Carter, Ben Webster, and Chu Berry, some of the top names in jazz. His first record date with the Goodman septet soon followed, and before year's end he had participated in four more Goodman recording sessions, and recorded as part of another all-star band that backed blues singer Ida Cox. During this period Christian also took part in Goodman's second Carnegie Hall concert and Hammond's widely-acclaimed "From Spirituals to Swing" concert presentation at the same hall. He had arrived – with a vengeance. Within a few short months he had become a sensation.

Bebop is Born

As a member of the popular Goodman organization, Christian, in addition to recording, performed, broadcasted, and toured extensively. Beyond this, he sat in with kindred spirits whenever possible. He was, in short, one of the busiest, most popular, and in-demand musicians in jazz; his fluent, exciting, resourcefully imaginative handling of the much-maligned guitar became the talk of the music world. No one, literally, had ever played it like Christian, his long, flowing lines bespeaking an all but limitless melodic fertility, an unerring, easy swing, and a harmonic awareness far in advance of its time. It was the latter that enabled him to perform with the young beboppers at Minton's, and it has been claimed that he and pianist Thelonious Monk largely were responsible for framing the new music's harmonic character. Perhaps even more important, Christian was a natural melodist, capable of improvising lines and phrases of such striking force and memorability that it seemed we'd always known them, a trait he shared with alto saxophonist Charlie Parker. Many of the ideas he tossed off so casually in his solos were later used as themes for the Goodman sextet: "Wholly Cats," "Seven Come Eleven," "Gone With 'What' Wind," "A Smo-o-o-oth One," and others (many bore the names of others as composers, however).

Recording Career

Considering how extensively he recorded with Goodman during his twenty-three months in the limelight, Christian, ironically, never was given a recording date of his own. His "official" recorded legacy consists almost wholly of the numerous sides he made while a member of the Goodman organization from October, 1939, to June, 1941, when illness precluded further recording. He was featured on about two dozen of them. Of no less importance are Christian's 1940 Minton's Playhouse recordings, made on cumbersome disc-cutting equipment by enthusiast Jerry Newman, to whom jazz fans will forever be indebted for capturing lengthy, representative samples of the guitarists's incendiary brilliance in such informal circumstances. While the recorded sound is primitive by today's standards, Christian's contributions are of a breathtaking, time-defying gloriousness.

His health never good to begin with, Christian was admitted to a hospital in the spring of 1940 for a checkup. At that time a spot on one lung was discovered and, tuberculosis suspected, he was advised simply to take good care of himself, to lead a normal, healthy life, and not exert himself. Given his hectic schedule of performing, touring, and sitting-in, even this simple regimen proved too difficult and his

health steadily deteriorated. In July of the following year, too ill to play, he was admitted to Seaview Sanitarium on Staten Island. Even there he partied, and friends reportedly smuggled him out of the facility to continue the festivities in more congenial surroundings. For a time his health had improved, but suddenly his condition worsened. When pneumonia set in, the end was inevitable. On March 2, 1942, Christian died.

Although that singular voice was stilled, its reverberations continue to sound to this day, carried in the music of literally every guitarist who's put pick to string since his time. All have been touched, directly or indirectly, by Christian's revolutionary, deeply personal, and totally original approach to jazz guitar, which rendered obsolete all that had preceded it and set the instrument – and jazz in general – on the course they have followed since. Many have followed in Christian's footsteps but none has filled his shoes. He was, and remains, one of the music's authentic, true originals; the fountainhead of modern jazz guitar whose innate genius has yet to be equalled, let alone eclipsed.

CHRISTIAN'S LEGACY

In the years immediately following Charlie Christian's appearance, jazz saw an ever-increasing number of players drawn to his fleet single-string hornlike approach, which has dominated the way the instrument has been perceived and played since his time. Then too, with the declining fortunes of the big bands in the years after World War II and the rise of the small jazz ensemble, there was a corresponding decline in the art of rhythm guitar playing, always the major professional activity of plectrists during the previous several decades. Commenting on this in 1958, Barney Kessel observed, "In small groups today, the amplified guitar is hardly ever used as a rhythm instrument. It's used either to supplement the function of the piano, or to work sometimes instead of a piano, serving as the harmonic basis. Or it's used as an improvised voice in solos." Amplification, then, not only changed the sound of the guitar but a number of its basic functions as well.

So pervasive has been the Christian approach, so strong and inescapable its pull, that a number of players have been unable, or perhaps unwilling, to do anything more than offer approximations of it – just as alto saxophonists of the postwar period paid homage to the gripping power of Charlie Parker's music by slavishly imitating every aspect of

Barney Kessel

Oscar Moore

his approach, not excluding the excesses of his personal lifestyle. As far as jazz guitar was concerned it seemed as if there were little Charlie Christians everywhere.

Personal Voices

Some guitarists, of course, sought to develop personal voices by integrating compatible elements drawn from Christian's music into their own playing approaches. The most notably successful of such syntheses were those developed by, among others, Oscar Moore, whose bluesier adaptation of the Christian style was featured in the Nat "King" Cole Trio of which the guitarist was a member until the late 1940s (following which he involved himself in rhythm-and-blues with his guitar-playing brother Johnny); his successors in Cole's popular unit, Irving Ashby and Johnny Collins; the earlier-mentioned Mary Osborne, jazz's only important female guitarist (rivaled in recent years by the gifted young Emily Remler who might in time develop an individual handling of the instrument); the near-legendary "Jim Daddy" Walker, who made some strikingly forceful recordings with alto saxophonist Pete Brown in 1944 before slipping into near-total obscurity soon after; and, not least, Jimmy Shirley who, as a member of the Herman Chittison Trio, impressed listeners during the middle 1940s with an attractive Christian-based style of some originality, often employing a "Vibrola" attachment to give his guitar a novel, quasi-Hawaiian sound.

Barney Kessel

The most adept exponents of the Christian approach have been Barney Kessel and Herb Ellis, both of whom hail from the same part of the country as did Christian. Born October 17, 1923, in Muskogee, Oklahoma, Kessel has been involved with music, and the guitar in particular, since his earliest years. At twelve he bought his first guitar with money earned from selling newspapers, and over the next few years taught himself to play, read music, and finally to arrange and compose. At fourteen he replaced Christian in an otherwise all-black band in his hometown, an experience that stimulated his musical growth. Two years later the young guitarist met his idol in Oklahoma City where Christian was making a short visit. Christian sat in with the band the sixteen-year-old guitarist was performing with and, as Kessel recalled, "talked to me at great length, and was altogether friendly and helpful with advice."

The meeting strengthened Kessel in his resolve to become a professional musician, and in 1942 the twenty-year-old guitarist made his way to Los Angeles, where for the remainder of the decade he worked with a number of orchestras and engaged in radio and television broadcasting and other commercial assignments. Indicative of his early, authoritative command of the jazz idiom is the fact that he was the only white musician chosen to appear in the classic 1944 Gjon Mili film *Jammin' The Blues*. The early 1950s found him a member of the Oscar Peterson Trio for a Jazz At The Philharmonic tour, following which he returned to Los Angeles, teaching, recording, doing studio work, and performing clubs, and concerts. While he was involved largely in commercial music from the early 1950s on, Kessel continued to perform in a jazz context whenever his schedule permitted, leading his own critically acclaimed group through the middle 1960s, and in recent years has begun to perform jazz more and more frequently.

While generally considered, in Leonard Feather's apt phrase, "the most distinguished exponent of [the Charlie Christian] style since Christian's death," Kessel's mastery of his instrument is total, enabling him to undertake carefully orchestrated solo performances – 1954's "Love Is Here To Stay" and "A Foggy Day" are early examples – or fingerpicked contrapuntal pieces such as his "Barney's Blues" in addition to the deeply creative, infectiously swinging linear playing for which he has been justly celebrated.

Herb Ellis
Replacing Kessel in the Peterson Trio was Herb Ellis, born August 4, 1921, in McKinney, Texas. After his music studies at North Texas State College, he joined Glen Gray's Casa Loma Orchestra in 1944, later switching to Jimmy Dorsey's band and attaining his first renown in 1947 as a member of the vocal-instrumental trio, the Soft Winds, for which he also composed a number of its more successful songs, including the well-known "Detour Ahead." Commercial work continued until he joined Peterson in 1953, and over the next half-dozen years Ellis toured widely with the popular pianist and recorded extensively under his own name, with

Peterson and other members of the JATP performing-recording family. Ellis then put in several years as accompanist to such vocalist as Ella Fitzgerald and Julie London, a lucrative but largely anonymous business, but one that requires deep resources of sensitive musicianship, which this guitarist possesses in abundance.

Like Kessel, Ellis has pursued a much more active jazz performing career in the last few years. He has introduced his fluently inventive, earthy linear style to a new generation of young and eager guitar listeners.

Modern Heirs of Christian
Important additional modern heirs of Christian's music have included, among others, the Detroit-born, largely self-taught Kenny Burrell (July 31, 1931) who, following graduation from Wayne State University in 1955, performed with Dizzy Gillespie, Benny Goodman, and others before forming the first of his own combos in the early 1960s. Burrell has recorded extensively, both as leader and sideman for a broad range of stylists, demonstrating in the process great facility and versatility on his instrument. These qualities are most fully represented on his critically-acclaimed *Guitar Forms* album of 1965, in which he performed on electric and acoustic guitars in a program that ranged from funky blues to carefully orchestrated, classically structured works. Burrell, critic Harvey Pekar noted, "offers imaginative and well-sustained solos, his lines clean and flowing, and he gets a pretty sound from his instrument."

Grant Green, born in St. Louis June 6, 1931, began his guitar studies at age thirteen and within a few years was performing in local rhythm-and-blues, rock 'n' roll, and jazz groups, making his recording debut with Jimmy Forrest in late 1959 while in Chicago enroute to New York City. Brought to the attention of Blue Note Records, Green was signed to the label and in the ensuing years appeared on a large number of albums, his own and others', playing with a singing, unpretentiously lyrical, always perfectly focused directness of expression that gave his ballad and up-tempo performances real freshness and vitality.

And the blues remained at the core of his approach. An economical, rather conservative player, Green was, in critic Robert Levin's estimation, "particularly concerned with the guitar's hornlike possibilities [who has] reduced certain elements of Charlie Christian's approach to their basics."

Tal Farlow

BEBOP AND EARLY MODERN JAZZ GUITARISTS

While still rather strong, the Christian influence was diffused somewhat in the middle to late 1940s when a number of young jazz guitarists began to temper and expand it through the incorporation of some of the musical innovations that had been set in motion by the bebop movement, primarily an expanded harmonic palette and an agile, complex handling of rhythm based upon eighth and 16th notes. One of the earliest and most successful to fruitfully meld the two was Chuck Wayne, born Charles Jagelka on February 27, 1923, in New York City, whose early studies of mandolin led him to the guitar in the late 1930s. A variety of musical assignments, primarily in the New York City area, culminated in his joining the highly popular, influential quintet organized in 1949 by pianist George Shearing, one of the earliest jazz combos to achieve commercial success with a deft, accessible, yet sophisticated approach in which bop figured prominently. Leaving Shearing in 1952, Wayne led a number of groups of his own, engaged in extensive freelance activity, and recorded a number of fine albums yet has failed to make much impact on the public beyond his impressively adroit work with Shearing.

Another important figure in the transition from Swing to post-bop modern jazz guitar was Bill DeArango, born in Cleveland, Ohio, September 20, 1921. Following graduation from Ohio State University he performed with local groups until drafted into the Army in 1942. Following his discharge, he settled in New York City and worked with a number of performers, including tenor saxophonist Ben Webster, with whom he performed for close to a year, following which he formed his own group. By 1948, however, DeArango had returned to his hometown, where he has lived since. One of the most accomplished early bop-influenced guitarists, possessed of a fleet, harmonically knowing and rhythmically incisive approach of striking individuality, DeArango recorded little before leaving the jazz limelight, but each of his few recordings with Webster, Dizzy Gillespie, Charlie Ventura, and Red Norvo is well worth seeking out. Easily the finest and most readily available sampling of his taut, gripping, linear style was the quartet session he undertook in 1954 for Emarcy Records, where his guitar was wonderfully and sympathetically seconded by pianist John Williams.

Other early transitional plectrists include Mundell Lowe (born Laurel, Mississippi, April 21, 1922), Sal Salvador (Monson, Massachusetts, November, 21, 1925), Billy Bauer (New York City, November 14, 1915), the self-taught Barry Galbraith (Pittsburgh, Pennsylvania, December 12, 1919), and Dick Garcia (New York City, May 11, 1931), among a large number of others.

Tal Farlow

One of the most compelling of all early modern jazz guitarists was the self-taught Talmadge Holt "Tal" Farlow. Born in Greensboro, North Carolina, June 7, 1921, Farlow came to the instrument somewhat late. Inspired by Charlie Christian's recordings, he took the instrument up in 1943, and over the next several years, guided almost solely by records, taught himself to play it. By the latter part of the decade he was able to adapt the brilliantly complex music of premier bop saxophonist Charlie Parker to guitar with striking results. Three years in the trio of vibraharpist Red Norvo, where he played with bassists Charlie Mingus and Red Mitchell, completed his education, bringing Farlow's arresting, muscular, and idiosyncratic command of linear playing to extraordinarily high levels, and leading him as well to develop a number of interesting techniques – notably artificial harmonics, a low-amplified playing of rhythm that approximated the sound of drums played with brushes, and so on – as a means of fleshing out the trio sound.

By the time Farlow started recording on his own in late 1953, he was formidably equipped to undertake some of the most seizing, rhythmically arresting, fluently agile guitar playing to have been heard in modern jazz, his lack of formal studies giving his music an audacious, greatly individualistic character. Technically Farlow was capable of incredible speed of execution, yet he never indulged in gratuitous display. His improvisations always possessed a strong ideational continuity, a refreshingly uncliched rhymthic vitality, natural swing, and an all but limitless imaginative fertility. Prior to his voluntary semi-retirement in the late 1950s he made a large number of exciting, nonpareil recordings; those with the remarkable trio he led from 1955 to 1958 with pianist Eddie Costa and bassist Vinnie Burke are particularly outstanding, and on occasion considerably more than that. Farlow has returned to fulltime playing in recent years and, if he no longer performs with the fiery, driving vigor of his early days, he still evidences plenty of the individuality of expression that has always marked his approach to modern jazz guitar. He is one of its undisputed masters.

Jimmy Raney

Contrasting with Farlow's fleet, supercharged approach to the instrument was the more sober, controlled lucidity of expression of Jimmy Raney (born in Louisville, Kentucky, on August 20, 1927), who brought to the electric guitar a stunning musicianship, a spare, thoughtful melodism, and an approach to improvising that was as intelligent, carefully modulated, and, in its quiet, understated intensity, as audacious as any in jazz history. Raney was the epitome of the "thinking" musician, creating improvisations that, despite their having been created spontaneously, possessed an abundance of logical, coherent development, intellectual-emotional continuity, and real clarity of expression. These qualities were evident in his playing from the start of his professional career, and have accounted for the extraordinary levels of his work with Red Norvo, Stan Getz, Artie Shaw, and, from 1953, on his own – his quartet and quintet recordings being among the very finest modern jazz guitar work, of the mid- to late 1950s. Retiring by nature, Raney withdrew from regular jazz performing during the 1960s, settling into supper club, cabaret, and theatrical work as well as accompanying vocalists, a task for which his marvelous technical mastery ideally equipped him. He did, however, continue to record in various jazz contexts during this period, with Eddie Harris, Zoot Sims, Dave Pike, Stan Getz, and others.

Following a stint with vibraharpist Gary McFarlane's sextet, Raney returned to his hometown of Louisville in the mid-1960s where, with only occasional stays in New York City, festival appearances, and other touring, he has lived since. Personal considerations as well as an undisguised disenchantment with the business side of music have been the major reasons for Raney's decision to forego the limelight. Happily for us, however, the guitarist has continued to record and, in recent years at least, resume live performing. His albums for Choice, Muse, MPS (Pausa) and, most notably, Xanadu Records have borne witness to his contributing growth in, and unexampled mastery of, modern jazz guitar. Among the last decade's most tasteful, eloquent, and creative demonstrations of the art of jazz guitar, these albums have unequivocally reasserted Raney's pre-eminence in a musical idiom he brought to lapidary perfection over his many years as an active,

ever-questing musician who steadfastly has refused to settle for artistic compromise or to rest complacently on past laurels. He has passed these qualities on to his son Doug who, following an earlier interest in rock, applied himself to the study of jazz guitar with such felicitous results that he now poses his father the only serious competition he's ever faced. Not only is the Raney saga not over but, thanks to Doug's appreciation and continuation of his father's work, it is beginning a whole new series of chapters.

Johnny Smith

Johnny Smith, born in Birmingham, Alabama, June 25, 1922, occupies a special place in jazz history. Smith is perhaps best known as the author of "Walk, Don't Run," a pop record hit by the guitar group The Ventures, and for his own hugely popular 1952 hit recording, "Moonlight In Vermont," with tenor saxophonist Stan Getz, the recording that brought the guitarists to the attention of jazz listeners. While many jazz critics have dismissed his music as lacking in spontaneity and rhythmic force, Smith's flawlessly surfaced music has exerted a tremendous, still continuing influence on other guitarists. His stunning technical command of the instrument and thoroughgoing harmonic sensibility are expressed in a series of finely-wrought, gemlike orchestrations whose every aspect, from overall conception to the smallest nuances of phrasing and accenting, has been carefully worked out.

Always a sometime performer most active in radio and recording studios, Smith occasionally led his own groups during the 1950s, when his popularity was running highest, but since the early 1960s he has lived in Colorado Springs where he teaches, operates a music store and studio, and in general eschews virtually all performing activities save the infrequent concert and music clinic. He is still considered the guitarists's guitarist, possessor of a flawless technique and the conceptual savvy to order it perfectly.

ACOUSTIC JAZZ GUITAR

The early 1960s also witnessed a rebirth of interest in the acoustic guitar, primarily through the activities of a pair of Washington, D.C.–based guitarists, Charlie Byrd and Bill Harris, both of whom played nylon-stringed classical guitars. Much of this activity stemmed directly from the popularity of bossa nova, a suave, modern version of the traditional Brazilian samba to which had been annealed a strong influence from modern jazz. One of the chief catalysts

Laurindo Almeida

to this development was the Brazilian Laurindo Almeida (born Sao Paulo, September 2, 1917), a solidly schooled classical guitarist who had come to the United States in 1947 to be featured instrumentalist with the Stan Kenton Orchestra. In 1954 and again in 1958 Almeida undertook a number of recordings with alto saxophonists Bud Shank, producing the first fruitful synthesis of jazz and Brazilian music. These recordings had a direct influence on the development of the bossa nova idiom over the next several years.

Bossa nova arrived in the United States as a fully shaped music in the early 1960s and achieved phenomenal popularity, triggered by the great success enjoyed by Charlie Byrd and Stan Getz, whose 1962 collaboration produced "Desafinado" and "One Note Samba," among other works, the first recordings of the idiom to draw wide attention to the bossa nova in the U.S. Byrd had been introduced to this appealing music while on a State Department-sponsored tour of South America the previous year, a direct outcome of which was his realization of the potential inherent in establishing the Brazilian samba rhythm in conjunction with jazz improvisation. "The combination of Getz's subtly graceful improvisation and Byrd's harmonic and rhythmic ingenuity was not only an artistic success," wrote Leonard Feather, "but also a commercial hit of such magnitude that the entire bossa nova craze in the U.S. may be said to have sprung directly from this album." Feather went on to note of the guitarist, who was born in Suffolk, Virginia, September 16, 1925, "Because of his firm roots in jazz, his thorough classical training, and his sensitive absorption of the sounds he heard in Latin America, Byrd developed into possibly the most versatile guitarist ever to play jazz." And indeed he has been remarkably successful in bridging the two worlds – and often irreconcilable esthetic values – of classical music and jazz, his impressive technique and deep knowledge of harmony helping to offset the occasional rhythmic stiffness and inability to shape cohesive, organically whole improvisations that are Byrd's major weaknesses as a jazz player.

He shares the latter deficiency with Bill Harris (born Nashville, North Carolina, April 14, 1925), like Byrd a solidly schooled instrumentalist who, following early experiences on electric guitar backing such R&B groups as The Clovers, during which he developed his approach to fingerpicked acoustic guitar, made his debut with the latter in 1956, revealing a harmonic orientation more consonant with the Swing Era than the post-bop modern period. Still, while he has had no followers, Harris has developed a pleasing, rhythmically resilient approach that is both charming and immediately recognizable as his alone.

In recent years acoustic fingerpicked guitar has been kept before the public through the efforts of young Detroiter Earl Klugh, a well-schooled player who earned his spurs in George Benson's backing unit. Striking out on his own in 1976, Klugh has enjoyed great success with a deft, accessible approach to pop song materials, which he mixes on his albums with his own appealing compositions, his two recorded collaborations with pianist-arranger Bob James, *One On One* and *Two Of A Kind*, being particularly noteworthy.

CHRISTIAN'S LEGACY CONTINUES

Byrd and Harris notwithstanding, the main thrust of jazz guitar activity during the late 1950s and early 1960s continued the post-bop, Christian-rooted linear style, which not only flourished but produced such major plectrists as Jim Hall, Wes Montgomery, and Joe Pass, among others.

Jim Hall

Jim Hall, born in Buffalo, New York, December 4, 1930, has followed an approach similar to Raney's in that he, too, impresses as a thinking improviser whose playing tempers a basic emotionalism with an incisive, directing musical intelligence. Unlike Raney, however, Hall, in the years since he made his recording debut with the somewhat effete quintet of drummer Chico Hamilton, has performed with an unusually broad spectrum of jazz performers, including Jimmy Giuffre, Lee Konitz, Sonny Rollins, Art Farmer, Gerry Mulligan, and others, and has recorded with an even greater number and much wider diversity of stylists, from traditional to avant-garde, complementing each and every one perfectly. Hall is, in fact, the compleat guitarist: a forceful and gripping soloist whose thoughtful, low-keyed melodism is always logically, coherently, and clearly developed, and a marvelously sympathetic accompanist who listens and responds. He has never made a bad recording but has made any number of superior, moving, and innately musical ones.

Wes Montgomery

Emerging in the late 1950s as a member of the family group The Mastersounds, John Leslie "Wes" Montgomery received quite a bit of critical attention through his commanding use of octave lines in improvised playing, a technique that had been used earlier, most notably by Django Reinhardt, but not to the extent nor with the finesse that Montgomery used it. It was merely one of several techniques in his quiver, but it focused a good deal of attention on him and it wound up, for better or worse, being closely identified with his playing. Born in Indianapolis, Indiana, March 6, 1925, he took up guitar under the stimulus of Charlie Christian recordings. This influence has remained at the core of Montgomery's approach even though he later fell under the sway of such players as Jimmy Raney and Tal Farlow, and at his best Montgomery impressed as something on the order of a latter-day Christian: a guitarist of singing warmth, unerring yet powerful swing, and unassuming emotional directness who was equally at home with popular standards, blues, and original jazz lines. His early work was his best, full of excitement and commitment, inventive and swinging, yet never straining for effect or mired in clichés (even of his own making), as some of his later, more commercial recordings were. His use of the thumb rather than plectrum prevented Montgomery's playing from attaining too much in the way of great speed, but he had more than enough for his purposes, and the use of his thumb had obvious tonal benefits in the dark, mellow sound that is one of the more pleasing and distinctive features of his original, heart-felt music. He died at age forty-three of a heart attack.

Joe Pass

One of the most agile, harmonically resourceful of all bop-influenced guitarists, Joe Pass was born Joseph Passalaqua on January 13, 1929, in New Brunswick, New Jersey, and raised there and in Johnstown, Pennsylvania. He has played guitar since the age of nine; a quick study, he made such sustained progress on the instrument that he was playing professionally by his fourteenth year. His early models, Christian and Reinhardt, soon gave way to his growing interest in bop through the recordings of Charlie Parker, Dizzy Gillespie, Coleman Hawkins, and others, which he heard in a local music shop. In 1949 he moved to New York City to learn the music firsthand but, following a brief period of playing casuals there, fell victim to narcotics addiction. This claimed the next dozen years of his life and it was only after his entering Synanon, the controversial drug and alcohol-rehabilitation center, that he was finally able to vanquish his addiction, reclaim his life, and resume his musical activities. While there, he was heard performing with several Synanon musician-residents by Pacific Jazz Records' Richard Bock who, as *Down Beat* reported at the time, "was convinced not only that the group should make a record but also that Pass was probably the most important jazz discovery in years." The resultant album, *The Sounds of Synanon*, the first recording to present Pass in a strict jazz context, was one of the successes of 1962, and on its release, Leonard Feather observed, "The album does more than merely present a group of good jazz musicians. It unveils a star. In Pass Synanon and Pacific Jazz have discovered a major jazz talent, I believe. His style is as fluent and as technically impressive as any guitarist's now playing jazz; his sound is the soft, easy tone of the Jimmy Raney school; his statements are confident, with superb melodic imagination and structure. Pass is also a composer to watch out for."

Following this debut recording which, incidentally, led to the first of his many *Down Beat* poll victories, the guitarist was heard in support of a number of Pacific Jazz artists as a means of demonstrating his versatility and adaptability, and undertook a number of well-received recordings of his own – notably his *Catch Me!* and *For Django* albums, stunning recordings both – as well as regular performing in the Los Angeles area with saxophonist Bud Shank. All of these activities secured his reputation, and since that time he's literally never looked back. In the intervening years Pass has gone on to earn great acclaim as one of the foremost guitarists in jazz, a superlative, immensely satisfying improviser who always gives his best, whose strong, strikingly distinctive playing always has been marked by flawless musicianship, deep harmonic awareness, an almost inexhaustible melodic fertility, and, not least, crisp, unerring swing. In recent years he's demonstrated these qualities on many recordings for the Pablo label, in international concerts with its regular stable of artists, and has come to be recognized as one of the most thrillingly, dependably creative guitarists in modern music. His solo acoustic recordings have received special accolades for the beauty, power, and totality of his command of the instrument. Too, he remains one of the undisputed masters of linear guitar playing, a forceful, gripping improviser of seizing, fiery creativity and rhythmic finesse.

George Benson

Nor should George Benson be overlooked, who emerged during the middle 1970s as the decade's equivalent to Nat "King" Cole, an instrumentalist of uncommon gifts who achieved phenomenal popular acceptance as a jazz-inflected vocalist. Born in Pittsburgh, Pennsylvania, on March 22, 1943, Benson first performed on ukelele as a youngster, taking up guitar in 1954, a year in that he recorded four vocal performances for RCA's "X" label. Rock 'n' roll claimed his energies during his high school years, a period that saw him performing in local bands, including his own, which he formed at age seventeen. After hearing recordings by Wes Montgomery and Charlie Parker, the guitarist turned his attention to jazz, making such rapid strides in its mastery that he was performing regularly in organist Jack McDuff's popular combo from 1962 to 1965, at which time he formed his first band. A keen, intelligent player influenced by Montgomery, Charlie Christian, and a number of jazz horn players, Benson made any number of striking recordings in a strict jazz context until his vocal performance of Leon Russell's *This Masquerade*, a Top 10 record hit in 1976, set him on the course he has since followed, mixing his smooth, urbane vocals with finely etched jazz guitar lines. Benson has developed great finesse in his practice of

George Benson

Charlie Byrd, Bertell Knox, Barney Kessel, Joe Byrd, and Herb Ellis (from left to right)

humming in unison with his guitar phrases, a technique that had been used some three decades earlier by jazz bassist Slam Stewart.

Other Guitarists

While a number of alternative approaches to the instrument have proliferated in recent years, this fundamental approach, rooted in Charlie Christian and incorporating many of the expressive devices of bebop and post-bop modern jazz, not only has continued to flourish but shows no signs of exhausting its potentials for generating committed, creative, original playing from those adept in its conventions. And, in fact, there is every indication that the most recent generation of guitarists – Pat Martino, Ted Dunbar, Doug Raney, Peter Sprague, Bill Conti, Ron Eschete, Joe Beck, Bruce Forman, and Martin Taylor, among a number of others – has found the approach both relevant and helpful in the forging of their own stylistic expressions. Far from being an outmoded idiom, bop and its disciplines, among the most formidably challenging in all of jazz, continue to provide such players a deeply stimulating, re-

warding, multifaceted outlet for the ordering of their artistic impulses, while demanding at the same time the utmost from their technical resources. It literally calls forth the best they're capable of giving at any time in their respective musical developments and provides the basis for further growth.

NEW APPROACHES: FUSION GUITAR

Given the spiraling, worldwide popularity of rock from the middle 1960s onward, it was inevitable that this music would exert a powerful influence on young guitarists. In fact it has, and from the late 1960s jazz has witnessed the development of a number of musical approaches in which the impact of rock, and rock guitar in particular, has bulked large. Several guitarists have played pivotally important roles in these developments, none so significantly as the British guitarist John McLaughlin. McLaughlin's seminal work with Miles Davis's iconoclastic electric ensemble of the late 1960s, particularly that involved in the celebrated *In A Silent Way* recordings, and soon after with the Tony Williams Lifetime's *Emergency* album, its first and by all odds best, effected a singularly fruitful synthesis of rock and jazz guitar that has stood as a watershed of sorts.

The major distinguishing elements of McLaughlin's approach involved the use of instrumental tonalities produced almost solely by high amplification, often overdriven, resulting in a guitar tonality that would have been considered distorted by conventional players of the instrument (virtually all of whom have preferred a warm, dry, lightly amplified sound as close to the natural sound of the acoustic instrument as possible). Other features involved a controlled handling of the note-sustaining capabilities of such powerful amplification, allowing the generation of an almost limitlessly sustaining tonal production, and the resulting changes in solo patterns such a device permitted which, along with the high energy levels produced by heavy amplification, imparted a feeling of great excitement and power to the music. Blended with the free approach to improvising developed by such jazz instrumentalists as Ornette Coleman, John Coltrane, Albert Ayler, and other young turks, this resulted in a radically different approach to jazz guitar than the music had traditionally borne in previous decades. Not only was the solo conception altered in this approach, but the very sound of the instrument changed almost beyond recognition in a chicken-or-egg relationship, tonality influencing conception, and vice versa, making for a very fluid situation in which matter and manner were often one and the same. The medium truly was the message, at least in post-bop, rock-derived contemporary jazz guitar.

Much of the stimulus to these developments came from the brilliant, self-tutored electric genius of the guitar, Jimi Hendrix, whose near-demonic forays into pure texture – in which distortion, feedback, sustain, and the like were turned into vital, integral components of the music he created with such abandon in the middle 1960s – opened up an exciting, hitherto unperceived world of musical possibilities. Like many untutored visionaries, Hendrix had an imperfect understanding of the conventional disciplines of music, with the result that his playing, for all its brilliance and originality, frequently was chaotic, sprawling and, in the final analysis, inconclusive. Still, warts and all, he showed us what electric guitar might be, and in a very real sense he is the true father of contemporary electric guitar, his experimental work leading to, and influencing in many of

Ted Dunbar

its important aspects what is currently described as "fusion" music.

It is the achievement of McLaughlin, Larry Coryell, Jerry Hahn, and several other early fusion guitarists that they took up the challenge of Hendrix's music and through their greater musical sophistication, no less than their understanding of so-called "free jazz," developed a number of viable solo and ensemble approaches in which Hendrix's searing, passionate iconoclasm was more fully shaped, and given coherence both by their intelligence and their greater awareness of the principles of musical construction. Without sacrificing the power and energy of his approach, they imposed a certain order to the chaos that characterized much of Hendrix's music, creating in the process the handling of guitar that has become so prevalent in recent years, initially through their own gripping work and later in the work of the young guitarists they have in turn influenced. While many of the conventional traditions of jazz were overturned by these developments,

James "Blood" Ulmer

they have generated their own conventional practices and procedures over the last decade or so.

Which is not to say, of course, that all such music sounds the same. It does not, and will not, for fusion guitar, like any other of jazz's several stylistic idioms, is as varied as the playing styles of those working under its umbrella. Such terms as "fusion guitar" or "post-bop rock-derived contemporary guitar" are necessarily imprecise, mere conveniences under which are grouped widely disparate players who share certain broad, often vague stylistic tendencies. The music of John McLaughlin, for example, is quite different in a number of important, perceptible respects from that of Larry Coryell, just as his is in the same relationship to John Abercrombie's, Ralph Towner's, John Scofield's, Philip Catherine's, Al DiMeola's, or Pat Metheny's, to cite several younger players who have come to prominence in recent years. Few, however, would mistake them for players of Jim Hall's or Joe Pass's generation, or they in turn with Eddie Lang's or Lonnie Johnson's.

WRAP-UP

Each generation of jazz musicians seeks to achieve its own expression by interpreting the past in reference to its own present time, and this is further compounded by the jazz artist's deep-seated tendency to fashion an approach of true, distinctive originality – this is, after all, what jazz is all about, what distinguishes it from all other forms of musical expression. There is in fusion music a particularly strong tendency toward this, for one of the major characterstics of a free jazz-based form of expression is that the music in effect creates itself only in performance, its thematic materials, such as they are, serving primarily as springboards for the sustained improvisational development that follows, and which provides the listener the greatest enjoyment he derives from the music. This is, of course, one of the signal characteristics of unalloyed jazz expression, and its restoration to a position of primacy is one of the more impressive and valuable features of the new music, developing in its listeners no less than its players a willingness to follow closely the unfolding drama of the performance. The creation of such a hazardous, risk-filled approach to music-making is breeding a whole new generation of guitar virtuosos of undoubted technical brilliance and imaginative resourcefulness, for to play the music well, with power and passion and real organic wholeness, demands players of uncommon gifts.

Not all that has been produced in the genre thus far has attained to these levels, but it is endemic to the music that it constantly asks of its adherents that they strive mightily to do so, to risk chaos in the pursuit of excellence.

Over the sixty-odd years during which its development has been documented by recordings, jazz guitar has evolved from a simple, almost naive music not far removed from its folk roots in the fin-de-siècle South to its current state of great musical sophistication and wide stylistic diversity. It has been enabled to do this in building-block fashion, each generation of performers building upon and extending the accomplishments of that immediately preceding it, learning from it the music's conventions and gradually expanding them to permit the incorporation of new techniques, broadened conceptual bases, altered melody-harmony-rhythm relationships and, not least, new developments in technology, all of which impinge, at various times and in various ways, upon the manner in which the music is perceived, shaped, and modified. In addition to the process of steady, sustained evolution through which any artistic discipline passes over time, there appear from time to time performers of such singular powers and advanced levels of expression that the music is enabled to progress even more rapidly. Jazz guitar has been blessed with several such visionaries – Eddie Lang, Lonnie Johnson, Django Reinhardt, and, greatest of all, Charlie Christian – whose daring, innovative and thoroughly original approaches have strongly affected the instrument's development. The impress of their distinctive artistry is everywhere evident in jazz guitar, even if later performers are unaware of their impact, thanks to the ongoing process of evolution that binds the advances of individual contributors into the unbroken lineage that comprises musical tradition. With each passing year and each new performer added to this continuum, jazz guitar casts its nets ever wider, incorporating all manner of personal and idiomatic expressions, some to be absorbed into and nourish the traditions, others to be discarded as ephemeral.The borrowings from rock, popular music, and, more recently, various ethnic and third–world musics that younger guitarists have been introducing are simply the latest manifestations of this vital, organic process and will ensure that the music remains fresh, vigorous, and relevent to the expressive needs of its performers, that jazz guitar will indeed continue to grow and renew itself.

DISCOGRAPHY: JAZZ GUITAR

OSCAR ALEMAN
Swing Guitar Legend
Rambler 106

After Reinhardt, the only non-American guitarist of the prewar period to develop a mastery of the idiom comparable to his, the Argentinian-born Aleman is, unfortunately, much less known than his considerable achievements should warrant. Rambler's 16-selection survey of the best of his European and Argentinian recordings from 1936–45 goes a long way to redressing this imbalance, for it well illustrates the guitarist's formidable gifts as an improviser of uncommon power, possessed of a harmonic sense even more advanced than Reinhardt's and a supple, driving rhythmic impetus that allowed him to outswing Django. A stunning album whose imaginative, audacious playing will come as a revelation to those unfamiliar with Aleman's wonderful music.

GEORGE BARNES
Blues Going Up
Concord Jazz 43

Plays So Good
Concord Jazz 67

With the exceptions of the several cuts included in the two Yazoo compilations cited earlier, there are no examples of Barnes's influential early acoustic chorded and chord-supported work currently available. These two 1977 albums do, however, go a long way to redressing this oversight, as they offer excellent well-recorded examples of his warm, well-crafted playing at its easygoing best. The fine quartet he co-led with cornetist Ruby Braff earlier in the decade is represented on the Chiaroscuro and Concord Jazz labels with several excellent albums each offering generous samplings of Barnes's fetchingly elegant guitar.

GEORGE BENSON
The George Benson Collection
Warner Bros., two-record set 2HW-3577

Like Nat Cole before him, Benson started off as a jazz instrumentalist but achieved his greatest success as a popular vocalist with an effortless-sounding approach in which jazz phrasing plays no little part. This 18-selection compilation brings together a representative sampling of the singer-guitarist's recent work in this area, including the major vocal successes but not stinting his fine, always tasteful and interesting instrumentals, which are scattered throughout the collection. The earlier, pre-pop phase of the guitarist's career is amply documented in the 2-LP sets *George Benson & Jack McDuff* (Prestige) and *Benson Burner* (Columbia). Many other recordings of his are available on the Prestige, Columbia, CTI, A&M, Polydor and Warner Bros. labels.

KENNY BURRELL
Guitar Forms
Verve 2070

One of the most completely satisfying recitals by this talented, versatile jazz guitarist, *Guitar Forms* is the one Burrell set that comes closest to encapsulating the full range of his artistry. The performances run the gamut from blues-inflected linear electric work à la Christian to poised acoustic set-pieces (on nylon classical guitar) with lush orchestral accompaniments, and everything in between, every one a model of its type, the guitarist giving each its due and playing at peak abilities throughout.

CHARLIE BYRD
Latin Byrd
Milestone, two-record set 47005

LAURINDO ALMEIDA
Chamber Jazz
Concord Jazz 84

EARL KLUGH
One on One
Columbia 36241

Two of a Kind
Capitol 12244

That the acoustic gut-stringed classical guitar enjoyed something of a renaissance in jazz during the mid-1960s was due primarily to the Washington, D.C.-based Byrd, who demonstrated the instrument's potential for lyrical jazz expression in a series of lovely performances of bossa nova, the modern Brazilian samba form that enjoyed a several years' vogue at the time. Some of Byrd's finest efforts in this vein are contained in this sampling of his highly acclaimed Riverside recordings of the period. Numerous other examples of his polished, adroit playing are available on the Fantasy, Columbia, Milestone and Concord Jazz labels. The Brazilian-born Almeida has been a fixture on the U.S. jazz scene since the late 1940s, when he joined the Stan Kenton Orchestra. His early 50s collaborations with saxophonist Bud Shank, fusing Brazilian music with jazz, eventually led to bossa nova a decade later. In recent years Almeida has continued the practice of recording his poised classical-styled guitar with jazz players of a lyrical bent, with such groups as the L.A. 4, and the listed set offers his fine, easy jazz settings of a number of attractive classical works. More recently the most consistent and accomplished exponent of jazzy classical guitar has been the young Detroiter Klugh whose numerous Liberty albums contain his fetching original compositions as well as versions of popular song hits in an accessible commercial format. His two recorded collaborations with pianist-arranger Bob James are particularly outstanding examples of contemporary crossover jazz performed with taste, power and elegance. Klugh, in particular, turns in some of his most interesting playing.

CHARLIE CHRISTIAN
Solo Flight: The Genius of Charlie Christian
Columbia, two-record set 30779

No hyperbole in this album title. Christian, the shy, self-effacing Texas-born guitarist, has been jazz guitar's only authentic figure of genius, responsible for synthesizing the best elements of the instrument's previous history into a seamless, totally original approach of such great melodic-harmonic resourcefulness that it has served as the basis for literally all subsequent developments in the instrument's usage in jazz. As is suggested by this set of 25 of his 1939–41 recordings, most made while he was featured soloist with the Benny Goodman Orchestra, the key to Christian's enduring influence resides primarily in his astonishing imaginative fertility, which allowed him to frame improvisations of real substance, organic wholeness and easy-sounding inevitability, creating mobile, singing lines of unforced naturalness. Once heard, it's as though we've always known them. A stunning, absolutely essential album. While jazz guitar didn't start here, it was brought to perfection in these recordings.

LARRY CORYELL
The Essential Larry Coryell
Vanguard, two-record set 75/76

JOHN MCLAUGHLIN
Al Di Meola/Paco de Lucia
Friday Night in San Francisco
Columbia 37152

PAT METHENY
80/81
ECM, two-record set 2-1180

JAMES "BLOOD" ULMER
Free Lancing
Columbia 37493

More recent developments in jazz guitar are charted in these several albums by contemporary performers who have left their mark on the instrument and the music. The post-Gary Burton stage of rock-influenced jazz guitarist Larry Coryell's troubled career is well surveyed in the Vanguard compilation of 12 lengthy selections from his well-received albums for the label. British guitarist McLaughlin joins forces with two of the instrument's leading younger lights, DiMeola and DeLucia, in this free-wheeling acoustic guitar recital, recorded "live" in concert. Two trio performances combine with duets by the participants in which the differing, yet compatible approaches of the three are shown in bold relief. McLaughlin's characteristic work on electric guitar is well showcased on numerous other recordings, solo recitals, with his Mahavishnu Orchestra, as well as with Tony Williams's Lifetime. Pat Metheny's pleasingly eclectic brand of contemporary melodism is particularly well demonstrated in the 8-selection set listed, with others of his ECM releases not far behind in interest. At the opposite end of the contemporary spectrum is Ulmer's spiky, intense, hyperkinetic approach, which simultaneously fuses electric blues, funk, Jimi Hendrix, free jazz and electronic musics, among other influences, making for a stylistic amalgam perhaps best described as spaced-out rhythm and blues. It possesses an undeniable rhythmic fervor and a raw urgency that, when well realized, as is often the case here, can be as compelling as it is unsettling.

TAL FARLOW
"Tal"
Verve 2565

In the early to middle 1950s the self-taught Farlow developed one of the most strikingly original of all approaches to modern jazz guitar. Learning well his lessons from Christian, his first and chief model, Farlow developed an approach notable for its great speed of execution, harmonic savvy, coloristic variety and, most important, a quirky, wholly idiosyncratic handling of rhythm and accenting that gave his playing its highly distinctive sound. All of these characteristics are well displayed in the eight selections in this album, made with the marvelous trio he led during the middle 1950s, one of the finest features of which was the stunning interplay between the guitarist and his pianist Eddie Costa and which charged the group's work with such incendiary brilliance.

JIM HALL
Concierto
CTI 8012

Hall, one of the finest, most commendably versatile of all modern jazz guitarists, combines in his deft, lucid, always musical approach elements of Raney, Christian, and other post-bop players. Noted as a deeply thinking musician, he has performed with a wide range of jazz players over the last quarter-century, and has enhanced every encounter to which he's been part. Like Burrell's *Guitar Forms*, this lovely 1975 recording illustrates perhaps better than any other the full breadth of his gifts, for the performances range from his ardent, feelingful rendition of Rodrigo's *Concierto De Aranjuez* to straightahead jazz performances in his distinctive, carefully modulated style. Other examples of his crystalline playing may be found on the Milestone, Verve, Pausa, A&M, and Concord Jazz labels – and they're all good.

LONNIE JOHNSON
Lonnie Johnson in Jazz, 1925–65
Origin Jazz Library, two-record set OJL 8104-5

This 28-selection set is the definitive representation of Johnson's work in a strict jazz context, It offers all of his groundbreaking, late 1920s recordings with Louis Armstrong, Duke Ellington, Charlie Creath, Clarence Williams, and the Chocolate Dandies, as well as a number of solos and several duets with pianist Jimmy Blythe or Eddie Lang (appearing as Blind Willie Dunn). In these recordings Johnson staked his claim as one of the seminally important early jazz guitarists. In addition, his few later efforts in this genre are included, a few sides with clarinetist Jimmie Noone and several made with a Canadian Dixieland group several years before his death. Again, an essential album.

BARNEY KESSEL
The Poll Winners Ride Again
Contemporary 7556

Poll Winners Three
Contemporary 7576

On his numerous Contemporary Records albums of the early and middle 1950s the Oklahoma-born Kessel established his reputation as the foremost Charlie Christian disciple of modern times, with a particularly satisfying extension of Christian's earlier linear guitar approach that was totally modern in harmonic character while retaining the easy swing and appealing melodism of his model. This claim is validated to a fare-thee-well in these two still fresh-sounding recordings from the period, on which he is superbly seconded by bassist Ray Brown and drummer Shelly Manne, with the guitarist winners of Down Beat jazz polls on their respective instruments (and hence the album titles). Another fine Kessel set from the period is Let's Cook where he is joined by such stellar players as saxophonist Ben Webster, pianist Hamp Hawes, trombonist Frank Rosolino, and others. In recent years the guitarist has undertaken an admirable album series for Concord Jazz Records, which indi-

cated there has been no diminution of his abilities.

EDDIE LANG
Jazz Guitar Virtuoso
Yazoo 1059

Lang's widely admired technical fluency, melodic resourcefulness, harmonic savvy, and superb touch – qualities that led to his dominance in jazz recording of the late 1920s and early 1930s, as well as bringing his instrument into the mainstream of jazz practice and setting it on the course it has since followed – are handily underscored in this well-chosen program of 14 performances from 1927–32. Included are several solos, including his adaptations of Rachmaninoff's Prelude, duets and trio performances with pianists Frank Signorelli, Arthur Schutt, or Rube Bloom and, most important to jazz guitar history, three of his fabled 1929 duets with Lonnie Johnson as well as two with guitarist Carl Kress from 1932. An absolutely essential album, for jazz guitar truly starts here.

WES MONTGOMERY
The Incredible Jazz Guitar of Wes Montgomery
Fantasy Original Jazz Classics 036

Thanks to the continuing interest in Montgomery's music, there are currently available large numbers of recordings from every stage of the guitarist's career, none more compelling than this modestly priced reissue of his second Riverside album. Made in early 1960 with a topnotch rhythm section in support, Montgomery soars effortlessly, playing with unfettered creativity in his distinctive extension of Christian's linearity, leavening his fresh-sounding lines with generous doses of his patented octave work and chorded playing as well. Another excellent set is Liberty's 2-LP Beginnings, which brings together the best of his late 1950s recordings for Pacific Jazz Records. Many other sets are on the Verve, Riverside, and A&M labels.

JOE PASS
The Complete "Catch Me" Sessions
Liberty 1053
JOE PASS-HERB ELLIS
Two for the Road
Pablo 2310714

With Catch Me, his first date as a leader after his discovery as part of the Sounds of Synanon group, guitarist Pass established his reputation as one of the major post-Christian electric guitarists. Two decades later, it remains one of the signal recordings of his career, his playing charged with an electric excitement, plentiful invention and a palpable sense of urgency he has yet to surpass. Pass has recorded extensively since, most notably for Pablo Records, making any number of exemplary albums over the past decade, of which the set of duets with kindred spirit Herb Ellis is a particularly satisfying example of the art of jazz guitar at its spark-producing best, the meeting stimulating both men to some of their finest, most gripping playing. Pass's several Virtuoso solo recitals for Pablo are likewise well worth seeking out.

JIMMY RANEY
Jazz Classics
Prestige 7434

The Influence
Xanadu 116

It can be truly said of Raney that he never made a bad record but some, of course, are better than others. The Prestige album, made with Stan Getz, among others, contains some of the guitarist's finest playing from the important early stage of his career. Four classic performances from 1953, with Getz featured on tenor saxophone, are included – "Motion," "Lee," "Signal," and "Round 'Bout Midnight" – each containing some of the guitarist's loveliest, most perfectly shaped playing. More tasty examples of his playing from this period may be heard in the earlier listed Johnny Smith Album, *Echoes of an Era*, where Raney performs as part of the Stan Getz Quintet. A more recent illustration of his still continuing mastery is offered in Xanadu's splendid *The Influence*, the first of several excellent Raney albums from the late 1970s. Raney's son Doug, his chief musical legatee, is heard performing with his father in the attractive Steeplechase album *Duets*.

DJANGO REINHARDT-STEPHANE GRAPPELLI
Quintet of the Hot Club of France
Angel 36985

A dozen of the finest recordings made by the unique string ensemble formed in late 1934 by the Belgian gypsy guitarist and his musical alter ego, violinist Grappelli, comprise this immensely satisfying program, one of the best introductions to Reinhardt's effortless-sounding, warmly lyrical, imaginatively fertile and, above all, strikingly original acoustic guitar style, at once rhythmically incisive and almost rhapsodic in its melodic-harmonic expansiveness. There are currently available, happily, many other albums of Reinhardt's singing, singular playing for those wishing to investigate his distinctive music further, including a number of modestly priced reissues on the Everest label. Any of them are well worth seeking out, for Reinhardt truly never made a bad recording, only varying degrees of good, better, best.

JOHNNY SMITH
Echoes of an Era
(with Stan Getz)
Roulette, two-record set 106

Smith's suave, harmonically sophisticated guitar instrumentals, arranged with lapidary perfection yet bearing solid jazz values, exerted a powerful influence on other guitarists during the early 1950s. Most of the best and most

memorable of his important early work in this vein, including the greatly popular "Moonlight in Vermont," a true jazz guitar classic, is contained in this set, shared with his frequent collaborator from this period, tenor saxophonist Stan Getz. Thus, while only half of the set contains Smith performances, it offers the only sampling of his groundbreaking guitar work currently in print.

Collections:
50 Years of Jazz Guitar
Columbia, two-record set 33566

In attempting to survey the entire historical development of jazz guitar through 28 representative selections, spanning the years 1921–71, this set almost achieves the impossible. Its ambitious, intelligently chosen program spans the early prejazz playing of Sam Moore (heard performing on an 8-string octocorda), through the early work of Lonnie Johnson and Eddie Lang (solo, duet, and with jazz ensembles), the Hawaiian guitarist Benny Nawahi, blues players Bobby Leecan, Oscar Woods and Memphis Minnie, guitarist-entertainer Otto Heimal, country guitarists Leon McAuliffe and Hank Garland, and jazz performers Dick McDonough, Carl Kress, Joe Sodja, Teddy Bunn, Eddie Durham, Charlie Christian, Slim Gaillard, Django Reinhardt, George Van Eps, Kenny Burrell, Herb Ellis, George Benson, Charlie Byrd and John McLaughlin. An interesting, provocative and immensely enjoyable compilation whose cross-genre approach is tellingly effective, and quite instructive as well, making it a model of its type.

Guitar Player
MCA, two-record set 2-6002

This fine sampler, prepared under the aegis of *Guitar Player* magazine, offers a fairly comprehensive representation of a number of guitarists and jazz guitar styles,

from vintage to contemporary. Blues is represented by two characteristic performances by the titanic B.B. King; swing by a pair of spirited duets by Irving Ashby and John Collins; classical guitar in a jazz context by three fine selections by Laurindo Almeida; while the mainstream of post-Christian, bebop-influenced jazz guitar is well served by three Joe Pass performances and an equal number of Barney Kessel-Herb Ellis collaborations, More recent developments in the instrument's use are signaled by three selections apiece by Larry Coryell and young wizard Lee Ritenour, making for a pleasing, well-balanced program that surveys much of the guitar's history in jazz performance. All the recordings, incidentally, were undertaken in 1976 specifically for this set and are unavailable elsewhere.

Pioneers of the Jazz Guitar
Yazoo 1057

Fun on the Frets
Yazoo 1061

These two fine samplings of acoustic jazz guitar concentrate on the pioneering work of Eddie Lang (three duets with Lonnie Johnson, one with Carl Kress), Nick Lucas (two solo performances), Dick McDonough (two solos and two duets with Kress), and the duo of John Cali-Tony Guttoso (two performances) in the first listed album, which spans the years 1928–37. In the second are offered two more mid-1930s McDonough-Kress duets, two fine Kress solos from 1939, 10 duets by Kress and Tony Mottola from 1941 radio transcriptions, and four exemplary single-string and chorded solos by the impeccable George Van Eps from 1949. There is, it would seem, little real improvising in these carefully arranged performances, yet the spirit of jazz phrasing and rhythm informs all of them, making the two compilations of inestimable value to the student of jazz guitar.

Country Pickin'

by Dan Forte

Despite the enormous popularity of country music, and its phenomenal endurance in the face of changing fads and fashions (even its own), country guitar is treated somewhat like the bastard son of the guitar family. Nearly every major college and university in the United States has a classical guitar program, and most offer courses in jazz guitar; sociologists trace the evolution of the blues; and the entire guitar industry seems geared toward the young heavy metalist; but country guitar continues to be viewed as slightly illegitimate. The image most people have of country music remains one of Roy Clark and Buck Owens, clad in overalls, sitting on well-placed hay bales on the set of television's *Hee Haw*. Meanwhile, Chet Atkins has performed with symphony orchestras all over the world; the fingerpicking style bearing the name of Merle Travis has influenced players of all styles; pioneers like Hank Garland and Jimmy Bryant made the unthinkable transition from country to progressive jazz; and country music's trademark sound, the steel guitar, continues to advance at an ever accelerating rate, both harmonically and electronically. Maybe it's time for country's image to catch up with its reality.

The advances in country guitar picking are indeed impressive when one considers that, like most pop musicians, nearly all of the genre's influential players, past and present, learned the instrument without "formal" training – teaching themselves, listening to records or the radio, swapping licks with other players, perhaps learning some chords from a Chet Atkins book. Partly because no one showed them the "right" way to play, and because of the individual requirements for some highly individualistic styles, numerous unorthodox techniques developed – from Maybelle Carter's method of playing lead bass lines with her thumb while strumming the rhythm with her fingers to James Burton's simultaneous use of flatpick and fingerpicks.

Kitty Wells

Crockett's Kentucky Mountaineers,
with their Gibson instruments

The Guitar in Country

Surprisingly, the entire evolution of the guitar in country music – from Riley Puckett and Maybelle Carter to Buddy Emmons and Jerry Reed – is less than a century old. Though the medieval ballads and Celtic music of the British Isles that formed the basis of country music became part of the American life style as soon as the first settlers arrived in the New World, the guitar did not enter the picture until the 1890s. The fiddle and the mountain dulcimer with its drone strings provided a closer approximation to the sound of highland bagpipes, so if a vocal was accompanied at all (and as often as not they weren't) it was usually by one of the two. The banjo, which was brought to America by African slaves, was also uniquely suited to British and early country music, especially when a Viriginian named Joe Sweeney added a fifth drone string to it.

The guitar entered this music at about the same time black musicians began to use it, during the 1890s. It filtered into old-timey music through three channels. Upper-class ladies saw the guitar as a parlor instrument, on which they could play light, pleasant tunes. In the Southeast, black railroad workers introduced the instrument to coalminers and mountain people. In the Southwest, the guitar music of the Spanish settlers was adopted by cowboys north of the border, who used the six-string to accompany their ballads of life on the plains, usually sung to the tune of an Irish or English melody.

The Crook Brothers

"HILLBILLY" MUSIC

During the 1920s radio began to shape musical tastes and talents in a more immediate and dramatic way than had ever happened before, and country music was one of the primary beneficiaries of the long electronic reach that radio could offer recordings. And so was launched the radio barn dance, first on WLS in Chicago, then on WSM in Nashville, where the Grand Ole Opry began in 1925. These programs covered enormous areas of the U.S., and featured what was known as "hillbilly" music, mostly string bands dominated by fiddlers and banjo pickers. Nevertheless, radio is also where country guitar came to prominence, beginning with the likes of Riley Puckett and Sam McGee.

The first "hot licks" guitarist in country music was a blind singer/guitarist from Georgia named Riley Puckett, who recorded on his own as early as 1924 ("Rock All Our Babies To Sleep") and formed the Skillet Lickers with fiddlers Gid Tanner and Clayton McMichen in 1926. Puckett established a national reputation for himself through his Columbia recordings and radio broadcasts over WSB, Atlanta. His experimental, syncopated guitar runs were often in conflict with the Skillet Lickers, which was actually a studio band – with extra personnel appearing and disappearing on different sessions – revolving around the old-timey style of Tanner and the pop and jazz leanings of McMichen. E.C. Ball, a fine old-timey guitarist who recorded briefly in the 1940s, recalls the effect Puckett had on him and a great many guitar players of that period: "I always liked his style of playing. He did a lot of runs and stuff that you heard very little of in those days." Indeed, the only guitarists playing "out front" besides Puckett were on black "race records" – recordings of black artists, targeted specifically at the lucrative black market. The influence of blues players can be heard clearly on Puckett's "The Darkie's Wail" (actually "John Henry"), played bottleneck style, and "Fuzzy Rag," exhibiting his syncopated bass lines and rhythmic chording (both available on *Old Time Greats, Vol. 1*, Old Homestead, OHCS 114).

On much of the Skillet Lickers' recorded material, Riley's guitar is confined to the bass run-and-strum role that was the standard for old-time string bands. The instrumentation for most of these dance bands consisted of fiddle(s), banjo, and guitar(s). The guitar wasn't freed from holding down the bass until bluegrass music introduced the upright bass.

Field Recordings

It was during the 1920s that the record companies discovered that "hillbilly" music, like the blues, had a large and previous untapped audience; and so they began sending agents to record local musicians on the cumbersome field-recording equipment of the time. These "field recordings" were usually made with portable equipment in homes, stores, or hotel rooms, since there were no recording studios in the rural South. In August of 1927, Victor Records' Ralph Peer went on just such an errand to Bristol, Virginia, where he discovered two "hillbilly" guitar heavyweights in the same week – Maybelle Carter and Jimmie Rodgers.

Maybelle Carter

The Carter Family – A.P., his wife Sara, and his sister-in-law Maybelle – came from nearby Maces Springs, Virginia, but A.P. had done quite a bit of traveling (he spent a year working on a railroad gang in Indiana) and had collected dozens of songs and written several about his home on Clinch Mountain. The Carter Family played an enormous part in adding to the repertoire of country songs ("Keep On The Sunny Side," "Wabash Cannonball," "Wildwood Flower," to name just a few), while Maybelle's innovative guitar work influenced scores of future pickers.

In the liner notes to *Legendary Performers, Vol. I: The Original Carter Family*, Maybelle's son-in-law, country star Johnny Cash, explains: "Maybelle's style of guitar playing was unique, and evidently she came up with it on her own. What she did was play the melody on the bass strings while maintaining a rhythm on the treble strings, fingering a partial chord. Later, she developed some intricate melody runs on the bass strings. Of course, such runs were not new, but they were used differently by Maybelle; they were being used not only as a part of the lead instrument, but as fills and also for the 'bottom' of the song. Throughout it all, the strong emphasis on the bass was a must, and this was gained in part by the use of a thumbpick and two steel fingerpicks." Cash also points out that Maybelle's family (by no means wealthy) must have been quite confident in her musical abilities to let the eighteen-year-old buy a Gibson L-5 archtop, which was extremely expensive in those days, selling for $125.00. Most photographs of guitar players of that period show them playing round-hole, flat-top guitars, usually cheap mail order models or Stellas that could be obtained for ten dollars. This investment by the Carters in Maybelle's musicianship turned out to be an investment in country music's future as well, since her guitar style had a wide impact on future pickers.

The Singing Brakeman

Jimmie Rodgers – known variously as "The Singing Brakeman," "America's Blue Yodeler," and finally "The Daddy Of Country Music" – was born in Meridian, Mississippi, in 1897. The son of a section hand, he worked on the railroads until he took ill in 1924 and turned to music, having learned some guitar and banjo from black section workers as a water boy. When Ralph Peer came to record country musicians in Bristol, Rodgers had planned on auditioning his string band, the Jimmie Rodgers Entertainers. But an argument over billing divided the group the day before the audition, so Jimmie went alone with his guitar, and thus, musical history was made.

At his first session, Rodgers recorded "The Soldier's Sweetheart" and "Rock All Our Babies To Sleep," but the record was not an immediate hit. For his second session, however, he went to New York and recorded "Blue Yodel #1" ("T For Texas"), which combined blues phrasing and structure with the white tradition of yodeling. It was an instant success, and soon Rodgers was recording "Waiting For A Train," "In The Jailhouse Now," "My Rough And Rowdy Ways," and several more "blue yodels." Some songs, such as "Any Old Time," featured full band backing, complete with brass, while others, like "Blue Yodel #8" ("Muleskinner Blues"), consisted of simply Jimmie and his guitar. On "Muleskinner,"

The Carter Family

Rodgers accompanies his vocal with a syncopated, stop-and-start bass line and strumming pattern, and then proceeds to take off on a single-note guitar solo. Oddly enough, he breaks from the verse-verse-yodel pattern of the rest of the song by singing a verse, rhyming it, and then playing his solo for an entire stanza through the next turnaround. While country blues players of the period would play leads or fills in the treble while keeping a steady rhythm going in the bass, the bottom drops out completely for Rodgers's solo until the tag.

Rodgers began the vogue for cowboy songs so important through the history of country music and guitar players – including Ernest Tubb, Hank Snow, Bill Monroe, Merle Haggard, and Gene Autry – long after his death of tuberculosis on May 26, 1933.

Blues Influences

Jimmie Rodgers was obviously not the first or only country guitarist influenced by black blues – in fact, Maybelle Carter was one of the *few* innovators in country music with almost no discernible blues influence – and there were black country singers long before Charley Pride. In the Depression years and before, blue-collar whites and blacks worked side by side, especially in the South, and there was much cross-pollination of musical styles. This give-and-take helps explain why black songsters like Mississippi John Hurt seemed so out of place geographically when compared to the black blues singers of their region. Hurt's smooth fingerpicking and relaxed, melodic vocal style (similar to Libba Cotten and Etta Baker) more closely resembled white coun-

The Delmore Brothers

try players from Tennessee and the Eastern Seaboard than the rhythmic drive and emotional intensity of Delta bluesmen such as, say, Charley Patton or Son House. On the other side, country guitarists as diverse as Merle Travis and Sam McGee drew on the black styles in order to adapt them.

Sam McGee

Sam McGee's fingerstyle guitar playing is a telling example of a black-influenced artist changing the course of country music. Born in Franklin, Tennessee in 1894, "Mr. Sam" developed his fingerpicking method listening to black railroad workers and an older white guitarist named Tom Hood. In an interview with *Guitar Player* magazine, conducted a month and a half before his death in 1975, he told Bob Krueger: "Where we learned the most about the style was from the black people. My daddy ran a little store, and these section hands would come over from the railroad at noon. After they finished their lunch, they would play guitars. Two of them, the Steward brothers, played real good, and that's where I learned to love the blues tunes. Black people were about the only people that played guitars then. It's a little different than I do, but it's the same kind of picking, using your fingers."

McGee's fingerpicking style was exactly the opposite of Maybelle Carter's; he would play intricate melodies on the treble strings with two or three fingers while maintaining an alternating bass with his thumb (similar to John Hurt). Although he and his banjo-playing brother, Kirk, backed Fiddlin' Arthur Smith and were members of the Fruit Jar Drinkers – and Sam backed banjo great Uncle Dave Macon for twenty years – McGee was the first to exploit the guitar's possibilities as a self-contained *solo* instrument. A portable mini-orchestra, Mr. Sam became an original member of the Grand Ole Opry radio show in 1925, and stayed with the show until his death almost fifty years later. Although many people have been credited with being the first to play an electric guitar on the Opry, McGee experimented with an electric lap steel guitar on the show back in 1926 – before Judge George D. Hay, the Opry's founder, told him to "hold it down to earth." That kind of conservatism continues to dominate the Opry even today, as we shall see.

THE HIGH LONESOME SOUND

During the 1930s guitar-mandolin duets were very popular, such as the Monroe Brothers (guitarist Charlie and mandolinist Bill, before the latter went on to invent bluegrass), the Blue Sky Boys (Bill and Earl Bollick), and the Callahan Brothers. As in the earlier string bands, the guitar was confined to strumming rhythm with some bass-run fills. One exception was the Delmore Brothers duo. While Alton played rhythm on six-string guitar, brother Rabon played lead on a Martin four-string tenor guitar, on songs like "Freight Train Boogie" and "Brown's Ferry Blues" (both later recorded by Doc Watson, the most obvious example of the influence they exerted). Still, it was Bill Monroe who took the next step in adapting "hillbilly" music to the changing demands of its audience. Though he started calling his group the Blue Grass Boys in the late thirties, after splitting from brother Charlie, the sound that we have come to identify as bluegrass music was not fully realized until the formation of Bill's classic bluegrass band in 1945. Mandolinist Monroe described his fast-paced, bluesy music as "the high lonesome sound" and named it after his home state of Kentucky. With young Earl Scruggs on banjo, fiddlin' Chubby Wise, Cedric Rainwater on upright bass, and singer/guitarist Lester Flatt, he boasted an all-star line-up that has rarely been equalled in the history of country music.

In bluegrass, the guitar again served as timekeeper, not unlike its role in the guitar-mandolin duets, but through the strong, rhythmic playing of Flatt it gained a new dimension. Although the terms "bluegrass" and "flatpicking" have almost become synonymous for the type of guitar playing later pioneered by Clarence White and Doc Watson, early bluegrass players, including Flatt and Mac Wiseman, played with a thumbpick and seldom if ever soloed. As Tony Rice, probably the most advanced flatpick soloist on the scene today, details, "Lester wore a thumbpick and one fingerpick. And compared to Lester, none of the others were very ept at that. He was a driving player – he knew how to use that technique. Jimmy Martin, I guess, was the first significant guitarist in Bill Monroe's band who used a flatpick, and that, of course, started a whole new thing. Back then a guitar solo was as rare as a bass solo in bluegrass. And maybe it was good that it was, because sometimes that time just feels so good you don't want to break it up. The tempo is real important. If you're a bonafide bluegrass guitarist, working with some bluegrass cats, you've got to be able to get off your ass and keep time. If the banjo player wants to kick off 'Train 45' at 300 miles an hour, you've got to be able to accommodate him."

Along with his rhythmic drive, Lester Flatt left his indelible imprint on the vocabulary of bluegrass guitar with his famous G-run, repeated, modified,

Bill Monroe

and transmogrified by virtually every subsequent picker in the genre. The G-run was developed initially because Flatt had trouble keeping up with Bill Monroe's demon mandolin solos; and so he picked up at the end of the solo by playing this run, which went from E to F# to G on the low E string, B to C to C# on the A, D to E to F# on the D, and finished up with the open G string. This little lick became *the* classic bluegrass move. One of the players who relied on this technique was Don Reno, who could play the G run upside-down or inside-out. Though primarily a banjo player, Reno played superb bluegrass guitar with Reno & Smiley, shown to full advantage on the duo's gospel recordings.

Rarely did a guitarist move from bluegrass timekeeper to electric soloist. One of the few bluegrass guitarists to successfully make the transition to electric guitar and rockabilly music was Joe Maphis, who also played fiddle, banjo, and almost anything with strings on it. On his electric albums, utilizing a custom-made double-neck Mosrite solidbody with a short-scale neck tuned an octave above standard pitch, Maphis sounded as though the record was playing at fast speed – but in actuality it was his *fingers* that were moving at fast speed. One such LP was appropriately titled *Fire On The Strings*.

133

STEEL GUITAR RAGE

In country music, as in blues, vastly different styles, from primitive to sophisticated, were simultaneously developed in different parts of the U.S. Just as Delta blues legend Robert Johnson was moaning "Hellhound On My Trail" at approximately the same time as T-Bone Walker was pioneering electric, swing-style Texas blues, so Bob Wills and his Texas Playboys (complete with drums, fiddles, horns, and electric guitars) were recording jukebox hits like "Steel Guitar Rag" (1936) only a couple of years after the Delmores cut "Brown's Ferry Blues" (1934). And nearly a decade passed before Bill Monroe's vision was actually realized in the classic bluegrass band.

The Big Band era and Swing music had their heyday during the 1930s, and it was then that a powerful musical amalgam of country and western styles and the big band sound was born. The western swing sounds of Wills, Hank Penny & his Radio Cowboys, Adolf Hofner and his Orchestra, Milton Brown & his Musical Brownies, and the Light Crust Doughboys came from Texas and Oklahoma, just as the blues from those states leaned heavily toward boogie–woogie. Acoustic Hawaiian guitar was an integral element of early western swing groups, but it didn't take long for Bob Dunn (of Milton Brown & his Musical Brownies) to electrify his lap guitar with a crude homemade pickup to amplify his horn-like steel lines, recording with it as early as 1935. Leon McAuliffe of Wills's organization followed suit shortly thereafter, recording his classic "Steel Guitar Rag" (an adaptation of Sylvester Weaver's "Guitar Rag") on electrified steel in 1936.

Leon McAuliffe

Western swing's high point was the middle and late 1940s. At one point in 1944 Bob Wills's band included no less than twenty-two instrumentalists (twelve of them horn players) and two singers. But the format was fertile ground for the burgeoning steel. Easily the most famous steel guitarist of the period (and for a long time to come) was Leon McAuliffe, immortalized by Wills's familiar intro, "Take it away, Leon!" McAuliffe began playing in the Light Crust Doughboys at the age of sixteen and joined Wills a couple of years later, in 1935. In 1940 he began playing a double–neck electric Rickenbacker, so that he could play in both *A6* and *E13* tunings without having to retune. Adding more tunings (while others added pedals), he has remained a purist of the pedal-less steel, currently using a four-neck Fender. Leon was not the improviser Dunn was, and he has been criti-cized by some for "choppy execution," but there is no denying he was a primal influence, recording some 200 sides with the Wills band. His technique was easily eclipsed by those who succeeded him in the Playboys, but at his best McAuliffe exhibited a powerful rhythmic sense and decidedly electric tonal range. On his early recordings, his tiny amplifier almost seems to scream under the force of his steel's pickups.

Noel Boggs

Oklahoma-born Noel Boggs joined Bob Wills in 1944, having previously played with the Jimmy Wakely Trio and Hank Penny's Radio Cowboys. His style was very chordal and complex, and he had technique to spare. On his early Rickenbacker double-neck and later Fender four-neck, he would keep all the guitar's switches open so that he could jump from neck to neck (from tuning to tuning) in a single song. With Wills he recorded "Texas Playboy Stomp," a steel guitar standard almost of the stature of "Steel Guitar Rag." In 1946 he left the Playboys to work with Spade Cooley and later went back to work with Hank Penny. Boggs, Jimmy Wyble, and guitarist Cameron Hill worked out harmonized, three-guitar lines that became a trademark of the Texas Playboys and singer Tommy Duncan's subsequent band.

Herb Remington

Replacing Boggs in the Wills band was Herb Remington, from Mishawaka, Indiana. Remington joined Wills in 1946 and recorded classics like "Boot Hill Drag" and "Playboy Chimes." Known for his chordal work and raw, driving sound, Herb always displayed an abundance of taste. His famous "Remington Ride" was recorded in 1950 with Hank Penny, following his departure from the Playboys. Later adding pedals to his setup, Remington has remained active, recording several albums of swing and Hawaiian music.

Joaquin Murphey

At the same time that Boggs and Remington were playing with Wills, a West Coast player named Joaquin Murphey was becoming a steel guitar legend through his work with Spade Cooley's Orchestra (which he joined in 1942) and Tex Williams & the Western Caravan (which he joined in 1946). Murphey's name is seldom mentioned without being prefaced by the words "enigmatic" or "mysterious," due to his eccentric, moody temperament and unique style of playing. Murphey was clearly ahead of his time, far jazzier than the steelers mentioned thus far, relying heavily on fast single-note riffs. His "Oklahoma Stomp," recorded with Cooley in 1946, is now a standard in the steel guitar repertoire, played religiously by greats like Buddy Emmons and Sneaky Pete Kleinow. Joaquin also played on Tex Williams's million-selling version of Merle Travis's "Smoke, Smoke, Smoke (That Cigarette)," in 1947. Pioneer that he was, Murphey was slow (more accurately, stubborn) to take to the *pedal* steel, which was where the instrument's future clearly lay. Pedal steeler Bobby Black recalls: "I saw Joaquin with Tex Williams in San Jose, California, when I was just a little kid, around 1948. And he was playing a Bigsby steel with three or four pedals. Recently, I got a chance to back up Tex on a show, because it was the only night Joaquin ever played that guitar. He just didn't like it, never used it again. He was having problems with it, I remember, and was swearing and cussing. But whatever he was doing sounded great to me; he was my hero."

But as Black puts it, "Guys like Joaquin who never depended on the pedals for their sound, I guess that was one of the reasons they were so distinctive in their styles. You could tell immediately who it was. Nowadays it's harder to differentiate, because the pedal setups are very similar. Also, the steel tunings have become standarized; there's really only two – E9 and C6. About 95% of the stuff you hear on records today is E9 tuning, so it all gets to sounding the same. Back in the old days, everybody had their own tunings – there was no limit. There was a book popular in those days called *52 Tunings For The Steel Guitar!*"

Other Steelers

In the late forties and early fifties several other steel guitarists came to prominence, either through their association with famous artists or because of their idiosyncratic playing styles. Don Helms's whining steel perfectly complemented Hank Williams's heartfelt lyrics; Cousin Jody's baggy overalls and slapstick antics were a familiar novelty act on the Grand Ole Opry circuit; Speedy West's fiery performance style, bouncing the bar up and down the neck, made country steel fun to watch and, teamed with Jimmy Bryant's guitar on studio dates, generated some of the hottest pyrotechnics ever heard in country music. The steel guitar had arrived.

WESTERN LEADS

Once amplification came to the guitar, western swing pickers contributed mightily to the revolution in sound and sensibility that inevitably followed the technological breakthrough. Lead guitar became, as in jazz and blues of the period, a possibility, but a possibility that needed defining. Muryel Campbell of the Light Crust Doughboys and Eldon Shamblin of the Texas Playboys electrified their six-strings in the late 1930s, at exactly the same time that another Texan, Charlie Christian, was setting Benny Goodman's sextet (and the entire jazz world) on fire with *his* electric guitar. Shamblin, for instance, developed a fine technique for solos and parts, but his real strength remained his rhythm playing. It was left to other talented hands to create a musical idiom within country for this new instrument.

Jimmy Wyble

Probably the most advanced of the western swing lead players was Jimmy Wyble. Though country artists like Hank Garland and Buddy Emmons would make the transition from country to jazz years later, Wyble was the first to embrace both genres. After stints with Wills, Hank Penny, and Spade Cooley, he went on to play with Benny Goodman, jazz vibraphonist Red Norvo, and even Frank Sinatra. Wills discovered Jimmy in 1943, playing alongside guitarist Cameron Hill in the Houston-based swing band, the Village Boys, and hired the pair on the spot. As Rich Kienzle points out in his article on Jimmy in *Guitar World* magazine, "Wyble and Hill, playing lead and harmony, respectively, were the Duane Allman and Dickie Betts of their time." The "twin guitars," as Wills dubbed them, were featured on several Playboys' sides, including "Roly Poly" and "Smoke On The Water." Today, Wyble continues his work as one of the most respected and prolific guitar educators and originators of a unique polytonal, contrapuntal fingerstyle method.

Junior Barnard

By the time Wyble and Hill joined Wills, the leader had trimmed his horn-filled big band down to a funkier octet or nontet centered around electric and steel guitars. This format was perfectly suited for Wyble's successor in the group, Lester "Junior" Barnard. Though not so sophisticated a guitarist as Wyble, Barnard was no less forward-thinking, anticipating the blues-rock lead sound of players such as Eric Clapton, Freddie King, and Mike Bloomfield twenty years before the style was in vogue. Unfortunately, Junior died in a car crash in 1949, but the recordings he made with Wills between 1942 (when he joined the group briefly) and 1947 (when he left the band permanently) document the Oklahoman's fiery, no-holds-barred approach. Barnard played an arch-top Epiphone Emperor, which he customized by installing a Fender steel guitar pickup along with a DeArmond pickup. The result was a fat, sometimes distorted tone that was decidedly electric. Junior was obviously influenced heavily by the blues and (to a lesser degree) by Charlie Christian's innovative electric work. He can be heard to full advantage on "Blackout Blues" from the *The Tiffany Transcriptions, Vol. 1*, which captures Wills and the Playboys in a loose, relaxed jam-session mood (lead singer Tommy Duncan even stumbles over the lyrics, laughing at Wills's antics). As Barnard rips into his solo on "What's The Matter With The Mill," Wills shouts, "Grind it out, Junior" – an appropriate description of the Junior Barnard style.

HONKY TONKIN'

In the 1940s, the Grand Ole Opry took its place as *the* country music radio show and helped make Nashville, Tennessee, the C&W capitol of the world.

In their *Listener's Guide to Country Music*, authors Bob Oermann and Doug Green write, "The 1940s were the end of the age of innocence in country music. During this decade the form made the transition from rural music with regional appeal to big-money polished entertainment. It moved from being acoustic-based to being electrified. It moved from amateur to professional. It became modern.... Nearly all the performers who thrived in the 1940s straddled the old and the new. All were firmly grounded in old-time music styles of the 1930s, but all had the ability to adapt to the new commercial reality. The modern country song publishing business was born in Nashville in this decade, as was the recording studio scene that concentrated, centralized, and homogenized country music." Starting in 1938, when Roy Acuff joined the Opry's regular cast, the Opry became in effect a showcase for singing stars with string bands, like Acuff, Bill Monroe, and Minnie Pearl. This change of musical emphasis from old-timey instrumentals left Opry founder George D. Hay unhappy and relatively powerless, but it also made the Opry the most popular barn dance in the country, and defined in the process the Nashville Sound that would soon dominate country music.

Ernest Tubb

One of the artists who helped make the Opry and the town indelibly synonymous with country music was Ernest Tubb, with his appearances on the Opry,

Earnest Tubb

the Ernest Tubb Record Shop, and his "jamborees" broadcast from the store. Tubb was a honky-tonk singer in the tradition of his biggest influence, Jimmie Rodgers, but one of the essential elements to his band's sound was the lead electric guitar. On hits like "Walking The Floor Over You" (1941), his slurred, slightly off-key vocal style was perfectly offset by the simple single-note melody lines of guitarist Fay "Smitty" Smith. Tubb obviously favored Smith's decidedly unflashy lead style (and the record's success didn't hurt any), because every guitarist that succeeded him in the group followed the same spare, no-frills stance. Jimmie Short played on several sessions in the mid-forties, including "Answer To Walking The Floor Over You," before Billy Byrd joined the group in 1949. Again, Byrd's playing was a study in economy but became an integral part of the Ernest Tubb sound in the ten years that Billy, his cowboy hat, and Gibson Byrdland electric were fixtures in Tubb's Texas Troubadours.

Hank Snow

One of the most underrated country guitarists is Canadian singing star Hank Snow, whose hard-driving acoustic flatpicking can be heard on nearly all of his hit records (he rarely used a session guitarist on

Hank Snow

Merle Travis

lead), including "I'm Movin' On" and "A Fool Such As I." He also recorded several all-instrumental LPs in the 1950s and teamed with Chet Atkins for the RCA album, *Reminiscing*, in 1964. Like Tubb, Snow's biggest musical influence was Jimmie Rodgers, but his main guitar influence was Karl Farr of the Sons Of The Pioneers. As he told Dennis Hensley in a 1976 interview for *Guitar Player*, "I tried to copy the runs and ad-libs that Karl did on their recordings and in their stage act. He was a super talent. Trying to imitate Karl's technique is what made it necessary for me to practice the guitar so much. He was especially good on fill-in riffs, something I've developed and used on my own vocals through the years."

TRAVIS PICKIN'

It isn't every country guitarist who can avoid Nashville *and* have an entire school of playing named after him, but then there have been very few (if any) guitarists like Merle Travis. The son of a coalminer, Travis was born in Muhlenberg County, Kentucky, in 1917. His first instrument was five-string banjo, but he soon switched to guitar, inspired by the bluesy fingerpicking styles of two Drakesboro coalminers, Mose Rager and Ike Everly (whose sons, Don and

Phil, later sang their way to international fame as the Everly Brothers). "I never had enough nerve to ask them to show me anything," Merle says of his mentors. "I'd just hang around them and watch how they done it and then go home and try it myself."

Though Merle played with fiddler Clayton Mc-Michen (late of the Skillet Lickers), banjoist Grandpa Jones, and the Delmore Brothers, he is best known for his solo work, both instrumentally and vocally. His style of "Travis picking" – playing the melody primarily with his index (and sometimes middle) fingers while his thumb maintains a bouncy, alternating bass – influenced (and continues to influence) scores of players, from Chet Atkins and Doc Watson (who each named children after him) to blues great Mike Bloomfield and English rocker Steve Howe. As Atkins has stated on more than one occasion, "The first time I heard him, I couldn't figure out why *everybody* didn't throw away their straight picks and start playing guitar like that. I'd probably be looking at the rear end of a mule if it weren't for Merle."

Travis continues to perform today, but his heyday was in the early fifties. Fortunately, he was captured on film several times during this period – since he headed for Hollywood when every other country artist had his sights set on Nashville, he even appeared in a few feature-length motion pictures, including *From Here To Eternity*. One of many Snader Telescriptions he made (in 1951) shows him sitting in an easy chair with a Bigsby acoustic guitar, playing "Lost John." His method seems effortless, but his technique is flawless, his musicianship no less than dazzling.

While albums like *Walking The Strings*, *Strictly Guitar*, and *Merle Travis – Guitar* featured Merle's picking, other recordings spotlighted his singing and songwriting. Tex Williams's version of Travis's "Smoke, Smoke, Smoke (That Cigarette)," recorded in 1947, became Capitol Records' first million seller, while Merle scored his own hits with "Divorce Me C.O.D." and "So Round, So Firm, So Fully Packed." He also penned such folk and country standards as "Dark As A Dungeon," "I Am A Pilgrim," and "Nine Pound Hammer," and wrote lyrics to Leon McAuliffe's "Steel Guitar Rag." But by far his biggest success came when Tennessee Ernie Ford sang Travis's "Sixteen Tons," in 1955.

As if his songwriting and guitar playing accomplishments weren't enough, Merle Travis was also one of the pioneers of the solidbody electric guitar. He and Paul Bigsby designed one of the first electric solidbodies, circa 1947 (the idea of having all six tuning pegs on one side of the headstock was Travis's innovation, later adopted by Leo Fender); that guitar, with Merle's name emblazoned across the pickguard, now resides in the Country Music Hall of Fame in Nashville, along with another of the "first" solidbody six-strings, Les Paul's "Log." Dissatisfied with the "Vibrola" tailpiece on his L-10 Gibson, Travis also got Bigsby to design the vibrato bar that would become synonymous with the name Bigsby. Merle's unit, which can be seen on his customized Gibson Super 400, has a longer handle than most, with a ring at the end, through which Travis would slip his little finger, for the chord-bending sound he made famous.

Perhaps the greatest testimony to Merle Travis's unique talent is that it has scarcely diminished with time. His 1973 appearance on the Nitty Gritty Dirt Band's cross-generational album, *Will The Circle Be Unbroken*, is nothing short of magical. Recorded in 1979 at the age of 62, *The Merle Travis Story* (on the CMH label) contains four sides of Travis picking, singing, songwriting, and joking – still up to the extremely high Travis standard.

MISTER GUITAR

In their October 1979 cover story, *Guitar Player* magazine proclaimed Chet Atkins "popular music's most influential fingerstylist," and that may still be an understatement. While Chet's biggest influence, Merle Travis, remained more or less a musician's musician, Atkins gained international stardom as an ambassador of the guitar, dabbling (and eventually mastering) country, pop, jazz, and even classical styles. The basic fingerpicking style both players employ may bear Travis's name, but the name Chet Atkins is synonymous with the instrument itself, and his eclecticism represents the best of Nashville's qualities. He is truly Mister Guitar.

Chester Burton Atkins was born June 20, 1924, near Luttrel, Tennessee. Growing up in a family full of musicians (including older brother Jim, later one-third of the Les Paul Trio), Chet began playing ukulele when he was four or five. By the time he moved to Georgia in 1935, to live with his father, Chet was already spending most of his spare time playing guitar. In 1942, he got his first professional gig – ironically, as a fiddle player with Archie Campbell and Bill Carlisle, who had a radio show on WNOX in Knoxville, Tennessee. The job also entailed a couple of solo spots on guitar, though, and soon he was the station's staff guitarist. In 1945, Chet switched stations, replacing Merle Travis (who had just left for California) at WLW in Cincinnati.

In 1946, Atkins joined singer Red Foley, who brought the guitarist to Nashville and the Grand Ole Opry. Chet's acoustic guitar was usually featured on a short instrumental during Foley's set, but when the network decided to cut out his solo spot, Atkins quit the band and the Opry. When he returned to the Opry in 1949 playing electric guitar with the Carter Sisters (led by "Mother Maybelle" from the old Carter Family), the response was considerably better.

Nashville

Chet's reputation spread quickly in Nashville, and the fact that his fingerstyle approach made him a bit of an oddity resulted in sessions backing Hank Williams, Eddy Arnold, and, eventually, most every major country artist who recorded in Nashville. The studio scene was a hotbed of activity and talent, and Chet came in contact with several other fine pickers. As he told *Guitar Player* in a February 1972 cover story (he has appeared on the magazine's cover more times than any other artist): "There were a lot of good guitar players in Nashville at that time. Grady Martin was playing fantastic guitar then, and so

Chet Atkins

was Hank Garland, two of the greatest guitar players I think I have known. Thumbs Carlille came to town a few years later, and there was Billy Byrd. A lot of good guitar players. We would get together every Saturday night in the dressing room at the Opry and have jam sessions, and show each other licks. It was great fun."

In 1947, RCA's Steve Sholes signed Atkins to his first recording contract as a solo artist. His first significant instrumental recording was "Galloping On The Guitar," cut in 1949. In the years following, Chet has recorded an estimated six dozen or more LPs, some featuring him in tandem with other guitar heroes, including Doc Watson, Merle Travis, Hank Snow, Jerry Reed, Les Paul, and jazz fingerstylist Lenny Breau. He has also recorded and performed with Arthur Fiedler and the Boston Pops and released a couple of nice Christmas albums, not to mention items like *Chet Atkins Picks On The Beatles* and *Teensville*, a 1959 release featuring his rock and roll hit, "Boo Boo Stick Beat."

Techniques

"Boo Boo Stick" was one of many sides showcasing electronic innovations Atkins had come up with – this time a volume pedal on which he replaced the volume circuit with a tone control: a crude wah-wah pedal. His penchant for using the guitar's vibrato arms can be heard over and over, on tunes such as "Trambone" and "Yakety Axe." "Slinkey" employs an extremely slow tremolo unit, "Chinatown, My Chinatown" utilizes tape reverb, and the dazzling "Little Rock Getaway" is rendered even more overwhelming by Chet's expert use of echo.

Of course, a guitarist of Chet Atkins's ability needn't rely on gadgets or gimmicks, as he proved time and time again with nothing more than his two hands, a guitar, and sometimes an amp. "Main Street Breakdown," cut in 1949 with Homer & Jethro, is a tour de force of the Atkins style at an early stage – featuring full-chord bends, descending pull-off flourishes, and some extremely hot single-note soloing. "Oh! By Jingo, Oh! By Gee" couples all of the above with Chet's patented muted alternating bass. As if mastering one tune weren't enough of a challenge, Chet later recorded "Yankee Doodle Dixie," which, as the title implies, features Atkins playing both songs simultaneously – sort of a demonstration of the advantage of playing fingerstyle.

Influence

But Chet Atkins's influence on country music was not limited to his guitar playing (though that would

seem more than enough to ensure immortality). In the early 1950s, Steve Sholes began to rely on Atkins to organize and oversee sessions that he couldn't attend himself. And when RCA built their new studio in Nashville in 1956, Sholes put Chet in charge. The first artist Atkins signed to the label was Don Gibson; their first release as a team yielded a two-sided smash hit, "Oh, Lonesome Me" and "I Can't Stop Loving You." Chet also produced and played rhythm on Elvis Presley's first RCA sessions (including "Heartbreak Hotel" and "I Want You, I Need You, I Love You") and played lead on nearly all of the Everly Brothers' hits, which he also produced. He also brought Jerry Reed and Waylon Jennings to RCA and helped pianist Floyd Cramer and saxophonist Boots Randolph become the most identifiable Nashville session men on their respective instruments. Though it is not an accomplishment he is especially proud of today, Atkins was instrumental in creating the polished, "uptown" Nashville sound and was among the first to use horns and violins on country records.

As if Chet's guitar artistry, sonic innovations, and A&R track records weren't enough, he also tried his hand at designing his own models of electric guitars for the Gretsch company, and, again, he was very successful. By 1959 there were four Chet Atkins models in the Gretsch catalog: the Country Gentleman, the Tennessean, the Chet Atkins Hollow Body (6120), and the Chet Atkins Solid Body (6121). Features varied, but most featured DeArmond pickups and a Bigsby vibrato tailpiece. These were favored by numerous country players as well as some notable rock 'n' rollers, including Eddie Cochran, George Harrison, and Pete Townshend. Gretsch later introduced the Super Chet and the Super Axe. In 1982, the Gibson company celebrated its recent association with Atkins by introducing the Chet Atkins solidbody electric classical guitar, designed for them by Chet himself, at a time when it appeared there were few, if any, challenges left for him to take on.

THE NASHVILLE SOUND

Along with Chet Atkins, three other guitarists set the high standards of creativity and versatility the Nashville studios were known for in the late forties and fifties – Hank Garland, Harold Bradley, and Grady Martin. Bradley played on the first session ever recorded in Nashville (a jingle for Shyer's Jewelers), in 1947, with his brother, Owen, on piano. The brothers built the first Nashville studio designed specifically for record-making in 1952, and two studios later built their famous "Quonset Hut" studio, in 1955. Like Atkins, Owen began producing sessions almost immediately, while Harold remained on the other side of the glass, playing guitar. Having spent three years at Peabody College in Nashville as a music major, Harold was primarily a pop guitarist before he joined Ernest Tubb in 1943. His early influences were Charlie Christian, Django Reinhardt, Les Paul, and his Nashville colleague Billy Byrd. Bradley is still active in the studios, as is Martin, who in recent years toured as part of Willie Nelson's band. In the early 1950s, Martin recorded a classic guitar instrumental called "Pork Chop Stomp," featuring Bud Isasac's pedal steel, on the flip side of a Red Foley single. Photographs from this period show Grady playing a one-of-a-kind Bigsby double-neck solidbody.

Hank Garland

Sadly, Hank Garland's recording career was cut short after fifteen years when he narrowly survived a 1961 automobile accident. Though he was only thirty when brain damage resulting from the accident impaired his motor skills, Garland had already proven himself the most progressive player in town.

Garland hailed from Cowpens, South Carolina, and was inspired to play guitar by hearing Arthur Smith over WSBA radio in nearby Spartanburg. He got a job with Paul Howard's Georgia Cotton Pickers (necessitating the move to Nashville) when he was only fifteen. Already, Garland was notorious for his speed with a flatpick, although there were still a lot of rough edges in his playing. He was exposed to jazz via Nashville players like Atkins, Bradley, and Billy Byrd, who played jazz in jam sessions but never on the job. Garland, however, incorporated everything he learned into his session work, having absorbed elements of Charlie Christian, Django Reinhardt, Les Paul, Barney Kessel, and later Tal Farlow, Barry Galbraith, and Wes Montgomery. Hank's ear and rapidly developing technique made learning new licks and styles easy. As Chet Atkins told *Guitar Player*, "He was one of those guys who you could play a lick for, and he'd come back like an echo."

Hank cut a few of his own records, like "Sugarfoot Rag," which went to number five on *Cash Box* magazine's country charts in 1949 as the B-side of "Chattanoogie Shoe Shine Boy" by Red Foley. He also toured with singer Eddy Arnold, but mostly stayed in the studios, where his soloing and arranging skills

Hank Garland

sparked hits by Don Gibson ("Sea Of Heartbreak"), Jim Reeves ("He'll Have To Go"), Kitty Wells ("Jealousy"), Ferlin Husky ("Gone"), Webb Pierce ("Tupelo County Jail"), and several by Brenda Lee. Often he, Bradley, and Martin played sessions together, with Harold soloing on the more pop-flavored tunes, Grady handling the funkier material, and Hank playing anything that required speed.

Like Atkins, Garland tried his hand at designing his own model of guitar. In 1955, he and Billy Byrd came up with the Gibson Byrdland thinline hollowbody (the name a combination of Byrd and Garland).

New Directions

In 1960, Garland and some of his Nashville cronies

(including Atkins, Floyd Cramer, Boots Randolph, drummer Buddy Harmon, and bassist Bob Moore) were teamed with seventeen-year-old vibraphonist Gary Burton and invited to play the prestigious Newport Jazz Festival in Rhode Island. Unfortunately, rioting on the festival grounds cancelled the show, but the musicians used the get-together to record *After The Riot At Newport*, which gave Garland a chance to stretch out in a jazz context. Later that year, with Grady Martin producing, Hank turned even more heads with his Columbia LP, *Jazz Winds From A New Direction*, with Burton, bassist Joe Benjamin, and Dave Brubeck's drummer, Joe Morello. The album proves Garland to be among the most creative bebop guitarists of the day and has been sighted by jazz/pop star George Benson as a major influence. Ironically, the LP's cover photo shows Hank and his guitar sitting in a convertible; less than a year later a violent auto accident ended his career and nearly took his life.

ROCKABILLY REBELS

Oh, well, I woke up this mornin', and I looked out the door.
I can tell that old milkcow by the way she lows...
"Hold it, fellas! That don't *move* me. Let's get real, real gone for a change."

"Real, real gone for a change" is one of the great understatements in rock 'n' roll history. After interrupting the bluesy intro to Sleepy John Este's "Milkcow Blues" at a January 1955 session at Memphis' Sun Studio, Elvis Presley – along with guitarist Scotty Moore and bassist Bill Black – got real gone indeed and changed pop music.

As we have seen throughout the history of country music, most of the idiom's prime movers relied heavily on a mixture of white rural music and black blues influence. Rockabilly, as its hybrid monicker indicates, was no exception. Elvis Presley's first Sun single coupled a hepped-up blues by Arthur "Big Boy" Crudup entitled "That's All Right" with a boogie-woogied rendition of Bill Monroe's "Blue Moon Of Kentucky." Nearly all the rockabilly that was to follow in that narrowly defined genre was a blend of country roots, black blues, boogie–woogie, youthful energy, and unabashed sexuality.

Surprisingly enough, it was country radio stations and listeners (normally stereotyped as the most conservative in pop music) who were the first to accept Elvis's avant-garde sound. His single of "I Forgot To Remember To Forget" and "Mystery Train" hit the top of the country charts in 1955, the same year that Bill Haley's "Rock Around The Clock" edged its way to the top of the pop charts alongside Mitch Miller's recording of "The Yellow Rose Of Texas," Perez Prado's "Cherry Pink And Apple Blossom White," and Bill Hayes's "Ballad Of Davy Crockett." The following year saw Elvis virtually dominate the country and western charts with "I Want You, I Need You, I Love You," "Don't Be Cruel," and "Heartbreak Hotel" – the latter two songs also topping the pop charts.

As Peter Guralnick points out in his chapter on rockabilly in *The Rolling Stone Illustrated History Of Rock & Roll*, "Rockabilly is the purest of all rock & roll genres." This is because, according to Guralnick, "it never went anywhere. It is preserved in perfect isolation within an indistinct time period, bounded on the one hand by the July 1954 release of Elvis's first record on the yellow Sun label and on the other by the decline and fall of Elvis, Jerry Lee Lewis, Carl Perkins, and Gene Vincent."

But dated though rockabilly may sound today, the fanaticism of its players and listeners (purists both) has seen it rear its greasy head more than once in the decades that followed its heyday. The fact that the music *didn't* evolve or change is part of its charm – like taking a trip (via time machine) to the neighborhood malt shop, circa 1958.

Scotty Moore

While the R&B-oriented hits of the 1950s by artists like Fats Domino, Little Richard, and the Coasters featured the saxophone or piano as the prominent instrument, rockabilly was nearly always based upon the lead and rhythm guitars (with the exception of Jerry Lee Lewis's "pumping piano"). During its prime, rockabilly produced several monster guitar players, ranging stylistically from the rawness of Paul Burlison (with Johnny Burnette's Rock 'N' Roll Trio) to the sophistication of Scotty Moore (backing Elvis) and Cliff Gallup (with Gene Vincent's Blue Caps). Like the records they were cutting, each guitarist's style was based on an amalgam of country and blues licks played at a furious pace. When Sun Records' Sam Phillips called on Moore to back up an unknown balladeer named Elvis Presley, the guitarist was leading a group called the Starlight Wranglers, with Bill Black on upright bass. "We played primarily country," Scotty recalls, "but from playing honky tonks and what have you, we had to play everything – even though you did it with basically a

country band. We just called it honky tonk music."
Backing Elvis's wild vocals, Moore coaxed a variety
of influences – Merle Travis, Chet Atkins, B.B.
King, Tal Farlow – out of his Gibson ES-295 hollow-
body. "This was the first opportunity, without my
really knowing it, that I had to really mix it all up,"
he explains. "I mean, it wasn't a planned thing. But I
loved blues and I loved country, and I played *some*
fingerstyle à la Chet and Merle, and with the few instruments we had you just did everything you could
to make it sound bigger, you know."

Carl and Luther Perkins

Another country-bred player, who exhibited a
punchier attack, was Carl Perkins, composer of
"Blue Suede Shoes," "Matchbox," "Honey Don't," and
"Boppin' The Blues." Like many rockabilly players,
Perkins borrowed more than a few ideas from
Chuck Berry. (It should be pointed out, however,
that Berry was obviously influenced by rockabilly
and straight country music; for example, his hit
"Promised Land" sets his lyrics to the tune of "Wabash Cannonball." Chuck could doubtless sit in on a
rockabilly session as easily as most rockabilly bands
could cruise through "Johnny B. Goode.") Perkins's
trebly, biting tone was derived in the early days
from Fender Stratocasters and Telecasters (some
early promo shots show him holding a 1952 Gibson
Les Paul). Later he popularized the Gibson ES-5
three-pickup "Switchmaster" hollow-body and Epiphone's version of the same concept. Guitarist Luther Perkins was not related to Carl, although both
were closely associated with singer Johnny Cash.
Carl wrote several songs for Cash, including "Daddy
Sang Bass," and was later a featured performer on
the country star's TV show, while Luther played
lead on virtually all of Cash's hits (as one-half of the
Tennessee Two, then one-third of the Tennessee
Three) from the Sun days of "Get Rhythm" until his
tragic death in a fire in 1968. His rhythmic, muted
bass lines were as identifiable an element of the
Cash sound as the singer's craggy voice.

James Burton

The only guitarist of this period to make the unlikely
transition from teen rocker to high-paid session
man was James Burton, who took up guitar at thirteen, was in the house band of the *Louisiana Hay-
ride* radio show a year later, and cut his first hit record, backing Dale Hawkins on "Suzy-Q," at age fifteen. Louisiana-born and trained on Dobro and steel
guitar, Burton combined bluesy bends with a unique
style of fingerpicking and flatpicking simultaneous-

ly. His tasteful fills and glassy tone can be heard on
numerous Ricky Nelson hits, including "Hello, Mary
Lou," "Travelin' Man," and "Believe What You Say."
Throughout the sixties, Burton and his Telecaster
were first-call on any country-flavored session
emanating from Los Angeles. The range of styles
Burton has encompassed is as varied and impressive
as the list of artists who have utilized his services – from straight country (Merle Haggard's
"Lonesome Fugitive" and "Workin' Man Blues") to
country-rock (Gram Parsons, Emmylou Harris,
Rodney Crowell) to soft pop (anything from Johnny
Mathis to John Denver). But when good old rock 'n'
roll is the order of the day, Burton can still rock like
nobody's business. In 1969, when Elvis decided he
was ready to return to active duty, he called James,
the most logical choice to fill the guitar seat, and
asked him to lead the new band. Burton stayed with
Presley until the King's death in 1977.

Maphis and Garland

The raunchy lead guitar heard on Ricky Nelson's
earlier hits, such as "Stood Up," "Waitin' In School,"
and "Bebop Baby," was supplied by Joe Maphis. In
an interview with *Guitar Player* magazine, Maphis
explained how he made the transition from C&W to
rock 'n' roll: "I would put that old guitar [referring
most likely to his custom-made Mosrite], on the
back pickup and romp on it, playing rock or anything they wanted. I tried to put in some specific
rock licks, but it was basically Joe Maphis. A lot of
lines I was playing were just country licks." Another
"legitimate" country player who made the transition
to rockabilly was Hank Garland, who recorded with
Jerry Lee Lewis, Charlie Rich, and can be heard on
such Elvis hits as "Are You Lonesome Tonight,"
"Little Sister," and "It's Now Or Never."

Paul Burlison

Easily the most primitive (and one of the most exciting) rockabilly guitarists was Paul Burlison, who
along with Johnny and Dorsey Burnette comprised
the Rock 'N' Roll Trio, one of the wildest groups of
the mid-1950s. Again, Burlison's Telecaster lead approach was a combination of C&W and Memphis
blues (in fact, he backed blues singer Chester "Howlin' Wolf" Burnett over KWEM radio in West Memphis, Arkansas, in 1951, because Wolf's regular guitarist, Willie Johnson, had to work in the fields by
day, while the show was being taped). Burlison's
style was lean and basic, relying on a lot of volume
and occasional distortion, as on the group's searing
version of "Train Kept A-Rollin'," later covered by

the Yardbirds with Jeff Beck – one of the first records to feature "fuzztone," which Burlison arrived at when one of the tubes in his Fender Deluxe amp was accidentally jarred loose.

Cliff Gallup

At the other end of the stylistic spectrum was Cliff Gallup, whose sophisticated, complex leads propelled the hits of Gene Vincent, such as "Be-Bop-A-Lula," "Cruisin'," and "Race With The Devil." In a recent interview in *Record* magazine, country-rock star Albert Lee said, "The best influence I had was trying to copy the solos by Cliff Gallup on Gene Vincent records. He had listened to Les Paul and Chet Atkins and played an amalgam of their styles. It was a good exercise to learn his solos, because he used a lot of the guitar, as opposed to copying blues solos, which are often hanging around two or three notes and going for effect."

Transitions

Rockabilly guitar gradually drifted further from its country roots and became a purer rock strain – in the form of Buddy Holly's rhythmic, Bo Diddley-inspired Stratocaster chording, Eddie Cochran's bluesy bends and pull-offs on his Gretsch Chet Atkins model, and eventually George Harrison's homages to Carl Perkins on early Beatles sides. Early instrumental rock stars like Duane Eddy and Link Wray obviously had deep country roots but played in a sparer, more melodic style (in Eddy's case) or more driving and bare-knuckled (in Wray's).

Though rockabilly could never be declared legally dead, it wasn't until the late seventies and early eighties that it made its commercial comeback, with groups like the Blasters, Rockpile, and the Stray Cats. There are probably more rockabilly guitarists active today than ever before, and "cat music" is once again on the airwaves. Rockabilly has even wedged its way into the punk/new wave movement, most prominently in the hands of X's bleached blonde guitarist Billy Zoom, who sees his role in the progressive L.A. band as more or less playing rockability licks at extremely high volume on his Gretsch Silver Jet.

Rockabilly's caretaker, England's Dave Edmunds, is a virtual encyclopedia of 1950s guitar licks and studio techniques. In addition to the one and only Rockpile album and his solo LPs, Edmunds produced the Stray Cats, featuring Brian Setzer on guitar, vocals, and tattoos. But the most overwhelming player in the idiom today (possibly the most accomplished rockabilly guitarist ever) is Danny Gatton,

lead man in Robert Gordon's band. Gatton can do it all – 32nd-note boogie-woogie, complex Chet Atkins pull-offs, uncanny pedal steel impersonations (a tricky technique using bends and the Tele's volume knob), and perfect-pitch bottleneck (in Danny's case played over-the-neck with a Heineken beer bottle). Gattons's lead concept seems to boil down to a rock 'n' roll version of his biggest influence, Les Paul. If Les had played rockabilly, he would have sounded like Danny Gatton. Unfortunately, Gatton's formidable reputation has mostly been word of mouth, because he is criminally underrecorded. His self-produced *Redneck Jazz* LP was released in 1978, but has already become an impossible-to-find collector's item. Onstage, though, Gatton continues to make jaws drop and aspiring pickers retire.

THE BLUEGRASS REVIVAL

On the shoulders of the early sixties Folk Music Boom that brought groups like the Kingston Trio and Peter, Paul, & Mary to the Top Ten and hootenanies into Suburbia, bluegrass music enjoyed a renewed popularity and mass exposure. Thanks to the revolutionary work of two guitarists, Doc Watson and Clarence White, bluegrass guitar stepped out of the shadows and into the spotlight. Prior to this time, there were a few isolated examples of lead guitar in bluegrass, such as Don Reno or George Shuffler, guitarist with the Stanley Brothers. But never before had the guitar been given equal billing with the fiddle and banjo, let alone been *the* lead instrument in a bluegrass band – or, in Doc's case, a solo instrument.

Doc Watson

One has to wonder what went through folklorist/mandolinist Ralph Rinzler's mind when he "discovered" a blind guitarist named Doc Watson on a field trip to Deep Gap, North Carolina, in 1960; such a find would be akin to an archaeologist stumbling across a woolly mammoth grazing in a field – or, more accurately, unearthing a heretofore unheard-of species. Oddly enough, when Rinzler found Watson, while recording banjo player Clarence Ashley, Doc was playing *electric* guitar for a living (a Gibson Les Paul, to be exact) in a local dance band, Jack Williams and the Country Gentlemen. Doc had been playing with the band since 1953, and it was there – since the group had no fiddle player – that he developed his unique style of flatpicking fiddle tunes. Doc still played old-timey music around the house, with family and friends, but he viewed the two types of music as separate, distinct entities not to be mixed. As Rinzler told *Frets* magazine in 1979: "Doc was an incredible example of a performer living with and performing within both his local community tradition and in the artistic traditions of the regional Southeast. Doc had his community music that he played with [father-in-law/fiddler] Gaither Carlton – hymns and ballads, very deep, old regional music. That was his down-home music. Now outside of that, he knew a lot of other music he learned off records and radio. He knew a lot of contemporary music, from repertoires of people like Elvis Presley and Chet Atkins, and he could play that equally well. That was his face-to-the-world music. And, at the time, he saw an unbreachable wall between the two of them."

Rinzler brought the thirty-eight year old Watson to New York in 1961 to play a concert for the Friends of Old-Time Music with Ashley, Clint Howard, and Fred Price. Soon Doc was playing the Newport Folk Festivals and recording landmark albums for Vanguard Records, some solo, some backed by his guitar-playing son Merle (whom Doc named after one of *his* guitar idols, Merle Travis). As if his rapid-fire flatpicking weren't enough, Watson is equally adept at fingerstyle playing (à la Merle Travis, Chet Atkins, John Hurt, and Sam McGee) and old-time clawhammer banjo. He also possesses a rich baritone singing voice and an easy-going, backporch stage manner that has endeared him to audiences around the world.

In the past ten or so years, the division between popular and old-timey music that Rinzler spoke of has grown narrower, and Watson has added a wide variety of material to his live and recorded repertoire – from blues to pop, from Gershwin to Elvis. Merle Watson has also asserted himself as a formidable guitarist and added more modern influences to the Watson sound. He has also introduced slide guitar to acoustic country music, playing simulated Dobro lines bottleneck blues-style.

Clarence White

Clarence White has often been called the second link in the flatpicking chain that started with Doc Watson, but more accurately, both were working on the same concept around the same time. By the time Clarence heard Doc play at the Ash Grove in Los Angeles in 1962, he was already a flatpicker to be reckoned with, even at the age of eighteen. Tony Rice, often referred to as the third link in the same

Doc Watson

flatpicking chain, recalls, "I heard of Clarence long before I heard of Doc Watson. Doc wasn't even on the folk scene until Ralph Rinzler brought him to festivals like Newport in the early sixties. But I first met Clarence in about 1960, when I was nine and he was about sixteen, and he was already playing a different rhythm style, even at his age. He'd put a little more finesse or something in his back-up. I wouldn't say that Clarence White was doing intricate picking like that before Doc Watson, but I'll say this, he became notorious for doing so before Doc. He came into prominence faster than Doc."

Clarence's group, the Kentucky Colonels, have been called by some the greatest bluegrass band of all-time, and their recordings from the early sixties (available on various Rounder and Briar albums) leave few doubters. The original line-up consisted of Clarence, brother Roland on mandolin, Roger Bush on bass, and Billy Ray Latham on banjo, with all four singing beautiful harmonies. But above all it

Clarence White (center) and the Kentucky Colonels

was Clarence's dazzling technique and superior taste that set the Colonels apart from other groups.

Born in 1944 in Louistown, Maine, Clarence and his family moved to California while he was still a youngster. Clarence and Roland first performed in a family group led by their father, Eric White, who played fiddle and banjo. By his teens White was picking out fiddle tunes on guitar. But as overwhelming as his solo work was, his syncopated rhythmic sense set him apart from other players.

Only a handful of players can claim to be innova-

tors in one genre; Clarence White is the rare example of an innovator in two. In 1967 he recorded with Gene Parsons in a group called Nashville West, which in retrospect marks the first recording that could be categorized as country-rock. Around this time he also played electric guitar on the landmark *Sweetheart Of The Rodeo* with the Byrds, whom he later joined, in 1968. Shortly before his death in 1973 (when he was struck down by an automobile) Clarence had turned his attention back to acoustic music. Considering the fact that he was only twenty-nine when he died, one can only imagine what further advances and innovations he might have conceived.

Bridging The Gap

In 1971, bluegrass was given another shot in the arm when the Southern California country-rock group, the Nitty Gritty Dirt Band, gathered some of the greatest bluegrass and country musicians ever assembled and recorded *Will The Circle Be Unbroken*. The lavish triple-set featured the Dirt Band – Jimmie Fadden, Jeff Hanna, John McEuen, Les Thompson, and Jim Ibbotson – backing legends such as Mother Maybelle Carter, Doc Watson, Merle Travis (marking the first time the two guitarists had ever met face to face), Earl Scruggs, Roy Acuff, Jimmy Martin, and Vassar Clements, with special guests Norman Blake and "Bashful Brother" Oswald Kirby pitching in. The LP showed rock audiences that "hillbilly music" was more vital and potent than they'd ever imagined and demonstrated to hard-core country fans that those long-haired hippies were capable of more than just rock 'n' roll.

THE FASTEST GUITAR IN THE COUNTRY

Nowadays, the popularity of country music, no longer limited to rural areas or the South, has become universal. Stars like Willie Nelson and Emmylou Harris can fill just about any hall in any city in any state, and the audience at the Lone Star Cafe in New York City is not all that different from the crowd at the Soap Creek Saloon in Austin, Texas. But well into the late 1960s the idea of a country music club thriving in Manhattan (and competing with the city's bigger rock venues) was unheard of. Nashville was the town every aspiring picker gravitated to; that was where you either made it or threw in the cards. But there were other towns.

Jimmy Bryant

Due to its large population of transplanted Southerners, California also had an active country music scene, and thanks to Los Angeles's position as the nation's second biggest recording center (during the fifties) a few fine players carved their niche outside "Music City," Tennessee. The first to do so on a significant scale were Joe Maphis (mentioned earlier) and Jimmy Bryant, a Georgia fiddler who set up shop in L.A. in 1948, at the age of twenty-three. Bryant was brought up on the road, playing fiddle alongside his father, who played rhythm guitar. Jimmy switched to guitar when he joined the Army

in 1941, still playing country but listening more and more to jazz players such as Django Reinhardt. In a 1972 interview for *Guitar Player* magazine, Bryant recalled, "Nobody would give me jobs at first, because I wanted to play fast, instead of commercial." His dazzling speed eventually earned him one of the busiest schedules in the L.A. studios, recording with Tex Williams, Roy Rogers, Kay Starr, Tennessee Ernie Ford, and numerous Capitol artists while he was under contract to that label. He also backed Bing Crosby, Stan Kenton, and even appeared on records by the Monkees in later years. He recorded several mind-boggling LPs with steel guitarist Speedy West, including the classic *Two Guitars, Country Style*. Another of Bryant's albums, aptly titled *Fastest Guitar In The Country*, featured back-up by jazz greats Shelly Manne on drums and Barney Kessel on guitar, who stated, "Of all the guitar players I have known, Jimmy Bryant is the fastest, and the cleanest, and has more technique than any other."

"When I was learning to play guitar," says Larry Black, a disciple of Bryant's and brother of pedal steeler Bobby Black, "he was my idol. He had the first Telecaster ever made, serial number 1, and it had a clear pickguard on it, with his name in 'rope' letters. When I saw that, I just had to have one, too. I immediately ordered one, in 1952, from a music store, and it took two weeks to get there – arrived by train. Mine was serial number 37."

The Boys From Bakersfield

While the country records coming out of Los Angeles and Nashville continued to get slicker and more "uptown," Bakersfield, California, began to assert itself as another country music empire. Buck Owens and Merle Haggard both settled there and gave listeners a rootsy, blue-collar alternative to the polished Nashville productions. Both recorded primarily with their own back-up bands, Owens's Buckaroos and Haggard's Strangers, whose guitar players – Don Rich and Roy Nichols, respectively – helped define the Bakersfield sound, while adding some very tasty licks to the country guitar vocabulary.

Don Rich

Rich teamed up with Owens in Seattle, Washington, where Buck was enjoying success on local radio and TV in the late 1950s. (Don's immediate successor in the group, incidentally, was Nokie Edwards, who went on to rock guitar immortality as lead guitarist of the Ventures.) Rich played lead guitar in the

Buckaroos, sang harmony, and was also featured on fiddle. As Albert Lee points out, "I've noticed that several of those guitar players also played good fiddle – Jimmy Bryant and Joe Maphis, and also Don Rich and Roy Clark (not to mention Roger Miller). I guess it gets your fingers moving."

Unfortunately, precious little has been written about Rich, who died in a motorcycle accident in 1974. His carreer was almost exclusively confined to his work with Owens (including group LPs by the Buckaroos) and a couple of solo fiddle releases. But, thankfully, Owens recorded prolifically, and Don's glistening Telecaster can be heard to full advantage over and over – especially on Buck's early Capitol sides, such as "Love's Gonna Live Here" (featuring Rich's distinctive high harmony singing), "Act Naturally" (a perfect example of Don's ability to make a complete statement in only a few bars), "I Don't Care (Just As Long As You Love Me)," and "Waiting In Your Welfare Line" (a collaboration by Don and Buck, featuring Don on acoustic). Rich's showpiece was "Buckaroo," written by Bob Morris, which became a hit for Buck Owens even though it was an instrumental.

Roy Nichols

A bit more eccentric a player and personality than Rich is Roy Nichols of Merle Haggard's Strangers. On his earlier Capitol hits, Haggard used James Burton on lead (on "Workingman Blues," James plays a brilliant variation on the same figure he used on Ricky Nelson's recording of "Milkcow Blues"), but Nichols is featured on most of the cuts recorded after 1967, when he joined the Strangers.

Nichols came from a musical family and played with the Maddox Brothers and Rose when he was seventeen. During his formative years his favorite guitarists were Junior Barnard and Django Reinhardt, although, in his words, "None of it wore off; I don't play like them, but that's who I listened to" (*Guitar Player*, February 1972). Roy's Telecaster string bending and "chicken pickin'" are his most distinctive characteristics – a major influence on Roy Buchanan's guitar style. Above all, his playing is spontaneous and unpredictable. As the Strangers' steel guitarist, Norman Hamlet, told *Guitar Player*, "I think Roy plays a different chorus in everything we do. Every once in a while, he'll hit a few licks that are on the records, but usually when it comes time to do a turnaround, he'll do something a little different and then maybe go back. Well, it ain't just every guitar player that can do that."

PROGRESSIVE COUNTRY

Another reaching for country's musical roots came in the form of progressive country or, as it is sometimes called, "redneck rock." The movement's figureheads are Waylon Jennings and Willie Nelson, who defined the sound and image of progressive country when they became disenchanted with the Nashville establishment and recorded an album entitled *The Outlaws*, with Tompall Glaser and Waylon's wife, Jessi Colter.

Willie Nelson

After years as one of Music City's leading songwriters, Nelson moved back to his home state of Texas in 1972, frustrated that he was not more accepted in Nashville as an artist. That year he threw an eclectic Fourth of July picnic at Dripping Springs, near Austin, Texas, that has been referred to as the Woodstock of Country Music. He quickly became a pied piper for the fertile Austin music scene. "It's just a rock 'n' roll rhythm pattern with country lyrics, and then something else. And that third thing has to do with whoever's playing it."

That third ingredient, in Willie's case, is a healthy dose of western swing. On *Shotgun Willie*, Nelson's first progressive-flavored album, released in 1973, he includes two Bob Wills tunes, "Stay All Night" and "Bubbles In My Beer," alongside his own originals and two by Leon Russell. The native Texan's love for western swing asserts itself repeatedly on subsequent LPs along with blues and jazz influences – mirroring the eclecticism of all of the state's indigenous artists and subcultures.

Characteristics

Progressive country, be it Willie, Waylon, or Jerry Jeff Walker, is always based around the guitar. In Willie's case, he flatpicks snatches of Eldon Shamblin, Hank Garland, Johnny Smith, George Barnes, even Carlos Montoya and Andrés Segovia, with his own inimitable sound – derived from his trademark battered Baldwin gut-string, with a hole where his pick has worn the wood away.

Neither Nelson nor Jennings are guitar virtuosos, but they are both entirely original. Waylon's characteristic piercing sound is a combination of country and rockabilly licks (he was in Buddy Holly's band at the time of the rock singer's death) played on his hand-tooled Fender Telecaster, often with the aid of a chorus effect. Whereas Nelson's singing and playing leans more and more toward jazz, Jennings has stayed within the bounds of blue-collar country, with occasional nods to Buddy Holly.

Willie Nelson

Jerry Reed

Pop Goes The Country

By the mid-sixties, country music had become exceedingly commercial and unbearably homogenized, to the point where what passed for country was little more than pop with a southern accent. Glen Campbell crooned Jim Webb ballads like "By The Time I Get To Phoenix" and "Wichita Lineman," while Roger Miller scored with novelty ditties like "Dang Me" and "You Can't Roller Skate In A Buffalo Herd." In retrospect, it seems that country music had stooped to an all-time low, but in the process it bled into pop's mass market long before the term "crossover" was an buzzword for artists or songs that sold to more than one demographic audience.

Jerry Reed

Of all the crossover artists, the one who has most firmly retained his country foundation is Jerry Reed. A fine singer, writer, and entertainer (he also had his own TV show briefly and later successfully made his way into motion pictures), Reed is first and foremost a monster guitar player. His hybrid of country and funk, not to mention his sense of humor, accounted for hits such as "Amos Moses," "Ko-Ko Joe," and "When You're Hot, You're Hot"; his phenomenal mastery of the guitar and original "clawhammer" fingerpicking style made him a legend among guitar players. As Nashville session man Paul Yandell, who recorded and toured with Reed, told *Guitar Player*: "The major thing I admire about Jerry is that he was the first guitarist to come along in ten years with a completely new style of guitar playing. Just as you can pick out Les Paul's style of playing or Chet's style, you can listen to a Jerry Reed guitar instrumental and say, 'That's Reed.' His clawhammer method of picking on a nylon-string, amplified guitar, with his own series of licks, really sets him apart. It's so complicated, he has to show it to you, because you can never figure it out by listening to his records."

"Jerry never borrows leads from anyone," Paul continues. "His runs come straight out of his head. His technique is very classical in one respect, because he makes tremendous use of the low bass strings for lengthy runs. In another respect, it's bluegrassy, in that he gets those high, tinny-sounding leads from his high strings."

Chet Atkins – whom Jerry lists as a primal influence, along with Les Paul, Merle Travis, and Johnny Smith – signed Reed to RCA in 1965 and produced most of his early LPs. Atkins also encouraged Reed to play amplified gut-string guitar, seldom heard in country music. In a 1971 interview with *Guitar Player*, Reed explained his lead approach. "I never liked single-string picking too much," he said. "I like to hear a lot of stuff going on. Most of my stuff is built around lines, Ray Charles type of piano licks and things I've just naturally stumbled on from just diggin' and grindin'."

Reeds' early RCA albums, such as *Nashville Underground* and *The Unbelievable Guitar & Voice Of Jerry Reed*, are probably the best examples of his "swarming" fingerpicking style, but unfortunately they are almost impossible to find. Another collector's item, *Jerry Reed Explores Guitar Country*, spotlights the Georgia native in a backporch mood, playing bluegrass and folk tunes on acoustic guitar. "There's some of the most amazing stuff I ever heard on that record," declares Tony Rice. "His version of 'Georgia On My Mind' is like a complete course in timing, just in that one tune. Just leave all the fancy shit behind for a while and concentrate on time – that's the best lesson you could get right there."

Reed also recorded two albums with Chet Atkins, of which he is justifiably very proud. Entitled *Me and Jerry* and *Me and Chet*, they feature some of the hottest as well as prettiest guitar interplay ever recorded, on tunes ranging from "Tennessee Stud" to "Bridge Over Troubled Water."

PEDAL PUSHERS

Once the heyday of western swing had passed, pedal steelers began to adapt their instruments and sound to the burgeoning Nashville Sound and its musical and commercial requirements. As a result, they soon settled comfortably into standardized tunings, in contrast to the chaotic, highly personalized setups that dominated the steel's early years. The *C6* and *E9* tunings were rapidly producing the sweetening effect that so many Nashville tracks featured.

Buddy Emmons

One of the players who helped pioneer the *E9th* sound was Jimmy Day, who played with Ray Price's Cherokee Cowboys in the late fifties and early sixties. Day was very much influenced by western swing, as was Price during that period. He was succeeded in Price's band by the man who is universally regarded as the most formidable pedal steeler on the scene, Buddy Emmons. By the time he joined Ray Price – he is featured on the singer's hit version of Willie Nelson's "Night Life," among others – Emmons had already played with Little Jimmy

Dickens and Ernest Tubb's Texas Troubadours. Though both were conservative country singers (in the Roy Acuff and Jimmie Rodgers molds, respectively), each boasted young, hot bands. During this time, Buddy was featured on instrumentals like "Raisin' The Dickens"—which he wrote and recorded in 1956, at age nineteen—and the famous "Four Wheel Drive," which he recorded in 1958 (while with Tubb).

In 1963, when he was twenty, Emmons went to New York to record *Steel Guitar Jazz* (on Mercury), a landmark in steel guitar history. With arranger Quincy Jones and a back-up band comprised of bassist Art Davis, pianist Bobby Scott, saxophonist Jerome Richardson, and drummer Charlie Persip, Emmons broke all the rules of steel guitar—displaying his superior harmonic knowledge and jazz chops on standards like "Cherokee," "Where Or When," and Sonny Rollins' "Oleo." Emmons may not be the most prolific session player on his instrument, but he is easily one of the most versatile, having recorded with such diverse names as Judy Collins, Ray Charles, Duane Eddy, John Sebastian, the Everly Brothers, Linda Ronstadt, George Jones, and Fairport Convention.

Pete Drake

The most recorded steel guitarist of the 1960s was Nashville session man Pete Drake, who appeared on virtually all the hits (and there were quite a few) by George Jones and Tammy Wynette, as well as on Bob Dylan's groundbreaking *Nashville Skyline* and George Harrison's *All Things Must Pass*. Sometimes criticized on a technical level (less than perfect intonation, an overdramatic vibrato), Drake nevertheless made some great records even greater and almost single-handedly opened the door for the pedal steel in Nashville. He also holds the dubious distinction of popularizing the "talking steel," wherein a mouth attachment enables Pete to talk or sing *through* his pedal steel. Just what the music world needs.

Bakersfield Steel

The two main purveyors of the West Coast/Bakersfield steel sound are Ralph Mooney and Tom Brumley. Mooney's bright, bouncy tone is one of the most easily identifiable in country music and can be heard on many of Merle Haggard's hits (including "Swinging Doors"), some of Buck Owens's early records (like "You're For Me"), and currently on tour with Waylon Jennings. Brumley's punchy tone came to prominence with Buck Owens's Buckaroos, before

he joined Rick Nelson's Stone Canyon Band. His great ballad style and use of the volume pedal helped make Owens's classic "Together Again" an enormous hit.

Country Rock

The West Coast was also incubator for the first groups that could be categorized as country-rock, who introduced a whole new audience and generation to the pedal steel. "Sneaky Pete" Kleinow of the Flying Burrito Brothers is probably the most faithful *and* progressive of the ilk. He has a firm foothold in country and western swing, but can go toe to toe with the hottest lead guitarists without giving any ground. The Burrito Brothers' "Christine's Tune" (also called "Devil In Disguise") exploits his range to its fullest, as he switches from a pristine Don Rich/Telecasteresque tone to maniacal fuzztone and back again. Pete's replacement in the Burritos was Al Perkins, a heavyweight on both electric and pedal steel guitar.

Rusty Young may not be the stylist Sneaky Pete is, but he received far greater mass exposure via his group Poco. Young, an accomplished songwriter and multi-instrumentalist, played pedal steel in the band, along with electric Dobro and Mellobar (a lap steel featuring a slanted fretboard, allowing steelers to play overhand slide while standing up). In Steve Fishell's words, "Rusty's distinctive style made me and a lot of other people my age—Hank DeVito, for one—quit school and buy a pedal steel. Rusty's E9 playing, especially early on, sounded very western, to me. It was so twangy, and he overemphasized the pulls. And he always played energetic as hell, at rock 'n' roll volume. He also had no qualms about doing *anything* to make the steel guitar sound different. He used every gimmick in the book, but in a constructive way—for instance, he used a Leslie [rotating] speaker quite often, and also played the Mellobar with a fuzztone. He spawned an entire generation of steel guitarists in the early 70s."

Bobby Black joined Commander Cody & the Lost Planet Airmen in 1970, where he stayed off and on for the next six years before moving on to the Moonlighters and Asleep At The Wheel. Bobby's impressive chordal vocabulary and tasty vibrato were the perfect complement to Cody's boogie-woogie piano and Billy C. Farlow's rockabilly vocals. He eventually moved to Nashville for a stint in the studios and a tour with Barbara Mandrell. He is currently back in the San Francisco area, where he plays in a band with his brother, Larry Black.

Before leaving the group and moving to Australia, Asleep At The Wheel's Reuben "Lucky Oceans" Gosfield earned a spot in the pedal steel annals, carrying the torch during the seventies that had been ignited by Joaquin Murphey and Noel Boggs three decades earlier. Though the Wheel is regarded as heir to the Texas Playboys' throne, Lucky and leader/guitarist Ray Benson (talented eclectics, both) could often be found backstage jamming on bebop, Latin, blues, or funk tunes.

COUNTRY GUITAR TODAY

Country music has shown phenomenal endurance in the face of changing fads and fashions – and that includes the recent country music fad. A number of nonmusical factors – a president with a Southern accent, a successor with a Love-It-Or-Leave-It, When-Guns-Are-Outlawed-Only-Outlaws-Will-Have-Guns stance, and, most of all, the media's appetite for a new trend – contributed to the *Urban Cowboy* climate of designer jeans and designer beer. Disco was out, country was in. Before the ashes quit smoldering from a thousand disco insurance fires, "Gilley bars," complete with mechanical bucking bulls, were erected on the same foundations – soon to be frequented by the same consumers who populated the discos, now wearing different clothes, learning new dance steps. That's show-biz.

But, aside from the fact that a number of people discovered that they really *did* like Willie Nelson, this latest fad is not a very accurate barometer of country music's strides or its enduring quality. Yes, bluegrass has enjoyed a renewed popularity and has expanded into "newgrass," "spacegrass," and "Dawg music." It seems like, having gone about as "uptown" as they could go, Nashville sessions have recently returned to basics a bit and, hopefully, will continue to do so.

But, this is a retrospective and not an obituary of country guitar – as for its prospects, the art form will continue to evolve and achieve new modes of expression. Two strong arguments for this optimism are Tony Rice and Albert Lee.

Tony Rice

At thirty-two, Rice is obviously the acoustic flatpicker that all others look up to, the successor to Doc Watson, the carrier of the torch ignited by Clarence White. He has been called the third link in that illustrious bluegrass guitar chain, but he is just as importantly the first link in the still developing style known generally as "new acoustic music."

Rice was born in Danville, Virginia, and raised in California, surrounded by a family of bluegrass musicians. When he was nine, Tony met Clarence White, then sixteen, and hearing him play his Martin D-28 had an indelible effect on Rice's development as a guitar player (Tony now plays the very D-28 he saw Clarence play that day). Like White, Tony mixes sure-handed flatpicking leads with innate rhythmic sense and a rich, warm tone, setting the standard for bluegrass guitar. He also never fails to surprise listeners, tossing twisted jazz figures into traditional tunes, Lester Flatt G-runs into bebop numbers.

Tony has recorded several albums, in both bluegrass and "spacegrass" settings (the best example of the former style is *Manzanita*; the most far-reaching of his progressive works is *Mar West*) and was a founding member of the influential David Grisman Quintet. He also recorded a heartfelt LP of old-time guitar-mandolin duets (on the Sugar Hill label) with Ricky Skaggs, featuring some of the prettiest singing ever.

Albert Lee

An alumnus of Emmylou's Hot Band, Albert Lee stands as country music's premier electric guitarist, probably the only player capable of filling the slot in that group vacated by James Burton with no noticeable drop in taste or intensity. Albert's sinuous Telecaster leads can be heard propelling records by Harris, Eric Clapton, Dave Edmunds, Rodney Crowell, Rosanne Cash, and Jerry Lee Lewis, among others. The fact that Lee had to learn country guitar second-hand, growing up in London, England, certainly doesn't seem to have hampered him much. "You did feel frustrated," he admits, "because you thought there'd be so much more over here. It was hard to get hold of the right records." Fortunately, he did get hold of some records by Jimmy Bryant and Cliff Gallup (of Gene Vincent's Blue Caps), his two biggest influences, and taught himself well enough to win *Guitar Player*'s readers' poll as Best Country Guitar Player two years running.

"A lot of people ask me, 'Living in England, how could you get into country?' It don't seem strange to me – I think it's more natural than anybody getting into blues in England. Country music is closer to the folk music of England than the blues is."

Albert Lee illustrates not only the advances made by English musicians but just how far country music has come. With him, country guitar has come full circle, back to its roots in British folk music.

Albert Lee

DISCOGRAPHY: COUNTRY GUITAR

Because the discography that follows is limited to albums that are still in print, such classics as Joe Maphis' *Fire On The Strings*, Jerry Reeds's *Nashville Underground*, and *Two Guitars, Country Style* by Jimmy Bryant and Speedy West are not included. These and a great many more are out-of-print, but are infinitely worth listening to for those willing to spend the extra time (and money) it takes to find them. One of the most extensive (and most reasonable) sources for rare records is Glenn Howard's Musician's Reference Library (Box 66550, Santa Cruz, CA 95066), which specializes in hard-to-find records in all styles, including country and bluegrass.

CHET ATKINS
Now And...Then
RCA, two-record set VPSX-6079

With twenty-five songs spanning twenty-five years, from 1947's "Canned Heat" to 1972's "Knee Action," this is the most impressive and representative of Chet's countless recordings. Sounds, settings, and techniques change from cut to cut, but each has Atkins stamped all over it – from the dazzling Django-like "Main Street Breakdown" to his 50s hit "Boo Boo Stick Beat," from the bouncy "Freight Train" to his almost baroque reading of Johnny Smith's "Walk – Don't Run" (which, incidentally, inspired the Ventures' hit version). Chet has dabbled in (and mastered) just about every style of music, but this is the real Chet, the classic Chet.

JERRY BYRD
Steel Guitar Favorites
Mercury, reissued by Steel Guitar Products, c/o Tom Bradshaw, Box 931, Concord, CA 94522

No lap steel guitarist has ever matched Byrd's incredible tone or unerring taste. Every cut is a mini-masterpiece here, especially "Limehouse Blues," "Jitterbug Waltz" (with Chet Atkins on lead guitar), and "Steelin' The Blues," Jerry's 1949 hit featuring Rex Allen on vocal. Who needs pedals?

THE BRYDS
Sweetheart Of The Rodeo
Columbia PC-9670

A sterling piece of fusion, with original Byrds Roger McGuinn and Chris Hillman joined by country journeymen Clarence White and Lloyd Green, with Gram Parsons mediating. Jaydee Maness also plays steel on some cuts, but Green's playing shines brightest, particularly on Merle Haggard's "Life In Prison."

THE CARTER FAMILY
The Original Carter Family, Vol. 1—Legendary Performers
RCA CPMI-2763

Maybelle Carter's famous bass-line-and-strum is shown to full advantage here on "Wabash Cannonball," "John Hardy Was A Desperate Little Man," and the classic "Wildwood Flower." A simple but revolutionary guitar style that inspired and influenced scores of country, folk, and bluegrass players.

SPADE COOLEY
Spade Cooley—Columbia Historic Edition
Columbia FC-37467E

Steel guitar genius Joaquin Murphey's eccentric style is featured throughout this collection of Cooley's tunes mostly from 1946. His classic "Oklahoma Stomp" is the LP's standout track, and his version of Leon McAuliffe's signature tune, "Steel Guitar Rag," provides an interesting comparison with the original. Noel Boggs shows up on one cut, "Swinging The Devil's Dream."

BUDDY EMMONS
Four Wheel Drive/Steel Guitar Jazz
Steel Guitar Products, c/o Tom Bradshaw, Box 931, Concord, CA 94522

Two landmark albums by the pedal steel's chieftain, reissued as a two-record set – what more could a steel guitarist ask for? *Four Wheel Drive* was cut during Buddy's tenure with Ernest Tubb, and the title track marks one of the earliest tunes to be recorded featuring pedals on the *C6* neck. *Steel Guitar Jazz*, recorded in New York in 1963, is the LP that blew everyone's mind. Emmons was only twenty-six at the time, but tunes like "Cherokee" demonstrate an unequalled harmonic knowledge and greater mastery of the *C6th* pedal changes.

FLATT & SCRUGGS
Flatt & Scruggs At Carnegie Hall!
Columbia PC-8845

This sounds as though it were recorded with one microphone (the liner photo actually shows two), but any high-fidelity shortcomings are far outweighed by the hot licks and pervasive energy of this live session. Lester Flatt plays strong rhythm and plenty of G runs throughout, while Josh Graves' Dobro darts in and out on standards like "Salty Dog Blues," "Flint Hill Special," and "Footprints In The Snow." Not surprisingly, Earl Scruggs's banjo playing steals the show.

MERLE HAGGARD
Songs I'll Always Sing
Capitol, two-record set SABB-11531

The consistency of Haggard & the Strangers is no less than amazing – nearly every cut (twenty included here) a classic. James Burton's instantly identifiable style is present on several tunes, including "Swing Doors" (with Ralph Mooney on pedal steel), "Working Man Blues," and "I'm A Lonesome Fugitive." Lead guitarist Roy Nichols and pedal steeler Norman Hamlet can be heard bending and sliding through "The Emptiest Arms In The World," and Roy turns on the afterburners for "Honky Tonk Night Time Man." No rhinestone Nudie suits here, this is blue-collar country at its best.

EMMYLOU HARRIS
Elite Hotel
Warner Bros/Reprise K-2286

A dream band backs Emmy's angelic vocals on what in retrospect reads like a Greatest Hits package from her onstage repertoire. Hank DeVito handles ballads ("Together Again"), shuffles ("Wheels"), and burners ("Ooh Las Vegas") with an abundance of taste, and Bernie Leadon contributes a beautiful acoustic lead break to "Sweet Dreams." And James Burton proves yet again that no one can touch him, be it his lyrical, understated melody on "Sweet Dreams," his Duane Eddy-tinged break on "One Of These Days," or his blistering picking at the end of "Las Vegas." Time and again, he can start a solo from left field and make total sense out of it.

ALBERT LEE
Albert Lee
Polydor PD-1-6358

"I was born to be a rock 'n' roll man," Albert sings, "playing guitar in a rock 'n' roll band." And, boy, he proves it – over and over. From the simple rock licks of "Real Wild Child" to the tight clusters on "Rock 'N' Roll Man," Albert's compact solo statements seem to jump out of his Telecaster. Truly a consummate guitarist.

SAM MCGEE
Grand Dad Of The Country Guitar Pickers
Arhoolie 5012

Even though this was recorded when McGee was well into his sev-

enties, he's in fine form, on guitar, banjo, and six-string banjo-guitar (featured on "Ching Chong" and his well-known "Buckdancer's Choice"). "Railroad Blues," composed by Sam, sounds like a perfect fusion of Jimmie Rodgers and Mississippi John Hurt.

WILLIE NELSON
Red-Headed Stranger
Columbia PC-33482

Willie's most ambitious work, progressive country's masterpiece. Nelson's amplfied gut-string guitar is the backbone of this song cycle, stating simple melody lines on "Just As I Am" and the hit "Blue Eyes Crying In The Rain" and adding jazzy flamenco-like flourishes to "Can I Sleep In Your Arms."

THE NITTY GRITTY DIRT BAND
Will The Circle Be Unbroken
United Artists, three-record set UAS-9801

With special guests Merle Travis, Doc Watson, Maybelle Carter, Earl Scruggs, Jimmy Martin, and Roy Acuff, the Dirt Band proves that there is no generation gap when it comes to musicianship. The *audio verite* presentation provides almost as many memorable moments as the songs themselves, such as the first face to face meeting of Watson and Travis. Thirty-seven songs in all, too many highlights to list.

BUCK OWENS
The Best Of Buck Owens And His Buckaroos, Vol. 2
Capitol ST-2897

Buck never sounded better than he did in the early-mid-sixties, where these tracks come from. Don Rich's Tele and Tom Brumley's steel shine on classics like "Together Again," "Love's Gonna Live Here," and the instrumental "Buckaroo."

RILEY PUCKETT
Old-Time Greats, Vol. 1: Riley Puckett
Old Homestead OHCS 114

Away from Gid Tanner and the

Skillet Lickers, Riley's guitar can be heard to full advantage, strumming rhythm, slipping in bass runs, and occasionally taking off on a solo, as on "Fuzzy Rag." "The Darkey's Wail" offers a rare glimpse of Puckett playing slide.

ELVIS PRESLEY
The Sun Sessions
RCA AYM1-3893

There's good rockin' tonight! This collection of Elvis' earliest recordings, 1954 and 1955, may amount to rock 'n' roll's greatest LP – certainly its most essential. Scotty Moore's revved up blend of Atkins, western swing, blues, and boogie formed the mold for future rock guitarists, and Elvis' driving acoustic rhythm helped define the rockabilly sound.

JERRY REED
Me & Chet
RCA ANL1-2167;

Me & Jerry
RCA LSP-4396

If all the loose instrumentals from Reed's vocal albums were collected on one piece of vinyl (or if Jerry just sat down in a studio for a day with nothing but his guitar) it would probably constitute the best country guitar LP yet. Short of that, these two discs find Reed and his mentor, Chet Atkins, in a relaxed, jamming mood but are filled with the energy of two monsters pushing each other to the limit.

TONY RICE UNIT
Manzanita
Rounder 0092

Rice has recorded several superb LPs, but this one features his finest bluegrass picking, accompanied by a band of all stars including Sam Bush, Ricky Skaggs, Todd Phillips, David Grisman, and Jerry Douglas. Tony's progressive side steps forward on the title cut.

JIMMIE RODGERS
This Is Jimmie Rodgers
RCA, two-record set VPS-6091E

The Singing Brakeman's very influential singing, syncopated guitar style, and original songs make this double-set a must. "Any Old Time," "T For Texas," "In The Jailhouse Now," "Peach Picking Time In Georgia," and more—every cut is a gem.

MERLE TRAVIS
The Merle Travis Guitar
Capitol SM-650

Merle's execution is sheer perfection, his tone crystal clear, his taste impeccabale on this set of a dozen solo instrumentals. Each tune, from "Blue Smoke" to "The Sheik Of Araby," is an advanced course in Travis pickin'.

GENE VINCENT & HIS BLUE CAPS
The Bop That Just Won't Stop (1956)
Capitol N-16209

The Blue Caps' Cliff Gallup was easily rockabilly's most advanced lead guitarist, both technically and harmonically, and although he stayed with Vincent for only about a year and a half, the sides he re-corded (such as "Crusin'" and "Race With The Devil" included here) have yet to be surpassed.

DOC WATSON
Doc Watson On Stage
Vanguard, two-record set T.9/10

Almost any of Doc's albums could qualify as an essential, but this double-set, recorded live, offers the widest variety of material in the least cluttered environment, backed only by Merle Watson's guitar. All of the Watson charm is here—the K Hzing flatpicking, the effortless fingerpicking, the rich baritone, and the back porch humor.

CLARENCE WHITE
Clarence White & the Kentucky Colonels
Rounder 0098

There are several Kentucky Colonels packages available these days, but this one places the spotlight on Clarence's guitar. Comprised of live tapes from 1964, 1965, and 1967, each cut paints a portrait of an artist who has already mastered more than most have ever at-tempted but is continually evolving and experimenting.

BOB WILLS & HIS TEXAS PLAYBOYS
The Tiffany Transcriptions, Vol. 1
Kaleidoscope F-16

These radio transcriptions, recorded in 1946 and 1947, capture Wills & Co. in a relaxed but swinging mood, with some of the hottest players he ever fronted. Junior Barnard burns on "Blackout Blues," while he and steel guitarist Noel Boggs play "twin" lines on "I Hear You Talkin'." Other tracks feature Herb Remington, Eldon Shamblin, and five-string mandolinist Tiny Moore.

VARIOUS ARTISTS
Steel Guitar Classics
Old-Timey 113

Not a lap steel album, but an anthology of some of the greatest Dobro and acoustic Hawaiian guitar players, including Cliff Carlisle, Jimmy Tarlton, and the great Sol Hoopii. The LP's highlight is Tex Carmen's playful "Hillbilly Hula."

Acknowledgements

For their help and encouragement in making this chapter possible, the author would like to thank Janice Azrak, Larry and Bobby Black, Evo Bluestein, Jimmy Bowen, Steve Fishell, Doug Green, Steve Hathaway, Glenn Howard, Tim Kaihatsu, Richard Kienzle, Bill Kirchen, Albert Lee, Tom Mulhern, Cathie Nelson, Tony Rice, Jon Sievert, and Tom Wheeler.

Rock: Kick Out the Jams

by Gene Santoro

In the beginning was the beat, but the guitar was not far behind. The electric guitar. From the jangling, broken chordings of Danny Cidrone in that first rock'n'roll hit "Rock Around The Clock," to the pungent stabs from Chuck Berry's semi-hollow Gibsons; from the psychedelic explorations of Jimi Hendrix and Jerry Garcia, to the blues-based fireworks of Eric Clapton, Jeff Beck, Jimmy Page; from the heavy metal of Van Halen to the inspired covers of Ry Cooder, rock guitar – its textures and its sounds, its posturing and its sexuality – has been the soul of the music. There is no way to imagine what rock would have been like without it.

If the guitar is the soul of rock, the faces that soul has presented have been fantastically varied and phenomenally eclectic. The music itself began, after all, as a fusion of influences, from rhythm'n'blues to blues to country music to jazz – Elvis's first recording and hit for Sam Phillips's Sun Records was, characteristically enough, an old Arthur Crudup tune called "That's All Right, Mama." As rock's principal instrument, the guitar has naturally mirrored that fertile and abundant heritage. Many of the greatest guitarists discussed in the other chapters of this book had a powerful influence on the best of the rock musicians. Some examples: Charlie Christian and T-Bone Walker, who pioneered the single-string, hornlike riffs that became such a fundamental part of first blues, then rock; Merle Travis, who brought the art of fingerpicking to its country peak; Muddy Waters and Howlin' Wolf, who pushed the urban blues with a relentless beat and a tight ensemble sound; Les Paul, whose oh-so-sweet country chordings were the proving grounds for an amazing range of technological experiments with tape speeds, overdubbing, echo

Jimi Hendrix

Chuck Berry

Bo Diddley

chambers, and the nature of the guitar itself; and so on, and on. The diverse wealth of influences virtually guaranteed that rock guitar would produce the variety of players and styles that it has.

Style isn't simply a matter of what notes to play and how. From the very beginning, rock guitar was as much theatrical prop as it was musical force. The tough adolescent sexuality that powered the sound found its perfect visual counterpart in the hipslung, pearshaped instrument. You could, if you wanted to, speculate almost forever about the Freudian or Jungian or whatever implications that charge the guitar with such sexual force; but the point, the real point, is that the best of the players have always understood that charge intuitively, and have translated it into physical expression. (See box on GUITAR AS PROP, p. 162.) In the end, its physical form, its sexuality, its variety of textures and sounds, its portability, and its relative accessibility as an instrument all guaranteed that the guitar would play the key notes of this new popular music.

CHUCK BERRY & BO DIDDLEY

There is just no way to talk about rock'n'roll guitar without talking about Chuck Berry. He dominated much of the early scene through his complete mas-

tery of all its aspects: songwriting, singing, playing, performing, and a shrewd sense of packaging. Berry's characteristic chops – the sharp, stinging three or two-note chordings executed by barring the high E , B, and G strings up and down the neck; the chukka-chukka rhythm that pushes the back beat and literally rocks back and forth on the lower strings between open fifths and sixths and sevenths; the twisted and bent "blue" notes, flatted thirds and sevenths that brought into rock the traditional country blues scales and attack – were soon being copped and duplicated in basements and garages across the U.S., and from there traveled around the world. As a showman, Berry has had few peers, with his "duck walk" on his haunches that sends him strutting across the stage, chugging and gyrating on his semi-hollow Gibson ES-335, turning the audience on with his inevitable showstopper, "I Wanna Play With My Dingaling." And the songs: "Maybellene," "Johnny B. Goode," "Roll Over Beethoven," and countless others tell the seemingly simple stories of teenage life and love, cars and disappointments, all through the ironic sensibility of a black country bluesman, propelled by the force of his personality and the staccato attack of his showcased guitar work. If there were a single fountainhead for rock guitar,

Chuck Berry would be it. Through him, rock'n'roll was fed on the rich and diverse legacies of Charlie Christian and T-Bone Walker, Nat "King" Cole and Louis Jordan, Carl Hoagan and Bill Jennings. He inspired Buddy Holly and John Lennon, Keith Richards and Eric Clapton, Bob Dylan and Jimmy Page. He is, quite simply, one of the masters of rock guitar.

If Chuck Berry had no real peer in the early days of rock guitar, the only man who might come close had a beat named after him that made everybody from Buddy Holly to Jerry Garcia, Keith Richards to George Thorogood sit up and take notice. Bo Diddley started by making his own electric guitars out of old acoustics and radio parts, and continued by wrenching his gutsy sound out of the most outlandish looking guitars ever made. Gretsch still custom-manufactures a wide variety for him: his favorite, a red, oblong-shape; a star; and triangles, one covered in purple carpet, another in fur; you get the idea. Out of this geometric array came percussive effects (often labelled "jungle rhythms" by detractors in the early days, because of their African overtones), heavy tremolo, and simple riffs, often played in open tunings. Elias McDaniel (his given name – he was adopted) may not have been as inventive a guitarist as Chuck Berry, but he wrote a number of rock'n'roll classics ("I'm a Man," "Who Do You Love?" and, of course, "Bo Diddley"), while his weird guitars and powerful stage presence combined to make him an influential model for early rock guitarists.

ROCKABILLY

The influences that shaped early rock'n'roll guitar may be traceable to a dozen different sources, but certainly rockabilly pulled together the most interesting and important. In fact, the names of the top rockabilly artists read like a Who's Who of rock'n'roll: Carl Perkins, Elvis himself, Buddy Holly, Gene Vincent, Eddie Cochran, Jerry Lee Lewis, Link Wray, Duane Eddy, the Everly Brothers. They really set the scene, at least until the early 1960s when the musical explosion in Britain introduced a renewed interest in more directly derived blues and jazz techniques. In terms of musical influences and early rock guitar aside from Berry and Bo Diddley, rockabilly was *the* sound around.

Carl Perkins

Carl Perkins set off a musical explosion with "Blue Suede Shoes" and "Honey Don't": his rippling chord-

ings, slyly bent notes, and twangy bass runs became the standard that other guitarists aspired to. One gauge of his influence is the Beatles' rendition of "Honey Don't" and "Matchbox," another Perkins

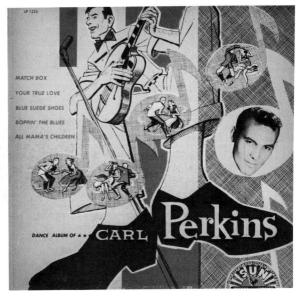
Carl Perkins

classic. The young George Harrison studied and honed his Perkins chops until he could reproduce and amplify the master's voice. If it hadn't been for the tragic car crash that incapacitated him right as his hits and sound were breaking in a big way, Carl Perkins might just have become the King.

Scotty Moore

Of course, things turned out differently – the crown was reserved for Elvis. But in those glorious days when Elvis really *was* the King, recording first at those echoey Sun studios in Memphis and then at RCA Nashville under the astute direction of no less a personage than Chet Atkins, Elvis's standard studio back-up included a guitarist named Scotty Moore. Moore, who also produced the recordings of several country blues artists like Big Bill Broonzy, set out on his Gibson 235 the stinging, spare, sinewy lines that toughened up the best of some of Elvis's most famous tracks: "That's All Right, Mama," "Heartbreak Hotel," "Jailhouse Rock," and "Hound Dog." In a way, Scotty Moore – together with Chet Atkins – was the direct ancestor of such guitarist-producers as Steve Cropper, whose own licks with Booker T and the MGs and Otis Redding revealed the same spare sense of melody that Moore used to fill in Elvis's sound.

Elvis Presley

Chuck Berry

The Guitar as Prop – I

The guitar, especially in rock music, has always had a strong sexual aura. In the hands of the most talented practitioners, that sexuality has played almost as important a role as the music itself. It certainly helped sell guitars.

Elvis Presley, as you would expect, was a major force in the recognition of the guitar's value as a prop. Like the music he helped pioneer, the roots of that recognition can be found in the country blues and minstrel show traditions, where musicians were also, necessarily, performers in the fullest sense. The audience in a Southern juke joint, for example, wanted to see as well as hear the enthusiasm behind the music; and so guitarists developed visual tricks to catch and hold their audience's attention (and save themselves from the probably violent form that a negative audience reaction would take). Peter Guralnick has described Delta bluesman Charley Patton's performing style succinctly in his *Listener's Guide to the Blues*: "His powerful rasping voice went along with a real propensity to entertain....He would rap on his guitar and throw it up into the air, his vocal asides have the air of vaudeville commentary....With his evident ability to make himself heard, his strong danceable rhythms, and his broad range of styles, he was the best kind of entertainer to play at the Saturday night dances and all-day frolics and picnics." With some minor alterations, that could be a description of The King himself. Elvis didn't so much play the guitar (though he could play quite competent rhythm) as use it to focus on his own tough sexuality: the sneering lips and twisting hips were punctuated by the female-shaped, phallic object hanging across his body from chest to crotch. It was dynamite, as *The Ed Sullivan Show* on US television inadvertently attested, by presenting Elvis's performance only from the waist up.

The other major champion in early rock'n'roll for the guitar's sexual nature was a more direct descendent of the blues traditions. Chuck Berry's famous "duck walk" illustrated how the prop's sexuality could be made physically apparent. As Berry crouched across the stage on his haunches, his big red guitar hanging between his legs, there was no doubt about just what other instrument the guitar was representing. It was an image that impressed itself on the succeeding generations of rock guitarists.

James Burton

And of course there was James Burton. "Hello, Mary Lou" and "Travelin' Man" are just two of the Ricky Nelson tunes that benefited from the unique sound Burton sprung from his Fender Telecaster. Trained on Dobro and steel guitar, the young musician developed a style of note-bending and combined fingerpicking and flatpicking that inspired generations of pickers. Burton's guitar has graced everything from *The Ozzie and Harriet Show* to *Shindig*, from Elvis (Burton led his band from 1969 to 1977) to Emmylou Harris and her Hot Band. His influence has been as wide-ranging as his playing.

Buddy Holly

Elvis and his music had a stimulating effect on young musicians everywhere, but on no one more than a singer-guitarist from Lubbock, Texas. Buddy Holly (he changed the spelling of Holley to conform to the misspelling on his Decca contract) not only wrote some of rock'n'roll's most outstanding tunes –"Peggy Sue," "That'll Be The Day," "Everyday," "Words Of Love," "Not Fade Away," "Maybe Baby," just to name a few – but was one of the first guitarists to use the then-new Fender Stratocaster. (Up to that point Strats were considered country guitars, but Holly changed that.) His leads, which prefigure the chordal-style solos that Keith Richards and Pete Townshend later built upon, were tasteful and effective, especially when backed by second guitarist Sonny Curtis or Niki Sullivan. There isn't any way of knowing how Holly would have developed his guitar and musical style if he hadn't died in the same plane crash outside Mason City, Iowa, that killed his friends and touring mates the Big Bopper and Rickie Valens – he was only twenty-two when he died, after all. But in less than two years he had become one of the major stars of rock'n'roll, close in popularity to his idol, Elvis; and virtually every major band or performer since has owed something to Buddy Holly's music.

Eddie Cochran

One of the first rock'n'rollers to feel that influence was Eddie Cochran. The author of "Summertime Blues" and "C'mon Everybody," Cochran had his musical roots in the raw country blues he heard as a boy in Oklahoma and Minnesota. When he was twelve, his parents bought him a guitar and his older brother taught him a few chords. He played along with the radio, and in the process picked up a taste for jazz and rhythm'n'blues and boogie woogie. Like Buddy Holly, Cochran decided to try for a recording

Buddy Holly

contract when he appeared on the same bill as Elvis – apparently the King's power in performance affected his fellow musicians as much as it did the audience. It also inspired Cochran to abandon country music for rockabilly, though he continued to play and sing from a range of material and styles. It was 1956; he was seventeen.

By the following year, Cochran had become an established session player on the West Coast, and had perfected on his semi-hollow Gretsch the classic chunky guitar riffs that, fed through heavy echo, would define his unique sound. Ricky Nelson (with James Burton behind him) was beginning to cover Cochran's tunes, even to appropriate his whole approach and sound. Out in Seattle, a kid named Jimi Hendrix was listening real closely to the string of hits that began with "Summertime Blues" in 1958. Cochran planned to tour with his pal Buddy Holly in 1959, but missed the tour – and the fatal crash that ended it – because of prior commitments. Grief-stricken, he swore off touring, and decided to perfect his command of the recording studio as producer and arranger. In 1960, though, his old friend Gene Vincent set up a tour of England, and Cochran decided he would go with Vincent again. It was an exciting trip – England was exploding with the rock'n'roll crazies, and Vincent and Cochran played to packed houses everywhere. (When the tour hit Liverpool, Philip Norman writes in his book on the Beatles, *Shout!*, "three would-be rock and rollers from a group last known as Johnny and the Moondogs strained their eyes to see the fingering of Eddie Cochran's guitar solo in "Hallelujah, I Love Her So!'")" The houses were so packed, in fact, that the promoters planned to extend the tour by ten weeks – but that extension was not to be. After completing the first half of their originally scheduled tour, Cochran and his girlfriend hired a chauffeured car to take them and Vincent to London Airport. It had a blowout at eighty mph, skidded, smashed into a tree or a lamppost, and smashed Cochran into the roof. He died from massive skull injuries on April 17, 1960, at age twenty-one.

Gene Vincent

Gene Vincent was severely injured in the crash as well, and though he never recovered, either personally or professionally, he survived and actually completed the tour scheduled for him and Cochran. It wasn't the first serious accident he'd had; in fact, his tough-guy, black-leather stage act depended for its added sinister note on the fact that when he was serving as a motorcycle dispatch rider in the Navy he had been knocked off his bike and received multiple fractures to his left leg. Always rebellious, Vincent wouldn't sit still long enough for the leg to heal, with the result that he had to wear leg irons – which certainly enhanced his image. (The same three members of Johnny and the Moondogs staring at Eddie Cochran's fingers bought Gene Vincent caps for their first Hamburg gigs.) Backed by a powerhouse group called the Blue Caps, with Cliff Gallup playing inventive, skittish Telecaster behind his echoey voice, Vincent sang hits like "Be-Bop-A-Lula" and "Bluejean Bop". His live performances were classic – his left leg anchored to the stage, dressed head-to-toe in black leather, snarling and raging, Gene Vincent epitomized early rockabilly.

Duane Eddy

Other rockabilly stars didn't fill in anybody else's sound: they created their own, in a long string of instrumental hits that ended only in the early 1960s. The most successful at mining and exploiting this musical vein turned out to be Arizona-born Duane Eddy. On his Chet Atkins-model Gretsch, Eddy "twanged" out a bass-note melody that rocked with his Bigsby vibrato bar. From his first hit, "Movin'n' Groovin'," cut when he was only nineteen, through the parade that followed – "Rebel Rouser," "Forty Miles Of Bad Road," etc. – Eddy followed the formula that spawned a whole school of soon-to-be-forgotten imitators. And so were born such garage-band standards as "Pipeline," "The Percolator Song," the theme from "Peter Gunn," and a host of others.

Link Wray

The other guitar star who blasted his way onto the charts in 1958 has only recently been resurrected by neo-rockabilly singer Robert Gordon. Link Wray's style, like Duane Eddy's, demanded the use – no, the drenching – of echo and reverb and tremolo. But unlike Eddy's single-string, bass-note melodies, which had arrangements built around them, Wray blasted his way through the band, working off chords and wrenching sounds out of his Les Paul or Danelectro that were nothing short of astonishing, especially for the time. Feedback, heavy distortion, lots of reverb and vibrato bar use, and slightly skewed scales were the trademarks of Wray's offbeat and often humorous attack; and his best-known cuts, "Rumble" and "Rawhide," remain classics of rockabilly guitar.

THE WEST COAST SOUND

The reach of the rockabilly sound and instrumental format extended far past the confines of Memphis and Nashville. Way out west, in Tacoma, Washington, two bricklayers named Bob Bogle and Don Wilson were inspired by Duane Eddy to put together a repertoire as a guitar duo and begin playing dances around the area. Once they'd built up a following, they began to think about cutting a record of their own, but were turned down by all the major labels. They hooked up with another guitarist, Nokie Edwards, formed their own recording company, and recorded a tune written by jazz guitarist Johnny Smith called "Walk Don't Run" that they got hold of by way of Chet Atkins. And so the Ventures were born. From 1960 on, they issued a string of instrumental hits – "Perfidia," "Lullaby Of The Leaves," "Hawaii Five-O," "Walk Don't Run '64," etc. – that dominated the market and defined the sound. ("Perfidia" and "Walk Don't Run" featured Bogle on lead; Nokie Edwards, hired as a bassist, traded with him and played lead on everything else since.) Covering hits with their Fender Strats (and later their own Ventures Models by Mosrite) played through blond Bandmasters and Jazzmasters, the Ventures shaped their attack around simple riffs that let them play with counterpoint and textures and harmonies. Until the Beatles blew them – and everybody

The Ventures

else – off the charts, they released some thirty albums that inevitably rushed to the top of the pops. Of course, a large part of the West Coast sound developed out of the beaches and cars that dominated teenage life in southern California. The Beach Boys, piloted by songwriter and (later) producer Brian Wilson, literally embodied the feel of that way of life in their music. They had listened to guitarist Dick Dale pioneering what he dubbed "surf music" in his appearances at the Rendevous Ballroom, picking furiously through 32nd note riffs on tunes like "Miserlou" and "Surf Beat." The Beach Boys absorbed that style well enough to be able to cover (with Brian's brother Carl on lead guitar) Dale's hit "Let's Go Trippin'." The fluid, Chuck Berry-based chops of this guitar-showcase tune were in effect the basis of the Beach Boys' early instrumental approach. Hits like "Surfin' USA," "Little Deuce Coupe," and "Fun, Fun, Fun" rolled out of Brian Wilson's talented hands and streaked to number one with predictable regularity. Then came the British Invasion of 1964, and suddenly the Beach Boys, like the Ventures, found their sound buried beneath a avalanche of British-born hits.

THE BLUES REVIVAL IN THE U.K.

Retrospectively – with the value of 20/20 hindsight – the early 1960s seem like a time when rock music very nearly died from a thoughtless overdose of Bobbies and other voiceless wonders with one

The Rolling Stones

name who had the same insipid background behind all their tunes. But underneath this placid, milk-drinking surface, other, more serious musicians were delving into the deeper tributaries that had flowed into rock'n'roll, giving it energy and shape. When their new, reformed, tougher music finally broke through the surface, it was powered by a new breed of guitar players who expanded the instrument's vocabulary, technology, and possibilities in a dozen different directions previously undreamt of.

Things broke in England first. The club scene there had been dominated since the late 1950s by Lonnie Donegan and skiffle music, a mixture of jazz, blues, and American folk played on homemade instruments. Skiffle music brought young musicians back to sources. But in March 1962, a singer-guitarist named Alexis Korner who led a band called Blues Incorporated opened the Ealing Club in London; and growing and enthusiastic audiences came to hear the blues of Muddy Waters and others, played by a parade of musicians that included Mick Jagger, Keith Richards, Brian Jones, Eric Burdon, John McLaughlin, Eric Clapton, Jack Bruce, and Ginger Baker. The British blues boom had begun, and soon

exploded into a constellation of star-studded bands.

The Rolling Stones

The Rolling Stones (named after a Muddy Waters tune) are a good place to begin the catalogue. Their first single, a cover of Chuck Berry's "Come On," fairly burst with rhythm'n'blues and straight blues styles, from cops of Berry's own standard licks to the use of harmonica and slide guitar. Those seemingly endless nights of playing at the Ealing Club for a pint of beer had finally paid off musically as well as financially. Drummer Charlie Watts and bassist Bill Wyman propelled the backbeat with a concentrated intensity that recalled, even as it derived from, Muddy's Chicago ensemble sound; and Keith and Brian on guitars meshed their rhythm work with a biting professionalism that drew on every source available, from Chuck Berry to Muddy to what was then called soul music. Richards especially learned to make his Telecaster modulate from bassy twanging to stinging treble runs, from the familiar Chuck Berry chordings to the fuzz-toned and overdriven distortions that heralded future developments in rock guitar. He also recaptured the chord-dominated lead line that Buddy Holly had pioneered, and made it an

The Yardbirds, with Eric Clapton (bottom right)

essential part of the band's unique and eclectic sound.

The Yardbirds

But the band that has to receive the notice as *the* home (however brief) of future superstars is, of course, the Yardbirds. Tasty as the licks of Richards or Hilton Valentine (the Animals' lead guitar) might have been, they were overshadowed by the sheer volume of finger wizardry that blasted out of the Yardbirds' ever-changing lineup. Clapton, Beck, and Page: a triad of innovative players, each of them stemming from the same roots in the blues and growing in increasingly divergent directions, all of them formidable influences with a legacy of music and followers that assures each of them a place in rock's Valhalla.

Eric Clapton

Eric Clapton spent a lot of his teenage life listening to the blues on the radio. Muddy, Big Bill Broonzy, Chuck Berry, B. B. King, and Freddie King were among the most formative influences. He played with the Yardbirds from 1963 to 1965, when they were evolving from doing only rhythm'n'blues covers to attempting a wide and gangling collection of styles. The shift was not to Clapton's taste, since he felt himself to be a committed blues "purist," and the breaking point came with the decision to release "For Your Love" as the band's first single. Clapton almost literally picked up his Telecaster, and his unique touch and sense of melody; within a short time he was playing "pure" (British) blues with John Mayall's Bluesbreakers, now on a vintage Les Paul through Marshall amps to get that trademark thick and overdriven sound. "Clapton is God" began appearing as graffiti around London.

It is easy to see why, listening to him play with John Mayall's Bluesbreakers on T-Bone Walker's classic "Stormy Monday," for example. The boy had it all. The characteristic hesitations and syncopations, the punching buildups toward chord changes, the lilting phrases punctuated by bent blues notes tumbling into abrupt finishes that accent the power and beauty of the line, the sure-fingered variety of attack, the breathtaking reaches up to the twelfth fret and beyond, the heavy sustain, the flawless timing – it must have been difficult to be a guitarist listening in the audience without being overwhelmed completely. Clapton was, if not God, the first real guitar hero; and legions would follow his every twist and turn, not to mention learning his every recorded lick. And so, by the time Clapton left the Bluesbreakers to form Cream, and help move blues-based music toward psychedelia, Mayall had literally hundreds of Clapton sound-alikes to audition.

Peter Green

The first Clapton replacement was Peter Green, who rapidly developed a reputation as the finest blues guitarist in England in the year or so he spent in the Bluesbreakers. Starting by duplicating Clapton's sound, Green soon displayed his honed intensity to good effect. For example, on "Looking Back" he starts off with near-feedback, scrambles up a really nice succession of riffs into a well-tempered lead, and closes the song out with fading feedback. When he left Mayall, it was with drummer Mick Fleetwood and bassist John McVie; together they founded Fleetwood Mac, which, in that early incarnation, evolved into a fantastic blues band – sharp-edged without rawness, steady in the Chicago blues mold, impressive and direct. Their biggest hit, "Black Magic Woman," from the LP of the same name, mixed snaky jazz-tinged guitar and insinuating vocal with other unusual textures: tremolo-laced rhythm work, Latin-ish percussion. It also marked Green's departure from the band for religious pur-

The Yardbirds, with Jeff Beck (holding guitar)

suits. He later released two solo LPs – the first entirely jazz-oriented, the second a return to his blues-based style.

Mick Taylor

Mick Taylor replaced Peter Green in Mayall's Bluesbreakers when he was just eighteen, but his guitar style was already apparent. Laid back and melodic, tasteful with a capital T, Taylor manipulated the now-standard blues guitarist's rig in subtle new ways. Take, for example, Mayall's classic *Bare Wires* LP. He took the wah-wah and played blues through it on "No Reply;" he played gutsy Chicagostyle blues on "Hartley Quits," but knew how to move the beat around, playing off the varying riff lengths to avoid a pat sameness to his format, wrenching the strings just enough to feel those blues; on "Killing Time" he played crying slide with just the kind of conviction that the Stones' later version of "No Expectations" would demand. No wonder when Brian Jones died in 1969, the Stones asked him to join – Taylor even had just the right choir boy face to offset Mick Jagger's "evil" routines.

Jeff Beck

A Clapton sound-alike wasn't what the Yardbirds wanted, and it certainly wasn't what they got. Even as early as Clapton's departure in 1965, they were making real musical moves in experimental directions, and they needed a guitar player that could fuel their flight. Jeff Beck was it. Combining feedback and controlled distortion, angular modal licks and jazzy scales, Beck created a sound that was about as different from Clapton's clean, vibrato-laced bluesiness as a sound could be. It really was, as Beck himself has claimed, an early stab at psychedelia, though that label is too confining for Beck's impressive array of techniques. From slashing slide guitar on "Evil Hearted You" through the growling ragalike licks of "Shapes Of Things" to the punk power chordings on "I'm A Man," the young musician was by himself a virtual guitar army; and when he joined forces briefly with Jimmy Page, his musical inventiveness overwhelmed the former session guitarist into playing patterns that would, not too much later, float Led Zeppelin on its own long flight.

For Beck, however, musical forums have to change regularly, no matter how successful they may be. And so, during the Yardbirds' 1966 U.S. tour featuring Beck and Page as dual lead guitarists, the band fired Beck when he claimed (once too often, in their view) to be sick and missed a string of gigs. The flurry gave rise to charges of unprofessionalism and egomania that have since returned periodically to haunt the man, if not his music; it also allowed Beck to form the first of his Jeff Beck groups with guitarist/bassist Ron Wood, vocalist Rod Stewart, drummer Mick Waller, and pianist Nicky Hopkins. At virtually the same time, Page took a band that had toured as the New Yardbirds, and went into the studio for thirty hours to cut an album called simply *Led Zeppelin*. The psychedelic sixties had, indeed, arrived in Britain.

Pete Townshend

That era had still another guitarist to help usher it in against an R&B background. He may have started out playing banjo in a New Orleans-style jazz band, but Pete Townshend has certainly revolutionized the way rock guitar is played – not only musically, but in terms of performance. (see GUITAR AS PROP, p.170) Clapton, Beck, Richards, Peter Green, Mick Taylor were all, to a greater or lesser degree, primarily single-string blues pickers; Townshend virtually invented the power chord to smash ahead the tune's rhythms instead of playing a lead around or on top of them. His whirling right hand rounds and pounds the heavy-gauge strings to punch out a throaty mass of distortion, harmonics, and controlled feedback: along with Beck, Townshend was both a harbinger of and a great influence on the psychedelic music that was to burst out of San Francisco's 1967 Summer of Love.

The Beatles

Of course, there was one group whose musical influence and growth paralleled those of other groups already discussed, and who also spanned the time between Lonnie Donegan and the Summer of Love – in fact, their growth determined much of the direction rock music took in those years. Their first incarnation played skiffle and was known as the Quarrymen; but by the time they'd forged their backbeat in the heat of Hamburg clubs, the Beatles had left amateurish skiffle – and most of their musical competition – far behind them. They toured enough to get roadburn, played enough dank cellar clubs to grow mold on their black leather jackets and new French–style haircuts. By 1961, they'd honed

Pete Townshend

their vocal and instrumental talents, their repertoire, their stage act, and they'd met Brian Epstein, who saw it as his sacred duty to launch a phenomenon upon the as-yet-unsuspecting world. He did, and the rest, as they say, is history.

None of the Beatles was exactly a guitar hero – no Jimi Hendrix or Eric Clapton, Eddie Van Halen or Steve Howe in their ranks. But they were *the* rock ensemble players, the models who had studied their sources and reshaped them and passed the modified influences on. They knew their instruments, and (a harder lesson) the limits of their instrumental abilities well. Lead guitarist George Harrison almost never took extended solos, preferring tasty morsels – a quick fill here, a carefully thought-out twelve bars there, a running riff to drive a song over there. A few examples will do. For quick fills, consider the chord climb and Chuck Berry punctuation in "I Want To Hold Your Hand," the choked Berry–style riff at the end of the chorus in "She Loves You," the fuzz-edged jab between verses in "I'm Looking Through You," the raunchy broken chords following the brass in "Got To Get You Into

The Guitar as Prop — II

Hendrix, Beck, Page all were masters of their own unique versions of the guitar as visual prop, but for sheer insane intensity onstage Pete Townshend has few peers. His leaps and cavorts are almost balletic, and when you consider his "windmill" strumming technique to smash out power chords, and his guitar-smashing finales, you've got a mesmerizing combination. The early Who, especially, were a highly visual act, with singer Roger Daltrey's prancing and preening and drummer Keith Moon's unpredictable insanity that led unerringly to the destruction of drum kit after drum kit. (In fact, Townshend's progressive loss of hearing seems partially due to a prank Moon played when the band appeared on the US television show *The Smothers Brothers Comedy Hour*: the irrepressible drummer finessed the Who's usual crowd-pleasing ending by setting off an actual explosion that blew right by Townshend's head.) To command visual attention in such a circus-like atmosphere required a dramatic approach, and Townshend's theatrics were one answer — not only for him, but for others, like Eddie Van Halen, who were clearly influenced by him.

Pete Townshend

My Life," the fiery grumblings between verses in "Sergeant Pepper." For sculpted solos listen to "Till There Was You," "Follow The Sun," "And Your Bird Can Sing," "She's A Woman," "Tax Man," "Michelle," and "Something." For running riffs – well, that was Harrison's special talent, and it's difficult to pick. Classics would have to include "I Feel Fine" (with what may be the first controlled feedback of the psychedelic era), "Day Tripper," "Birthday," "Helter Skelter," and much of the *Abbey Road* LP. Remember, though, that these are only selections – browse around almost any Beatles LP and Harrison will teach you something.

The same is true of bassist Paul McCartney, who began his days with the Beatles wanting to be a lead guitarist and ended by having freed up the electronic bass for almost anything in a rock context. Even on the earliest LPs, McCartney took his hefty Hofner violin-shaped bass and propelled songs instead of just anchoring them. There were many tunes – "Day Tripper," "Rain," "Paperback Writer," "A Little Help From My Friends," and countless others – where the bass was so far out in front as to be the lead instrument. But again, it was not McCartney's soloing but his contribution to the overall texture of the Beatles' sound that made him – and them – musically important even if they hadn't written a single song. Using their three guitars, Harrison, McCartney, and John Lennon managed to create a fabulous array of sounds and dynamics – especially before they became a studio band with other textures at their disposal. On almost any album before *Rubber Soul*, you can hear them playing with the building blocks of rock'n'roll. Acoustics, electrics, six strings, twelve strings, fuzztones, tremolo, vibrato bars – all found their way into and out of their tunes, with a dexterity and musical vision and coherence that can leave you breathless. Keep in mind, too, that the Beatles not only introduced some of the effects so important to the development of later rock trends, but also popularized lots of others that already existed. Including, for that matter, guitars themselves; especially electric guitars, and the idea of playing in a band and writing your own tunes. Certainly they had exactly that effect on many of the bands who made the sixties a musical feast.

U.S. BLUES

The blues found a great adoptive home in Britain and inspired some of the best pickers, but it is, after all, an American folk music. At no time since the advent of rock did the blues find such a wide audience, or wield such a broad influence, as during the early and mid-1960s. Along with the revival of the so-called protest music of the Depression, the music of Woody Guthrie, Pete Seeger, and others, the blues itself, especially at first the acoustic country blues, suddenly became a focus for great attention by young white musicians. Folk-blues guitarists like Dave Van Ronk, Stefan Grossman, Danny Kalb, David Bromberg, and hordes of other young pickers sat at the feet of Rev. Gary Davis and Mance Lipscomb, listening to their tunes, watching their hands, and transcribing what they saw and heard so they could try to duplicate it. Because the blues was looked at in the context of folk festivals, though, some interesting and instructive shuffling took place, altogether out of keeping with the revivalist emphasis on authenticity and integrity. Muddy Waters and Lightnin' Hopkins, both of them electric guitarists for many years, suddenly found themselves making the festival rounds playing acoustics *à la* Leadbelly, because electric music wasn't as "pure" as acoustic. The figure who became the sharp point of encounter between this perspective and another emerging musical sensibility was, of course, Bob Dylan; and the place was the 1965 Newport Folk Festival.

There are at least three versions of what happened there, according to James Sallis in his *Guitar Players*. The traditional one – the one that makes for the best story – has Bob Dylan slinging a Stratocaster over his shoulder to a loud chorus of boos from outraged and disappointed folk fans. The jeers reached such a chorus that the leather-jacketed Dylan and the electric band he was fronting were forced to leaved the hallowed Newport stage, but not before they had given birth to a new musical amalgam called folk-rock, and thus to a whole new direction in rock. Dylan was ably assisted at this birth by soon-to-be-luminaries Al Kooper and Michael Bloomfield, who even more than Dylan himself shaped in their subsequent careers and those they touched the future of the guitar in the new hybrid, and the course of the U.S. blues revival.

The folk music revival of the early 1960s had made the guitar accessible for the literally millions of white middle-class kids who picked it up to learn Woody Guthrie, Leadbelly, and Bob Dylan tunes. Among these students were Bloomfield, Danny Kalb, Clarence White, Robbie Robertson, Jerry Garcia, Jorma Kaukonen, Ry Cooder, David Bromberg, David Lindley, and too many others to list. Their names and music are, to all practical purposes, the history and music of the rock guitar in the mid- to late 1960s in the U.S., and they've all played their way back and forth around the roots of the music in endlessly inventive and assimilating ways. But that's getting a bit ahead of the story.

Michael Bloomfield

By the time he backed Bob Dylan at Newport in July 1965, Mike Bloomfield had been playing guitar for almost nine years in a collection of styles that ranged from acoustic ragtime, *à la* Blind Blake, to the hard-edged urban blues that came out of Chicago's South Side. Bloomfield himself was a rich kid from the North Side, but he drank up the atmosphere of "the bad side of town" with a thirsty vengeance. Like his friend Johnny Winter, Bloomfield became a guitar player with a mission: to revive and redefine the rich tradition of urban blues that was still, in the early 1960s, percolating in the Windy City. On his way, he did everything from manage a coffeehouse, where he staged old-time blues greats in concert, to doing studio and club dates behind the likes of Big Joe Williams, Sleepy John Estes, and John Hammond. He was devouring the recorded history of jazz at his friend Pete Welding's house. By the time he walked onto the Newport stage, Bloomfield had finished his apprenticeship and was ready to blow it all away. He did.

A young white harmonica player names Paul Butterfield had spent a lot of time on Chicago's South Side too, studying his musical craft with the best and putting a band together. Live, their guitarist was Elvin Bishop; but for the first Butterfield album on Elektra Bloomfield was asked to play slide on all cuts with Bishop backing him. The music was solid: funky, hard, moving, with Bloomfield's Telecaster skittering across the top of the arrangements like an agile angry bird. Then followed *Highway 61 Revisited*, where Bloomfield joined up with Kooper to back Dylan in a powerdriven combo that produced "Like A Rolling Stone," and led directly to the Newport confrontation. He turned down an offer to join Dylan's band to stay with Butterfield.

But it was *East-West*, the second Butterfield album, recorded in 1966, that helped rearrange the way rock guitar was played. It was literally a potpourri of possible guitar styles, a strutting of the stuff Bloomfield had absorbed. It was also the blistering announcement that his own playing had come of age. His slide on "Walking Shoes" opens the album with a strafing jab, as does the arching trebly lead with which he patches into Butterfield's harp solo; the minor key solo on "I Got A Mind To Give Up Living" is a modal marvel of chromatic feeling that builds and builds; his jazz-laced, airy feel on "The Work Song" alternates smooth seamless runs up and down the neck with offbeats that challenge the listener to avoid tapping a foot or two. The masterpiece, though, was the album's title tune (originally called "Raga"), which was so crucial to the development of subsequent rock guitarists that even FM radio jockeys found ways to program its thirteen-plus minutes into their playlists. Bloomfield's guitar seminally, neatly, ruthlessly lays out virtually every lick, musical influence, shade of feeling that would shape the guitar sound of San Francisco psychedelia. It is an amazing feat, no less for the prodigious musical assimilation than for the virtuoso performance. If Bloomfield had done nothing else, this would have guaranteed him a place among guitar greats. Of course, he did do other things: his album with the Electric Flag, and *Super Session*, which reunited him with Al Kooper and Harvey Brooks of the Flag, can delight and astonish even the most casual musician with their depth of feeling and technical range. But *East-West* will always be his moment in the sun.

Danny Kalb

Al Kooper became a much sought-after studio musician on the strength of the sessions he did with Bloomfield for Dylan; and in the course of his rovings through the New York music scene he hitched up with a band formed around a guitarist named Danny Kalb. Kalb had participated in the folk revival on the fringes, doing gigs and sessions, studying ragtime and fingerpicking blues guitar. In 1966 Kalb, who was by then considered one of the best guitarists around, put together a group that he named after a record he had appeared on with a few other New York folk musicians; and that was how the Blues Project came to be. Kooper came in later, and things broke for the group on the Thanksgiving weekend of 1966. Verve/Folkways sent a recording crew down to the Cafe au Go Go, then Greenwich Village's music headquarters, to record what was billed as a three-day "Blues Bag." The recording that came out of it was *The Blues Project Live At The Cafe Au Go Go*. Blasting off with Kalb's twitchy Danelectro runs – which sometimes sound like a talented spider being electrocuted on a set of guitar strings – and earnest vocals, their soon-to-be traditional set opener was a reworking of Muddy Waters's material called "Goin' Down Louisiana;" from there they charged through a variety of tunes that included Donovan's lyrical "Catch The Wind," Chuck Berry's "I Wanna Be Your Driver" and "You Can't Catch Me," Willie Dixon's sneering, menacing "Back Door Man," and Bo Diddley's "Who Do You Love." Their signature tune, however, was "Wake Me Shake Me," from their *Projections* LP, a kind of collage of spirituals and blues lines that Kooper created; it revolves around a funny key shift that Kalb climbs into screeching, Kooper's Hammond flattens it out into a melodic easygoing plateau, and finally Kalb backs the tune down into gear. It was a jammer's paradise; and like Butterfield's band on *East-West*, like the Yardbirds, the Blues Project presaged the age of the jamming supergroup fronted by a guitar hero. The group disbanded when Kooper left to form Blood, Sweat, and Tears (taking rhythm guitarist Steve Katz with him) and Kalb – literally – disappeared for months. He never regained the prominence he'd had as a musician.

Johnny Winter

Texas may seem a long way from Chicago and New York, but in 1969 the distance was bridged by Steve Paul, owner of New York's famed club The Scene, where every rock guitarist from Kalb to Hendrix either gigged or jammed regularly during the late 1960s. Paul had read in *Rolling Stone* magazine about an amazing albino guitarist who had hung

Johnny Winter

MONTEREY POP AND THE SUMMER OF LOVE

Forget whatever you've heard: Woodstock may have been the biggest and most hyped, Altamont may have marked the passing of an era in the music, but the festival at Monterey on June 16–18, 1967 was where the different trends in British and American music all shared a single stage and exploded with sheer power. Everybody who was anybody – especially any picker who was anybody – played there: Bloomfield with his Electric Flag; Jimi Hendrix with the Experience; Jerry Garcia with the Grateful Dead; Jorma Kaukonen with the Jefferson Airplane; Steve Miller with his band; John Cipollina with Quicksilver Messenger Service; and veteran Steve Cropper backing Otis Redding. The influences of the past were coming together and defining a new era for rock guitar, one that found a natural home in San Francisco. The Summer of Love spawned the psychedelic movement and its musical mirror, acid rock. The guitar players who fronted this sound relied on fuzz-tones; overdriven tube amps, often Fenders or Marshalls; blues-based runs with lots of bent notes, trills, hammer-ons, and pull-offs; frequent leaning on the vibrato arm; and drug-drenched, hypnotic extended solos. A new version of the guitar hero had arrived.

Jerry Garcia

In a very real sense, Jerry Garcia was the figurehead of the San Francisco rock scene, and he was certainly its premier guitarist. With the rest of the Grateful Dead, he defined the psychedelic sound from its earliest days, when the Dead were called the Warlocks and functioned as a sort of house band for Ken Kesey and his Merry Pranksters. To this day, Deadheads are a breed apart, a near-mystical sect that travels in packs braving changes in climate, country, and identity in order to fulfill their mission, which seems to consist of following the Dead members in their various permutations and musical venues. And their guru is Garcia.

He has certainly grown as a musician. His background was, unlike Bloomfield's, really more folky than blues: the early Dead often featured Dylan tunes like "It's All Over Now, Baby Blue," or Tim Rose's "Morning Dew"; but transmogrified by Phil Lesh's inventive and loping bass and Garcia's characteristic attack: offbeat, triplets, long slides up and down the neck culminating in hammer-ons and pull-offs. At parks on both coasts of the U.S., where they played for free, their standard opener was a hard-

around Chicago's blues joints with Mike Bloomfield, who'd jammed with B. B. King in a blues club called the Raven and astonished the audience – and B. B. – with his prodigious talent. Paul brought Johnny Winter and his bass player and drummer to Nashville and recorded them under the helpful eye (and ear) of Eddie Kramer, who was Hendrix's main engineer for the earlier LPs. The result: an album called simply *Johnny Winter*, and instant acclaim. Winter had listened to the blues and early rock'n'roll with the fervor of the fixated and the perception of the truly talented; and he assimilated into his licks and solos a range of influences that included Carl Perkins and Muddy Waters, early Jeff Beck and Robert Johnson, Chet Atkins and Jimi Hendrix. But mostly he played the blues, real driving blues that had the heaviness of Chicago pumping underneath it and his darting lines dancing melodically over it. Like Bloomfield's band and the Blues Project, he pulled blues classics, like "Mean Mistreater" and "When You Got A Good Friend," back into the mainstream of rock music and forced rock guitarists once again to pay attention to their musical heritage and draw from it.

driving cover of Martha and the Vandellas' "Dancin' In The Street." Their first album, called simply *The Grateful Dead*, showcases a lowdown smoking arrangement of "Good Mornin' Little School Girl" that fades out with a jumping boogie-style figure: Garcia opens it up low on the bass strings, punctuates with broken chords, and then stretches it out across the fretboard with breathless beauty. When he wants to, he has a sense of melody and a command of technique that is impressive and influential, drawing as it does on past masters as diverse as Chuck Berry and Django Reinhardt.

Still, the most interesting musical thing about the Dead is not Garcia alone, but rather what could be called their ensemble approach to the music: if Garcia's leads shine, it is at least partially due to the close-knit rhythm and melodic work that bassist Lesh and rhythm guitarist Bob Weir weave around his single-string runs. Lesh, along with Jack Casady from the Jefferson Airplane, took a cue from Paul McCartney and the Motown sound and radically redefined what the bass guitar meant in rock. Those Beatles tunes where McCartney doubled the lead guitar and counterpointed it, or played a kind of lead bass – "Day Tripper," for example – led Lesh, Casady, and other San Francisco bassists to play lines that were more than the bottom ends of chords. Instead they became independent melodies, much more complex than the straightforward if frantic boogie patterns of a Samwell-Smith in the Yardbirds or a Chas Chandler in the Animals. (Of course, Chandler had some incipient ideas that led in a more inventive direction as well: listen to "It's My Life" or "We Gotta Get Outta This Place." For that matter, the Stones' Bill Wyman's patterns – especially in "Satisfaction" – could get pretty offbeat at times.) The effect is that bass and lead intertwine, wrap around each other like threads in a fine tapestry. The Dead added a third independent voice: Weir's rhythm is hardly the chukka-chukka chording of your basic rock'n'roller. He listens carefully and blends his guitar's voice into the ensemble, so that he'll reach down if Lesh begins to climb, he'll cluster broken chords around a figure that Garcia vamps to build on, he'll hammer-on or slide or drop his work out entirely if the sound needs air. When it all works the texture is rich and layered. As Garcia tells it in *The Guitar Player Book*: "He's (Weir) like my left hand. We have a long, serious conversation going on musically, and the whole thing is of a complementary nature. We have fun, and we've designed our

playing to work against and with each other. His playing, in a way, really puts my playing in the only kind of meaningful context it could enjoy.... There are some passages, some kinds of ideas that would really throw me if I had to create a harmonic bridge between all the things going on rhythmically with two drums and Phil's innovative bass style. Weir's ability to solve that kind of problem is extraordinary. He also has a beautiful grasp of altering chords and adding color. Harmonically, I take a lot of my solo cues from Bob."

Jorma Kaukonen

The Jefferson Airplane strove for a similar density musically, though in their case the vocalists provided more of the muscle tone. They were nothing if not psychedelic, and their music had all the trademarks: heavily distorted lead guitar, odd accents and offbeats, intricate time signatures, drugged-out lyrics. In their heavy vocal arrangements, lead guitarist Jorma Kaukonen tended to use his guitar as another kind of voice against the choral, sometimes hypnotic effect that vocalists Marty Balin, Paul Kantner, and Grace Slick produced. Partly as a result, he did not use the guitar's range as fully as he did later with Hot Tuna, sticking more to the middle of the neck. Jack Casady, on the other hand, never stayed still for too long – at least on his bass's neck, since the only parts of his body that moved while he played, besides his hands, were his elfin eyebrows. His touch could range from slamming fuzz-tone chords to delicate single-string runs – a variety of tones he may have learned from the days when he played lead guitarist to Jorma's rhythm in their first teenage bar band. With Kantner on six- or more often twelve-string doing a variety of chording to hold the middle together, the Airplane pumped out one of the most densely layered sounds of the psychedelic era.

Moby Grape

Their first drummer thought so as well, but had his own ideas, even in those early days, of just how that psychedelic sound should be played. And so Alex "Skip" Spence put down his drumsticks, picked up an electric guitar, and founded the short-lived but legendary Moby Grape. They were San Francisco's quintessential weirded-out types, but the music they made was remarkable. Their lineup was three guitars, bass, and drums; and between those and their rich harmonies they blasted out a very complex, highly charged music made even more satisfying by its careful arrangements and ensemble work. With Spence and Peter Lewis coordinating their rhythm work, Bob Mosley's rolling bass, and atop it all, Jerry Miller's biting succinct guitar lines, the Grape created a sound that cut through the excesses of the psychedelic scene – excesses that, in the cases of bands like Big Brother or Quicksilver Messenger Service, could all too often turn psychedelic music into endless and aimless noodling. The Grape were tough and tight and very, very good; and the variety of musical styles they mastered were so formidable that they could function as a kind of musical introduction to the future of the California music scene.

Carlos Santana

One of the most unusual musical hybrids to emerge from the San Francisco era was Santana. The beat was Afro-Cuban, powered by a drummer, a conga player, and a timbales player, and soaring over it the Hendrix-inspired guitar of Carlos Santana. Lots of bent b strings to double notes played on the e' string, and lots of bluesy runs laced with psychedelic distortion were the staples of Santana's early guitar work; later, when he came under the influence of jazz guitarist John McLaughlin's guru Sri Chinmoy and played with McLaughlin, his guitar developed a jazzier voice. He has since played with a wide range of musicians, including jazz great Alice Coltrane and Stanley Clarke; but his most striking contributions to rock guitar are those of his San Francisco days.

JIMI HENDRIX

Psychedelia may have been San Francisco's musical stock-in-trade, but some of the key guitarists who powered that musical style were already familiar names: Clapton, Beck, Jimmy Page. Still, a new arrival in the galaxy eclipsed them all by the fiery magnitude of his performance at Monterey. Perhaps more than any other single guitarist since Chuck Berry in the history of rock, James Marshall Hendrix redefined the electric guitar as an instrument, and in the process changed the shape of rock'n'roll.

It wasn't exactly an overnight success story, but like that of many guitar heroes, it reveals an unerring, even uncanny sense of direction and dedication. From the time he was twelve, the young Hendrix jammed around hometown Seattle and Vancouver, playing sometimes righthanded, sometimes left. (Later, of course, one of his trademarks would be his righthanded Stratocaster strung upside down so he could play lefty.) There was a twenty-six month stint in the Army, where paratrooper Hendrix met and jammed often with Billy Cox (later bassist for his Band of Gypsies), and slept with his guitar because

Jimi Hendrix

he had read or heard that a lot of blues greats, like Mississippi John Hurt, had done the same thing. After he got out (on a medical discharge for back and foot injuries resulting from a paratroop jump), he began gigging again; by 1965 he had played behind a list of greats that included Little Richard, King Curtis, Ike and Tina Turner, and the Isley Brothers. All these influences flowed into his music; and when you add his knowledge of pioneer jazz guitarist Charlie Parker's licks, his respect for Chuck Berry (and deep understanding of Berry's guitar-based sexuality), his perfect pitch, and his huge ambidextrous hands, it's clear that the materials for greatness were gathered in one player.

Chas Chandler thought so too. The former bass guitarist for the Animals had become, like so many rock musicians, a record producer. He first saw Hendrix performing in Greenwich Village in 1966, when he was still calling himself Jimmy James, and his group the Blue Flames. At that time Hendrix was also lead guitarist for John Hammond Jr., who plugged him into the stellar circuit – which is why people like Dylan, Lennon, McCartney, Eric Burdon, and Chandler began showing up to watch him do his stuff. His stuff impressed Chandler immensely. He got Hendrix a passport and money, set up a meeting with Eric Clapton, picked up Mitch Mitchell and a lead guitarist suddenly turned bassist named Noel Redding to create Jimi's backup band The Experience. He then set up club dates around Europe, negotiated a record contract that resulted in instant hits with "Purple Haze" and "Hey Joe," and watched the Jimi Hendrix Experience burst beyond sensationalism into superstardom.

In Europe, that is: back home in the USA only a few fans had discovered the sound behind the rumor. All that changed when no less a personage than Paul McCartney recommended to promoters of the Monterey Pop Festival that they book the Experience. Part of what went down there was captured on celluloid for the movie *Monterey Pop*: Jimi's blasting, riproaring, full-tilt guitar chording in "Like A Rolling Stone" offset by his extremely understated vocal; the almost campy rendition of "Wild Thing;" and all of it leading to the feedback-drenched finale, where a worshipful, masturbatory Hendrix squirts lighter fluid on his unstrapped Stratocaster and sets it ablaze to the screams of the audience and amps.

Techniques

Dramatic as his performance was, the music he made was what captivated completely hundreds of musicians and record executives who heard Hendrix that Sunday evening. His fluid blues-based lines, his complex and funky chording, his obvious command of the entire fretboard were only the groundwork of his astonishing virtuosity. The man had obviously studied the blues and R&B, jazz and rock'n'roll, absorbed it all, and played it all with soul: his guitar spoke a staggering variety of languages that other pickers could only envy and try to emulate. The intense and supportive interaction between his voice and guitar recalled the great bluesmen, from Robert Johnson to B. B. King and his Lucille. The sweet broken chords he trilled came out of country, country blues, and early rock'n'roll via Chuck Berry, Carl Perkins, and Steve Cropper. The raunch and powerchords recalled Pete Townshend and Jeff Beck. The astonishing sense of melody rivalled Clapton and Bloomfield at their best. He also expanded the tech-

nical possibilities of the most mundane-seeming things. His extraordinary reach allowed him to develop odd fingering positions and jump around the neck with astonishing speed and effect. He picked up on Bo Diddley's technique, still revered by dozens of heavy metal guitarists, of grinding the pick against the strings while sliding it down sideways from the pickups toward the nut, creating a screeching slur that so aptly punctuated his transitions. Of course, everyone loved it when he picked with his teeth, or behind his back; or when he suddenly dropped into a deep kneebend while pointing the guitar up and out at the audience like some shrieking phallus. But prove as they did his seemingly total control over every aspect of his instrument, these techniques were still not the sum of his musical achievement. What Hendrix brought uniquely to rock guitar was his perfect understanding of it as an *electronic* instrument. In his adept hands, feedback – pure electronic sound – became playable for the first time, no longer just unwanted noise or the simple shriek of a psychedelic high. Hendrix shaped it into a range of tones, using his vibrato bar, the angle of the guitar to the amp, the proximity of his own body to the guitar, volume and tone controls, reverb and tremolo, wah-wah pedals, fuzz tones, and – maybe most importantly – an acute set of instincts.

So acute, in fact, that no one has ever managed to recreate his mind-boggling range of effects. At times it sounded like he had to be at least two or three separate guitarists, because he managed to produce a wall of sustained feedback that would serve as a kind of weirdly humming rhythm section behind his simultaneous lead lines. Even the road technicians who handled his equipment never understood just how his setup worked: only Hendrix could plug in and produce anything besides uncontrolled feedback at his soundchecks. It must have been an awesome feeling of control in his fingers, the itch of power known only to extraordinary virtuosos.

Setup

The power flowed first from Hendrix's modified Stratocaster. He rewound the pickup coils, bent the vibrato bar for hours until it would give him three steps down instead of one. Because he was playing a right-handed Strat restrung for a left – that is, upside down – the volume and tone controls, as well as the bar, were directly beneath his picking hand and palm, giving him a unique control setup. He generally outfitted his guitars with heavy-gauge low E, me-

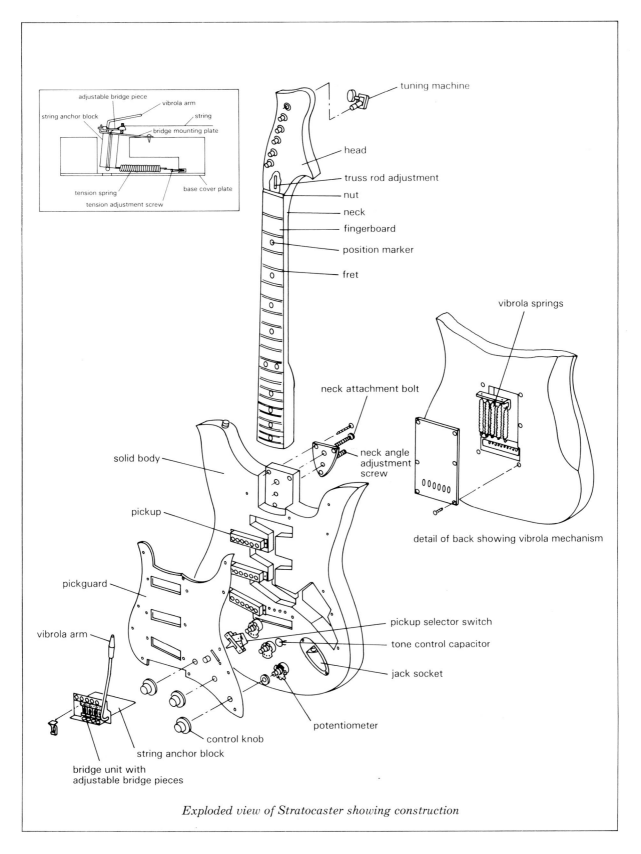

adjustable bridge piece
vibrola arm
string anchor block
string
bridge mounting plate
tension spring
base cover plate
tension adjustment screw

tuning machine

head

truss rod adjustment

nut

neck

fingerboard

position marker

fret

vibrola springs

neck attachment bolt

neck angle adjustment screw

solid body

pickup

pickguard

detail of back showing vibrola mechanism

pickup selector switch

tone control capacitor

jack socket

vibrola arm

potentiometer

control knob

string anchor block

bridge unit with adjustable bridge pieces

Exploded view of Stratocaster showing construction

Fender Guitars

Since the early rockabilly days, the odds are good that any guitarist who plays rock music will have at least one or another Fender guitar in his instrument arsenal. Outstanding Stratocaster users include Buddy Holly (whose use of it first made it popular for rock'n'rollers), Jimi Hendrix (whose use of it made it a must-have guitar), post-Cream Eric Clapton, mid-1970s Jeff Beck, the Stones' Ron Wood, and a host of others. The Telecaster can number country blues ace Roy Buchanan, the Stones' Keith Richards, and Bruce Springsteen among its many devotees. A Fender has truly become the sign of having arrived for an aspiring picker.

You have to wonder if Leo Fender foresaw all this when he began to manufacture steel guitars and amplifiers in his radio repair shop in southern California. In 1944, together with his partner "Doc" Kauffman, (who had worked for Rickenbacker, the developers of the electric Hawaiian guitar, and patented one of the first vibrato-bar attachments), Fender downsized the then-huge pickup magnets and built them into a solid-body guitar. The immediate reaction was a long waiting list of would-be renters.

By 1946, Fender and Kauffman split up, and Fender began manufacturing a guitar he called the Broadcaster. The main thing he was after — and that he achieved — was to get a clear trebly sound like a Hawaiian guitar, without the feedback problems that plagued the hollow-body electrics that dominated the market then. In addition, the Broadcaster had a detachable neck, in its case made of maple so that it could take a clear finish. The bodies that were naturally finished were made of ash, those that were painted were made of alder. In 1950 the model's name was changed to the Telecaster, in order to avoid trademark confusion with Gretsch's popular Broadcaster drum kits. Four years later production of the Stratocaster began, and the solid-body electric guitar was established.

Like the Broadcaster before it, the Stratocaster heralded a breakthrough in several areas of guitar design. It was the first solid-body to have three pickups, all single-coil and wired to a three-way switch (actually five-way: two positions between the three standard ones each engaged two pickups for a unique "out-of-phase" sound, which became so popular that Fender was soon manufacturing true five-way switches). Its simple yet brilliant vibrato unit largely solved the perennial problem with such units — namely, how do you keep them from pushing the guitar out of tune with each use? The answer Leo Fender came up with was a floating bridge, with adjustable and removable springs running *beneath* the unit *inside* the guitar's body under the pickups. The springs maintained a constant tension that pulled the bridge back to the proper position after each use, returning the guitar to tune. In addition, the body of the Strat was carefully contoured and bevelled to provide the guitarist with the maximum comfort possible. It should be obvious why the Stratocaster's appeal was so immediate and enduring.

In 1965, Leo Fender sold his company to CBS for 13 million dollars — and many guitarists felt that the quality of Fender guitars suffered as a result. In fact, there does seem to have been some dislocation following the CBS takeover, but given that Leo Fender himself was back on the scene within a couple of months as a design consultant, those fears seem to have been out of proportion. Nevertheless, the market for "vintage" (read pre-CBS) Stratocasters and, to a lesser degree, Telecasters, got quite heated up, and the quest for these models continues to be widespread — and for the sellers, quite lucrative.

1957 Fender Stratocaster

1955 Fender Esquire

1963 Fender Stratocaster

dium-gauge A and D, Hawaiian G, light-gauge B, and superlight E. He also used a number of open tunings, which allowed him to lay out the thick rhythm textures that he loved. Normally he fed the guitar through a combination of Univox univibes, a Dallas-Arbiter Fuzz-Face, Vox or Maestro wah-wah pedals, and a Leslie. It was, especially for the time, an impressive array of equipment; and Hendrix's use of it was not less pioneering than his assembly of it.

There is no way of knowing what other amazing innovations Hendrix could have come up with from his inexhaustible musical grab bag; dead before his twenty-eighth birthday, he left much of his genius unrealized. He was constantly broadening his musical horizons – jamming with people like Johnny Winter, Steve Winwood, Steve Stills, John McLaughlin, and Rahsaan Roland Kirk; setting up recording dates with jazz arranger Gil Evans; plotting films and cartoons and books. He was clearly a brilliant arranger and producer as well as a musician: his version of "All Along The Watchtower" became the standard rendition of that Dylan tune, and his use of the pan-pot effect to cruise voice and/or guitar across the stereo field refined the use of the studio.

Hendrix played like no other rock guitarist had, and everyone knew it. An entire generation of guitar players since has looked to Hendrix as the fountainhead of their effects. If Clapton was God – and he was, even to the early Hendrix – the remarkable achievement of the black guitarist's innovations is implicitly recognized by the homage of Clapton's elegaic rendering of "Little Wing" with Derek and the Dominoes. In fact, one story has it that Clapton and Pete Townshend sat through viewing after viewing of *Monterey Pop* just to see the sequence featuring Hendrix, both of them in awe.

ENGLAND ROCKS

Hendrix's arrival in England, and his subsequent catapulting to stardom, his recognition as a musician's musician, focused the creative juices building in many already recognized English players. As Eric Clapton put it: "What we were stretching to do then, Pete (Townshend) in his way and I in mine, and then to walk into a club and see someone that you'd never seen before who'd got it covered...! You see, we thought that we must be ahead of everyone else, so that if anyone's trying to do what we're doing they're nowhere as good as we are at doing it.

And then to have Jimi lay all that down was quite heavy."

Eric Clapton

He should know. Cream was formed about the same time as the Experience, but its direction into psychedelia was somewhat different. Clapton and bassist Jack Bruce had left John Mayall's Bluesbreakers and joined forces with drummer Ginger Baker to pursue the blues; in fact, one rumor had it that Clapton, after leaving Mayall, locked himself in a room for a year with only his guitar. Whether true or not, one thing seems certain – in the time between Mayall's band and Cream all the qualities that had made the young Clapton an arresting guitarist had deepened and broadened. His sense of melody was honed, his fingering was even smoother and surer, and his chording was evolving into something more complicated than a chukka-chukka rhythm. As it turned out, Cream – live at least – was not the ideal showcase for any of these qualities. Like the psychedelic bands of San Francisco, Cream in concert was a series of long and loose blues-based improvisations: like the worst of those bands, its improvisations too often degenerated into a kind of musical bar brawl, with everybody bashing away and nobody listening. Clapton's guitar work all too often sounds trapped: if you listen to the fabled live "Spoonful" on the *Wheels Of Fire* LP, for example, you can almost hear Clapton's confusion as the song lurches gracelessly from one transition to the next. Still, Cream had genuine moments of musical brilliance in concert, and they certainly had enormous influence. Uncounted imitators with Les Pauls and Marshall stacks learned every lick in "Sunshine Of Your Love." And in the studio, where producer Felix Pappalardi (later to found Mountain with Vagrants' guitarist Lesley West) seemed able to impose some musical discipline, they did some good versions of tunes that ranged from super psychedelia ("White Room," "Tales Of Brave Ulysses") to the inevitable Robert Johnson. Clapton tried out the wah-wah pedal Hendrix had introduced him to for the psychedelia, and took an approach completely different from Hendrix's – more regular, more on the beat, less against the grain of the rhythm: in short, more like himself. He perfected his blues playing – listen to "Sittin' On Top Of The World," where he sharpens one of the nicest, juiciest breaks any rock player has ever done, or "Politician," where his triple-tracked guitar lines float sweetly over, around, and through Jack Bruce's sneeringly ironic lyrics. There is

"Crossroads" on *Wheels of Fire*, where Cream pulls it all together and Clapton takes two classic solos. There is "Badge" on the *Goodbye* album, lyrics and bridge guitar figure courtesy of George Harrison, where his matchless melodic sense tells him how to squeeze raw pain and song out of about six notes played and replayed in ever-different configurations. And, for those who don't own a Cream LP, there is "While My Guitar Gently Weeps" on the Beatles' *White Album*, where he actually makes you believe it.

By the time Cream had ended, Clapton had had it with being cast as front man/guitar hero, even if his imitators hadn't. He hid as deeply as he could in Blind Faith, and burrowed in even deeper during the famous Delaney and Bonnie and Friends tour. Then he put together a group where the musicians would challenge him to be as good as he could be. Clapton had finally found a forum to suit him: Derek and the Dominoes was born.

And with stunning effect. Clapton had learned to sing – really sing – under Delaney Bramlett's tutelage, and his voice matched keyboard player Bobby Whitlock's with heartache. He had also found religion and lost it again; found love (in the person of Patti Harrison, his girlfriend, at the time his friend George Harrison's wife) and lost it again; and found drugs, in the form of heroin. In the meantime he had also found a guitar player who could challenge him to push at his musical limits, a session man from Muscle Shoals, Alabama, whom he had met through producer Tom Dowd. Duane Allman's slide contours the whole *Layla* album, and its spacey blues feel pushed Clapton to outdo himself on his own solos even while it took the pressure off him to constantly have to be "on." But there's no mistaking the searing pain that pours out of this record, whether in Big Bill Broonzy's "Key To The Highway," Clapton's own "Bell Bottom Blues," or most especially "Layla" itself. (The name comes from a Persian love poem, *Layla and Majnum*, which is about the obsessive love of a heartsick man for a married woman. Clapton had read the poem in the throes of his heroin addiction, and wrote the song for Patti Harrison.) Once the guitars hit that familiar opening lick in unison, the pain thickens the music into a mad swirl of slashing slide, power chords, and blues-drenched voices. "Layla" surges until the very end, when a kind of tranquility rides the theme initiated by the piano and picked up by Duane's slide. With that close, and his deepening addiction and heartache,

Eric Clapton virtually disappeared from public view until the mid-1970s.

Jeff Beck

While Clapton was finalizing his own version of the blues, the man who replaced him in the Yardbirds was putting the finishing touches on what was soon to become heavy metal, that stepchild of rock and blues. Jeff Beck had gathered around him a supergroup: Rod Stewart on vocals, Micky Waller on drums, Nicky Hopkins on piano, Ron Wood on bass. The two albums they made together, *Truth* and *Beck-Ola*, took Beck's highly individualistic guitar work and put it firmly in the context of psychedelia, in the process creating the heavy metal sound that Jimmy Page, Beck's old fellow Yardbird-in-arms, would pick up on and turn into a career. Beck and company, however, had two things that Page didn't: a well-developed musical sense of humor and an astonishing breadth. *Truth* has everything from an acoustic version of "Greensleeves" to a manic, feedback-riddled version of the old Yardbirds tune "Shapes Of Things." In addition, they threw in a blistering sendup of a couple of old standard blues progressions and the prototype for heavy-metal raunch that Page would follow – a truly revolting bit of work called "You Shook Me." Beck wrote in the liner notes, "Last note of song is my guitar being sick – well so would you be if I smashed your guts for 2:28." At times you feel as if he had. Beck's pyrotechnic genius still made him a musician's musician, but commercial success continued to elude him. After the group's breakup in 1969, he was in a serious car crash, and out of things until the early 1970s.

Jimmy Page

For many rock guitarists Jimmy Page quite simply *is* heavy metal guitar – and they're not necessarily wrong. Page had been a session guitarist of note before he hooked up with the Yardbirds, had listened to Beck's farsighted lessons and absorbed them, had understood the direction of the music in the late 1960s and how to capitalize on it. As Jim Miller once wrote in *The Rolling Stone Illustrated History of Rock*, "His playing lacked the lyricism of Eric Clapton, the funk of Jimi Hendrix, or the rhythmic flair of Peter Townshend. But of all the virtuoso guitarists of the Sixties, Page, along with Hendrix, has most expanded the instrument's sonic vocabulary. He exhibits a studio musician's knack for functionalism; unlike many of his peers, he rarely overplays, especially on record. Most of his solos instead evince the restraint and proportioned style of his avowed

Eric Clapton

Jeff Beck

influences: the brooding, involuted blues lines of Otis Rush; the finely filigreed acoustic approach of British folk artist Bert Jansch; the echoed, subliminally driving accompaniment of Scotty Moore (behind Elvis) and James Burton (behind Ricky Nelson) on their rockabilly records."

As a producer, Page learned very quickly how to shape his band's sound in the studio for maximum effect – bottom, bottom, bottom, and Robert Plant's screech riding atop it all, for a formula that's been aped countless times. Still, Page's technical abilities and self-discipline saved him from becoming a self-parody. The solo on "Whole Lotta Love," from *Led Zeppelin II*, is a wondrous mix of blues runs, extremely bent notes, dazzling speed, and just talent. "Communications Breakdown" displays the rare humorous side of Page's guitar work, as he simulates with his stuttering lines the feeling of near-aphasia. He knows exactly how to get the effects he wants.

Alvin Lee

As England's best known guitarists evolved from blues and early rock to full-blown psychedelics, there was one band that held the focus on the basics.

Ten Years After debuted in 1966, and featured a solid rhythm section (Ric Lee on drums, Leo Lyons on bass, and Chick Churchill on organ) that could move between blues, hard rock, and light jazz with competent ease. Atop it all flashed the fever-fingered Alvin Lee, who at times seemed able to compress several octaves worth of fingerboard into a single riff. Tunes like "Spoonful," "Help Me," (from the LP called *Ten Years After*) and, of course, "Goin' Home" feature Lee's hectic, if somewhat disjointed solos, which inspired young guitarists at the same time they caused despair. Speed was Alvin Lee's major asset. Lacking Clapton's melodic sense, Beck's out-and-out weirdness, Bloomfield's deep musical intuitiveness, Hendrix's sheer brilliance, he was not really of their stature among guitarists; but for a moment, appearing all over the world singing and playing "Goin' Home" to himself on a split screen in the movie *Woodstock*, he seemed to have it all. He didn't; and as Ten Years After tried to move from blues-rock into heavy metal, it faded away.

The Rolling Stones

No overview, however quick, of the continuing

Jimmy Page

evolution of rock guitar's blues roots in the 1970s would be complete without some mention of the Rolling Stones. When the Stones fired Brian Jones and replaced him with Mick Taylor from Mayall's Bluesbreakers, they did more than put an end to an internal personality and power struggle: they also changed some fundamental aspects of the band's sound. Taylor's single-string lead lines were a very different texture for the Stones. When Richards and Jones shared guitar duties, the line between lead and rhythm guitar had constantly been effaced, so tight was the coordination and conceptual attack. Like Buddy Holly, Richards chorded his lead lines as often as not, chugging out an intensified rhythm that kicked the tune forward. Mick Taylor's leads were, on the other hand, very clearly solo lines – there was no question of Taylor and Richards trading off rhythmic licks, or tossing each other's lines back and forth in a kind of balletic duet. The guitar chores were defined and divided, and the Stones' sound changed.

In 1976, when Ronnie Wood took over guitar chores following Taylor's departure from the Stones' lineup, the band's sound came back toward its original base: the intertwining of two tightly meshed, riffing rhythm guitars. Wood had a long list of credits: second guitarist and heavyweight bassist for Jeff Beck's original group featuring Rod Stewart, and then with Stewart again in another classic group, The Faces. He'd worked with Eric Clapton and Pete Townshend on *Rainbow Concert*, and picked up a lot of their tricks. Before he joined the Stones, Wood recorded a solo LP that Keith Richards (among others) played on, and the two hit it off musically and personally. It was easy, Richards later said, to choose who would replace Mick Taylor once Ron Wood was available. As he put it in a recent interview: "With Ron, if he drops his pick, then I can play his lick until he picks it up, and you can't even tell the difference." It seems somehow fitting that the "World's Greatest Rock'n'Roll Band" finished the 1970s by trying to get back to their roots.

L.A. ROCK

Maybe it's the climate. Maybe it's the beaches. Maybe it's the musical history of all that highly harmonized surfing. Maybe it's all those corporate entertainment headquarters. Whatever the reason, L.A. has created and sustained an eclectic blend of musical styles, always with a highly polished patina of production values. Most rock musicians become

aware very quickly how important it is for their sound to control, or at least have a significant way in, the engineering, mixing, and production of their recordings; in L.A., the studio has fulfilled its promise. But that is getting ahead of the story.

After the surfers and car songs, there was Ciro's, and the Byrds packed it starting in 1965. Piloted by Roger (Jim) McGuinn, the first of California's space cowboys, on twelve-string Rickenbacker, the Byrds moved from their individual folky roots to a spacey folk-rock hybrid, dominated by airy harmonies and chorded pickings that could range from straight folk ("Turn, Turn, Turn") to bizarre ("Eight Miles High"). The emphasis from the beginning was on the studio and success, the pattern that would hold true in L.A. rock for nearly twenty years. McGuinn's powerful and imaginative adaptation of the electric twelve-string to a rock beat inspired a continuing exploration into different sounds that could be grafted onto rock, an exploration that has now become a virtual L.A. tradition. Certainly with the *Sweethearts Of The Rodeo* album, the Gram Parsons–dominated Byrds defined the shape of L.A. rock for years to come: the lilting harmonies, country changes, Americana nostalgia, artsy folkiness, pop meaning, glossy production.

At about the same time, the Buffalo Springfield provided another set of possible approaches to the use of the guitar within the rapidly evolving L.A. musical format. One of the original "guitar armies," the Springfield boasted the twin lead guitars of Steve Stills and Neil Young, Richie Furay (later founder of Poco) on rhythm and twelve–string, and Jim Messina (also a founder of Poco) on bass. The richness of their vocal harmonies was beautifully complemented by the rich instrumentation that they grew to use. On a classic like "Bluebird," featured on the *Retrospective* LP, Stills and Furay weave airy acoustic and melodic electric parts around Young's raucous leads, balanced atop booming bass, with sweet harmonies thrown in. The seeds of the L.A. sound were well planted.

It wasn't long before they burst into a field of flowers. Like a kind of crazed musical bee, Gram Parsons had cross-pollinated almost every musician in L.A. with his sense of sound and druggie mystique, and his consequent influence far outweighs anything he did himself. The combination of urban irony and country licks and changes that shape and fill so many Eagles tunes, for example, is traceable directly to him. But however competent or inspired

Gibson's Les Paul and SG Guitars

The guitar most often identified with the heavier end of the rock spectrum is, of course, Gibson's Les Paul model, which has found its way into the hands of such heavyweights as Jimmy Page, Eric Clapton, Jeff Beck, Duane Allman, and literally legions of other real or imagined guitar heroes. Ironically, when Les Paul first showed his prototypical "log" to the Gibson company, they were so unimpressed they turned the idea down cold; but in 1950 they changed their attitude and sought him out, agreeing to pay him a royalty for every guitar made.

Two years later, the first Les Pauls rolled out of the plant as the famed "Gold Top" model, which la-

ter evolved into the Les Paul Standard. (Interestingly, Gibson initially left the company's name off the guitars because they didn't want their reputation to suffer.) In 1954 the Black Beauty, with extremely narrow frets and ebony finish, hit the market, followed in 1958 by the best-known model, the Cherry Sunburst. The body style that later became the SG model replaced the earlier models for the two years following its 1960 debut, and in fact had the Les Paul designation dropped, since the guitarist-inventor's contract with Gibson had lapsed. The original Les Paul format—body shape and designation—was not reintroduced until 1968, after the demand for vintage models had reached astronomical proportions. Today the Les Paul comes in a number of models.

The thing they all share, though, is that characteristic Les Paul sound—the thick, rich tone that sustains and sustains. (One of the driving forces behind Les Paul's

own experiments had been his search for a natural twenty-second sustain; with the Les Paul, he got that and some to spare.) Sustain is largely due to body construction; and to maximize it, the Les Paul guitars are all made from a solid mahogany body married to a carved maple top, which produces a brilliant and warm tonal mixture. The neck and headstock is made of three-piece laminated maple with either an ebony or a rosewood fingerboard, depending on the model.

Almost all Les Pauls have two pickups, usually a version of the Gibson humbucking type. (Early Les Pauls and the current Les Paul Pro Deluxe feature single-coil pickups.) Each of the pickups has its own volume and tone controls, and a three-way toggle switch allows you to select either or both pickups—a flexible arrangement that lets you mix the sounds you want. One of your very basic rock axes, the Les Paul really invites you to kick out the jams.

Gibson Firebird VII (c. 1964)

1953 Gibson Les Paul Standard

1959 Gibson Les Paul Custom

the playing of a Don Felder or a Joe Walsh, a Glenn Frey or a Bernie Leadon, the real guitar heroes of the L.A. music scene remain, appropriately enough, the studio musicians and the sidemen. The latter most outstanding have been Ry Cooder, David Lindley, Waddy Wachtel, and Lowell George.

Ry Cooder

Like many of the musicians he's backed, like the L.A. musical scene itself, Ry Cooder comes out of a folk music background. Born into a musical family, he was given his first guitar when he was around ten, and used it to master old-timey and ragtime fingerpicking styles of such masters as Blind Blake and Rev. Gary Davis and Leadbelly. Soon he was annexing Blind Willie Johnson's slide techniques and Joseph Spence's syncopations to his increasingly formidable arsenal. Nor has he stopped there: Hawaiian music, Norteño music, vaudeville, 1950s rhythm'n'blues – all found their way into this crazy quilt style of playing and co-exist quite comfortably. Given this background, it is interesting to note that the man who recorded rock's first digital album has as his current favorite guitars a few cheap Japanese Stratocaster imitations. It figures.

A guitarist's guitarist, Cooder has backed, among others, Taj Mahal and Captain Beefheart, Maria Muldaur and Randy Newman, John Sebastian and Rodney Crowell, the Stones and Little Feat. Certainly his presence on any piece has the personality of a signature, his trademark the relaxed and tuneful spareness of whatever he does. Above all, he has mastered the art of creating space around and in his lines and solos. His bottleneck solos display total command of the idiom – from arch and frightening in Randy Newman's "Let's Burn Down The Cornfield," to buzzing like a sick mosquito on his own "Never Make Your Move Too Soon" (from his *Borderline* LP). His distinctive chordal techniques – he still thinks of himself as primarily a rhythm guitarist – are real expansions of the rock guitar vocabulary, and venture into polyphonic textures. His array of tunings and cheap guitars offer a distinctive sound for his ever-acquiring musical sensibility. Quite simply, Cooder has managed to take fullest advantage of a number of guitar traditions and mix them into his own unique voice.

David Lindley

Like his pal Cooder, David Lindley started in folk music, spending a lot of time at the Ash Grove in L.A., listening, winning the Topanga Canyon Bluegrass Banjo And Fiddle Bakeoffs five years

David Lindley

straight. As might be expected from a musician whose first instrument was a baritone ukelele, Lindley had taught himself to play virtually anything with strings: violins, banjos, mandolins, bouzoukis, ouds, and, of course, guitars. Even more than Cooder, Lindley is what could be called a junk-guitar junkie. Besides cannibalizing and reworking bits and pieces into his own hybrids, he devours Silvertones and Danelectros and their ilk, using them as well as Strats and Teles for raw material. In fact, when Ry Cooder wanted to dig up some Japanese imitation Strats, it was Lindley he called for help.

But above all, Lindley can play. L.A.'s top musical attractions – Crosby & Nash, Linda Ronstadt, Warren Zevon, Rod Stewart – take whatever time his frantic schedule allows. But it was Lindley's nine-year association with Jackson Browne that produced some of L.A.'s outstanding sounds and redefined the art of guitar accompaniment in rock, even as it brought Lindley more and more attention outside studio circles. His sinewy, sinuous lap steel sang or snarled its way through virtually everything Browne did between 1971 and 1980, instantly recognizable from one tune to the next, yet perfectly adapted to whatever mood the song required. The mark of a talented session player, perhaps; but Lindley had stamped his unique mark on everything from the Youngbloods' "Darkness, Darkness" (that's his fiddle haunting the melody) to the theme for the TV show *The Rockford Files*. When he finally went on his own with *El Rayo-X* in 1981, his widely varied musical interests surfaced more clearly: reggae and African pop, calypso and ska, and good old rock'n' roll feed a complex riot of musical colorations. Lindley is one of the outstanding – and crazed – individual sensibilities behind the guitar today.

Waddy Wachtel

Unlike his fellow L.A. session fixtures Lindley and Cooder, Robert "Waddy" Wachtel specializes in the churning, badass end of the guitar's spectrum of sounds. His list of credits, though, is no less impressive for that: sessions for Warren Zevon (whom he has also produced), James Taylor, Maria Muldaur, J.D. Souther, Rod Stewart, Karla Bonoff, and Randy Newman, among others. Wachtel's strength is as an accompanist and arranger rather than as a front man, although his stage antics can entertain; and he can play fullblown gutsy raunch or sweet Mexican-flavored licks with equal ease. He is a high-energy player.

Lowell George

Lowell George was suddenly catapulted into the limelight he'd sought for so long when he died in 1979. Like his friend Ry Cooder, George was a musician's musician, with his focus almost entirely on slide playing, and he developed a unique and rich slide style. George's Stratocaster, usually tuned to an open A and played with a Sears Craftsman 11/16 socket on his little finger, could drone or sting, float or slash as it counterpointed Little Feat's lead guitarist Paul Barrere. One of the most outrageous moments in urban blues comes smoking out of "Cold Cold Cold/Trip Face Boogie (medley)" that concludes the classic *Feats Don't Fail Me Now* album. Starting slow and funky, then hovering high up around the twelfth fret, George finishes one of the most amazing boogie slide lines ever laid down by zipping somewhere over the pickups. He was a breathtaking picker whose musical resourcefulness lives on in his recordings.

SOUTHERN ROCK

As with heavy metal, this rock genre has produced more than its fair share of guitarists who play back humorless reruns of boogie licks, with obligatory flash excursions up and down the neck. Thanks to Duane Allman and Dickey Betts, there is frequently more than one soloist tightly harmonizing in formulaic patterns, but without that duo's fire and skill.

The Allman Brothers

Allman came by his chops the hard way: constant session work behind everybody who recorded at Muscle Shoals, including Wilson Pickett and Aretha Franklin. By the time he put together the group of musicians that became the Allman Brothers Band, he had already long since mastered the inventive slide that became his trademark. Combined with Betts's sparer melodic lines, trading off extended solos over a backbeat that made the late-psychedelic noodling of lots of San Francisco bands seem like the motionless musical hot air that it in fact was, Allman's guitar work created a whole new sense of possibilities for rock improvisation and technique. Like so many guitar innovators – Clapton, Beck, Hendrix, Bloomfield – he reached back to the roots and wrenched from them a new sound. The apparent ease with which his Les Paul could sing out a variety of blues-based slide runs has never been equaled, and the tight interplay, displayed prominently on tunes like the classic "Whipping Post", gave the Allmans a unique ensemble quality. Those glory days of the Allmans (captured on *Eat a Peach* and *Live At The Fillmore East*) revolved around the melodic harmonies that Betts and Allman finger together – now in thirds, now in fifths, now separate lines, now some completely unexpected twist, like two talented vocalists playing off their harmonizing. It was a monumental achievement, but not meant to be sustained. With Duane's death in 1971 the band's creative peak passed, as Dickey Betts became Richard and slid more and more toward playing unreconstructed simple boogie scales.

Lynyrd Skynyrd

Only Lynyrd Skynyrd, with their *three* guitar lineup, came close to generating the Allman's style of brash enthusiasm: Gary Rossington, Allen Collins, and Ed King drove the dense Dixie sound faster and fiercer than anyone following the Allmans. Doubled bass lines, thick chordings, clustered runs with quick syncopated moves made the sound unique and rich. Discovered by Al Kooper in an Atlanta bar in 1973, Lynyrd Skynyrd toured non-stop and knocked out Southern-rock stompers like "Sweet Home Alabama" and "Free Bird" until a plane crash in 1977 killed lead singer Ronnie Van Zent and guitarist Steve Gaines, effectively ending the band.

The Dregs

The ensemble approach to country blues led some Southern rockers in a different direction. A few students at the University of Miami, led by a jazz guitar major named Steve Morse whose primary instrument was classical guitar, formed a band called the Dixie Dregs. They gigged locally, playing covers of materials by the Allman Brothers and Mahavishnu Orchestra (fusion guitarist John McLaughlin's band) as well as some original tunes. All of it was instrumental, and it came from all over the musical map: rock, jazz, country, blues, classical, and folk influences pop up all over a Dregs LP without any apparent incongruity or discontinuity.

The multiple musical personality who produces the records, writes the songs, and plays guitar is an outstanding musician. Steve Morse is a methodical, highly trained picker whose instincts and ear are wonderfully intact, as his command of such diverse types of music proves. "Chicken pickin'," double picking, fingerpicking, and classical repertoire are all part of his working musical vocabulary. A lefty who plays right-handed guitar, Morse is deliberate, constantly looking for new musical challenges. At one point in his career, for instance, he decided to avoid playing hammer-ons and pull-offs entirely, claiming that those techniques so crucial to blues picking were in fact counterproductive for other musical genres. So, he bought himself a metronome, started by setting it at zero, and kept speeding it – and his clean picking speed – back up. That kind of thoughtful approach to his sound also enables Morse to edit his solos successfully from song to song, playing a short tasty bit to spice the tune ("Chips Ahoy" on *Industry Standard*) or stretching out for a few choruses ("Ridin' High" on *Industry Standard*).

Nor is he any less deliberate about his instrument itself. It is a hybrid of his own invention that, like the Dregs' music, seems to arise from a thousand little, oddly matched bits and pieces. A Stratocaster neck with Gibson Jumbo-style frets screwed to a Telecaster body with a Gibson humbucker, a stock Strat pickup, a cylindrical Tele rhythm pickup, a DiMarzio-modified Fender humbucker, and a 360-system hex pickup that wires him direct into their Slavedriver. This is not exactly factory-made, and Morse has another guitar exactly like it, in the event of theft or damage. He hates to change guitars, and with his rig he never has to, no matter what kind of music the Dregs are pumping out. With his instru-

ment's versatility he can move from the high lonesome sound of country guitars to synthesizer city just by juggling his pedals and his pickups. But, once he's set the sound just right, he still has to play those licks – and that is what Steve Morse is best at.

HEAVY METAL: 1970s

In the awesome wake of Led Zeppelin, literally hundreds of screeching lead vocalists joined forces with what seemed to be an endless army of guitarists to play Zeppelin-style music. Characterized mostly by its lack of subtlety, the music featured mainly raunchy powerchording, flash-type solos, and a lack of a sense of proportion or melody. Still, an army of guitarists was bound to produce from its ranks at least some truly powerful musicians, including Neal Schon, Rick Derringer, Todd Rundgren, Ronnie Montrose, Ted Nugent, Peter Frampton, and Eddie Van Halen. While the swaggering and sweating theatrics can seem tiresome at times, these are clearly intent players who take their craft seriously enough to reach for what they want. Of these, though, Eddie Van Halen is the single most innovative player to emerge.

Eddie Van Halen

Like so many rock guitarists, Van Halen cites Eric Clapton as his first and strongest influence, having absorbed the superstar guitarist's moves by learning his solos note-for-note. But having done that, Eddie has himself become a rock guitar revolutionary. Added to his super-fast heavy-metal licks are an astonishing mix of techniques; a use of the right hand for harmonics that derives from Ted Farlow, among others; a consistent leaning on the vibrato bar that whangs runs into an out-of-reach high; a touch with controlled feedback that recalls Hendrix; and an ability to compact all this into tight segments of sound.

His group's most recent LP, *Diver Down*, showcases Van Halen's virtuoso command of a wide range of styles. For starters, Van Halen (both band and guitarist) has no reservations about doing covers of old tunes, so their material is stronger and more varied than that of many bands. The lines and textures Eddie weaves through the songs reflect this variety. From the Spanish-sounding intro of "Little Guitars" to the tone-poemy structure (inspired by fusion guitarist Allan Holdsworth) of the solo in "Where Have All The Good Times Gone," from the muted, almost gentle solo of "Hang 'Em High" to the rhino/jungle feedback of the opening

The Guitar as Prop

BRUCE SPRINGSTEEN

Too much of rock was getting stale in the post-psychedelic era. On the one hand, it seemed to bump along its increasingly heavy metal pathways, blundering through licks and changes that were tired when the hills were young; on the other, it languished under the overartsy and oversensitive hands of singer-songwriters whose real roots were white folk music, and whose sense of the beat was, at best, a concession to the form. It was almost as if the music was waiting for somebody to shake it by the scruff of its neck until it came to its senses.

The Boss did just that. After two mixed attempts to break in big, after being billed (and rejected) as the new Bob Dylan, Springsteen honed his band and his sound. He tightened his wandering lyrics, reached back into the basics of rock, including Stax-Volt soul horns, Buddy Holly, and Phil Spector changes, Elvis Presley snarls and showmanship, and used his Telecaster like it was just another part of his body. By 1976, *Born To Run* had everybody listening.

As a guitarist, Springsteen has learned from almost everyone — like most rock and pop geniuses, he has a very eclectic ear. He can powerchord, play gut-wrenching or trebly solos, double Clarence Clemon's sax lines, thread a backing riff around a vocal. But as important as his musical prowess is his incredible use of the guitar as prop, where he outstrips virtually everyone else in the business, excluding only Hendrix and possibly Townshend. As the accompanying pix serve to indicate, to see a Springsteen show is to see a true performance, and the Tele gives that performance a shape by becoming a visual symbol of his communication with the audience. The intricate dance that he uses the guitar to choreograph is almost telepathically intense. Few performers have ever seemed so attached to their instruments.

Bruce Springsteen

Eddie Van Halen

riffs to "Pretty Woman," from the laid back six- and twelve-string melodies of "Secrets" to the thirties-ish "Big Bad Bill," Van Halen is continually proving himself able and willing to absorb an interesting and expanding repertoire of influences from the past, which he then assimilates into his own developing approaches to the guitar.

How he evolves some of his revolutionary techniques is a fascinating study in itself. For the intro to "Little Guitars," he had been listening to Carlos Montoya, was overpowered by the sound and the fingerpicking techniques, and decided to fake his own rendition of something approaching what he'd heard. Easy so far: but Van Halen's method of "faking" it relies on his intuitive grasp of the guitar's possibilities. He developed an almost mandolin-style tremolo on the high E string while slapping the low E with his middle finger to climb and descend on the bass. The results sounded overdubbed – they weren't, however much other guitarists might wish they were. Or on "Cathedral," where he's running a 1961 Strat through a preset echo and chorus, simultaneously cutting the volume in and out, and hammering-on a series of notes at the speed of the echo; the effect, as he intended, is a weird evocation of a church organ. These explorations of technique and sound exemplify how, one way or another, Eddie Van Halen is redefining the sound of rock guitar.

PUNK, ART-ROCK AND NEW WAVE

The extended soloing that took over rock music during the sixties and seventies almost inevitably created its own backlash. Punk music roared in, and stripped rock back to its basics with a vengeance. Johnny Ramone of the Ramones and Steve Cook of the Sex Pistols epitomize the stylistic results for guitar: raucous, bashing chords combined with Chuck Berry-style licks, all played at a blistering pace through heavy distortion and little or no dynamic modulation. Finesse and flash were out; fundamentals were in. And yet punk's demonic energies and fierce postures, as welcome and rejuvenating as they were for rock, also guaranteed that this musical style would have to burn itself out, at least in its primal form. But not before it had changed the direction of rock music in general and in particular inspired some future guitar stars to adapt its energies to new and exciting approaches to their chosen instrument.

Like most popular art forms, rock guitar has often seemed to express or focus a kind of identity problem for its outstanding heroes. Being a serious innovator often means forfeiting the mass appeal that popular art thrives on, and yet the allure of musical and/or technological wizardry creates its own audiences with their own cult figures. All of the players in this section have changed the course of rock guitar, sometimes dramatically, even though many, if not most, of their names are still virtually unknown outside the circles of the dedicated.

Lou Reed

Lou Reed has come a long way from the early days of the Velvet Underground. In that period, he spent much of his time on stage battling huge hunks of raw feedback that surrounded lyrics about sex and drugs and rock'n'roll, à la Andy Warhol. Sometimes he still plays lead guitar; more recently, he's given those chores over to Robert Quine (on whom more later). Reed has traversed the spectrum from the proto-psychedelic to the proto-punk, from the drugged-out masochist's musings to melodic representations of domestic bliss; but on his main ax now, a handcrafted clear plastic prototype created especially for Reed by Guitarman, his work can still cut with the edge of nightmare terror – it's almost as if his fingertips are always bloody while he plays. His lead lines on "Our House" from *The Blue Mask* are simple but slicing: they ironically counterbalance the scenes of apparent domesticity portrayed in the lyrics. The touch is still there.

Robert Quine

But so is a newly won sense of balanced judgement: and at this point enter Robert Quine. Reed lost a lot of musical momentum in the 1970s by playing with too many mediocre musicians; choosing Quine as accompanist made possible a brilliant recovery. An inventive guitarist who knows Reed's early work by heart, Quine has encouraged Reed (by word and example) to play more guitar again, and has enriched the texture of Reed's mood swings seamlessly – now brash and grating, now clear and melodic, always allowing a sense of space to wrap around the individual guitars and the bass lines by the inventive Fernando Saunders. From feedback screech to transparent song, Quine runs the gamut with an apparent ease not always deducible from his work with Richard Hell and the Voidoids. There, of course, the material's slant confines him more to punk power chordings and brash dissonant lines, more like early Reed or proto-art-rocker Captain Beefheart or, for that matter, the Gang of Four's clever guitarist Andy Gill. A minor master developing his own following,

Quine is sure to become better known as his abilities become better appreciated.

Tom Verlaine

Thanks to the groundbreaking efforts of Lou Reed, among others, the New York music scene in the early and mid-1970s fairly exploded with high decibel energy. The New York Dolls and the Ramones powerchorded their way into creating punk music in the style of the Velvets; Blondie grafted a disco beat onto a Warholian sensibility to help create new wave music; and Tom Verlaine came to New York from Maryland to found Television (from his initials) and become a guitarist of note. While his lyrics are a heady blend of irony, romantic imagery, verbal ambiguity, and melodic changes, his guitar, and the arrangements it weaves through, revolve around offbeats. Verlaine's scales are often modal, his timing eccentric and witty – he plays the guitar as if it were reaching toward some transcendental space where the complex rhythms and modalities can all be resolved. To keep you waiting, he rarely states the resolution, choosing instead to play a game of sweet-substitute with the tonic in his leads, veering away just as repose seems within his grasp. At his best, he can be an extremely unnerving – and instructive – guitarist.

Frank Zappa

For straight lunacy with an overlay of snide sophistication, L.A. remains unrivalled in many areas: food, architecture, entertainment, street life. Only in L.A., you can be sure, could Frank Zappa not only begin but flourish in a career that has been compounded of freakery and fanaticism. From the beginning, once he switched from drums to electric guitar at age nineteen, Zappa set out to skewer the pat sensibilities of Middle America; somehow he managed to wind up with Middle America as his audience. Suzy Creamcheese and Edgard Varese have combined to make a strange hybrid. Zappa's musical ideas are stimulating, if sometimes overblown. His guitar playing blends a kind of crossbred psychedelic overdrive with an assemblage of odd time and key changes – no small feat in itself. As Dan Forte points out, Zappa is practically the only rock guitarist there is who isn't soloing over 4/4 time day after day. Besides, he has had an enormous following and longevity, and the Mothers have become a latter-day Yardbirds, because so many first-class musicians have passed through the band's ever-changing configurations. Captain Beefheart, for example, got his start as a Zappa sidekick, and vocalists Flo and Eddie found a home in the Mothers for a while.

Adrian Belew

One of Zappa's most impressive alumni, aside from current sidekick/guitarist Steve Vai, is no less a picker than Adrian Belew. Zappa discovered him in Nashville, playing in the most recent of a long run of bar bands, and brought him to L.A. to audition him for the Mothers. On his second try, Belew made it, and his road has headed straight toward stardom since. His guitar has been featured on a growing number of classic cuts: the insane chopping and grunting of David Bowie's "Boys Keep Swinging" or the frenzied neck-jumping in Talking Heads' "The Great Curve" and "Cross-Eyed And Painless" is pure Belew.

In Belew, rock may have its first real electronic champion since Jimi Hendrix. A big claim perhaps, but Belew is no ordinary guitar player. When he gave up the drums he had been playing to switch to guitar, his goal was to duplicate the mindblowing effects of the early Hendrix. Ever since, he's had two sides from which to attack the guitar, percussive or rhythmic, and electronic – both areas in which Hendrix himself excelled. Belew's sense of rhythm is simply superb: even his vamps skewer the expected beats while they turn on the heat for the polyrhythms he so loves to work off. But the immediate impact of his playing is focused by the absolutely astonishing array of sounds and textures the guitarist wrings from his oddly painted 1957 Strat and footpedals, compressors, flangers, Roland synthesizers, and so on. Seagulls and rhinos, elephants and police sirens appear as if by magic, recalling some of Hendrix's best work on the *Electric Ladyland* LP. Belew also has control over the Strat's special blend of feedback and harmonic control (via the vibrato bar) as well as an edge-city, physical relationship with feedback and his guitar on stage – like virtually nobody else since Hendrix, Belew plays his over-driven sound with a deeply physical sense that shapes the technological triumph into music. He doesn't have Hendrix's intense attachment to the blues or funk, but his jagged sense of melodic line, derived as it is from Hendrix and from jazz sax players like Eric Dolphy, is developing rapidly into a trademark.

Robert Fripp

It does so even more starkly and searingly in the context of Robert Fripp's re-formed King Crimson. Fripp's own minimalist guitar, coupled with his elaborate outboard system of "Frippertronics" (two Revox tape decks and a Roland synthesizer guitar), makes for a regulated, linear sound. Against this measured format, driven and punctuated by bassist Tony Levin, Belew's oddly angled, charged solos soar and shriek, paint splashes of huge color across a hypnotic canvas. The growth between *Discipline*, the first album by the re-formed King Crimson and *Beat*, the second, is a direct result of the awareness and use of the stylistic tension between Fripp and Belew. On stage, the dichotomy is visual as well, with Fripp on his stool hunched near his equipment and Belew caroming around the stage, dancing his guitar to the controlled feedback, picking up at the head and beyond the pickups. This is, at least, one ongoing partnership that promises to deliver ever more interesting music.

This is not the case with some of Fripp's other partnerships. His work with Brian Eno is resolutely minimalist to the point of nervous exhaustion – the listener's, that is; while his recent collaboration with Police guitarist Andy Summers, which seemed promising because of their very different approaches to the guitar, didn't always seem to find enough common ground to take off from. Still, Fripp's guitar is a unique voice, and his highly inventive and insistent rhythms and patterns, not to mention his continuing development of Frippertronics, guarantee that his presence in the world of rock guitar will continue to be felt for some time. As with Belew, some of Fripp's best work has been for other people: witness his stunning accompaniment on "Fade Away And Radiate" from Blondie's *Parallel Lines* LP.

Andy Summers

The most visible guitarist dedicated to the electricness of the instrument is the Police's Andy Summers. His guitar soundscape includes steel drums and shrieks, floating chords and sharp-edged riffs. Trained as a classical and jazz guitarist, Summers is an unlikely candidate for electronic wizard, yet his usual onstage lineup includes an MXR phase 90, Electro-Harmonix player, MXR fuzz, an analog delay, an MN-TRON 111, a compressor, and two old tube Echoplexes. He normally runs all this from his 1961 Telecaster, fitted with Gibson humbucker, pre-amp, and phase-switching. Since his collaboration with Fripp, however, he has taken more to using a Roland guitar synthesizer (see SPECIALTY GUITARS box, p.196/197). From his long background in R&B bands, Summers really learned about

rhythms, and that education shows in the way the Police evolved. The group decided, quite rightly, that the world didn't need another power trio, and instead developed their own airy woven sound. Space is the group's main musical preoccupation, drawn partly, no doubt, from their being influenced by reggae. Steve Copeland's drums pound out a back beat, while Sting's bass – electric, stick, or stand-up, depending on the occasion – rides over and across it, humming from sustain or echo. As a result of these layers of sound, Summers's guitar work becomes an impressionist's palette of tone coloration, providing a chorded fill here, a few hot licks there, a bit of background drone in yet another place. As an example of flash, consider the jagged, atonal solo on "Driven To Tears," or the Indian modal runs on "Bombs Away", a musical pun on the "Bombay" rhyme of the following line. In this sense if in no other, Andy Summers is a guitarist who has broadened the sound of rock guitar to the scope of an orchestral instrument.

Phil Manzanera

In the chapter titled "Art Rock" in *The Rolling Stone Illustrated History of Rock*, critic John Rockwell wrote, "Roxy Music might be considered the leader of this particular pack." And so they might well be. Singer-songwriter Bryan Ferry, lounge lizard extraordinaire, is clearly the front man and dominant presence in the band, although the list of musicians who have played with him – Brian Eno, Paul Carrack, even Waddy Wachtel – is certainly impressive. But Ferry's chief collaborator has usually been guitarist Phil Manzanera, a widely respected musical innovator in his own right. A brilliant accompanist and arranger, Manzanera unfolds inventory of chops to complement Ferry's sobbing vocals with just the right degree of tension; and that inventory encompasses the tastefully melodic ("Still Falls The Rain" on the *Manifesto* LP) as well as snarling raunch ("Out Of The Blue" on *Greatest Hits*). When he stretches out in for a solo, or trades licks with Roxy's ace saxman Andy Mackay, he is almost always amazing, unpredictable. His own solo albums really showcase his full musical invention as writer, producer, and multi-instrumentalist. In his liner notes for the *Primitive Guitars* LP, Manzanera writes that he made a conscious decision at about age seventeen that his own guitar playing would be influenced not just by other guitarists, but would adapt its sound to examples like Miles Davis and Charlie Parker, Edgard Varèse and Erik Satie.

two-part interview conducted by Jim Schwartz in *Guitar Player* has Howe going through ASIA's first LP one song at a time, explaining his search for different sounds and textures, his switching around an array of guitars and effects to get them, his concentration on detail that leads – eventually, after a lot of hard work – to the tight and polished sound that is his trademark. Howe is a true professional whose success at generating a variety of sounds is due as much to the thorough understanding of each guitar and effect he uses as it is to any technical innovations that he may come up with. Certainly he's mastered a wide number of diverse styles: from the steel-string acoustic of "Meadow Rag" (the *Steve Howe* album) to the offbeat wrenching solo of "Roundabout" (Yes's *Fragile*), the Texas swing style version of "The Continental" (the *Steve Howe* album), and the layered power chords of "In The Heat Of The Moment" (ASIA), Steve Howe is at home everywhere, displaying the kind of idiomatic familiarity with differing styles that comes with study and work. He is an impressive picker.

Allan Holdsworth

Another musician who could easily qualify as a guitarist's guitarist is the lamentably underrecorded Allan Holdsworth. Championed by Eddie Van Halen, among others, Holdsworth's unique guitar is emerging from the (relative) obscurity that it lapses into periodically, despite the fact that he has played with – and been acclaimed by – musicians as diverse as Tony Williams Lifetime, UK, Jean-Luc Ponty, Soft Machine, Bruford, and others.

If there was one way to describe Allan Holdsworth's playing it would be "deadly accurate." He is inventive and fast, fluid and shimmery, rhythmically challenging and chordally dense. He has successfully fused the fat timbre of rock guitar with jazzy harmonies. His two-handed approach to the fretboard inspired Van Halen to perfect his own use of the Tal Farlow-inspired technique. Unlike most rock guitarists, Holdsworth claims never to bend notes anymore, substituting instead a classical-style vibrato by sliding; he also claims never to mute his strings with his right hand or use pull-offs. Like Adrian Belew he consciously avoids standard rock or blues licks, preferring instead to develop his unusual horizontal, up-and-down-the-neck fingering style that seeks to reproduce a saxophone's fluid sound. Finally, unlike most of the guitarists mentioned in this section, his array of technical tricks is not matched by a prodigious amount of equipment to help him

Andy Summers

Since his interests tended away from the blues (though he confesses to admiring Charlie Christian), he consistently reaches for unfamiliar sounds and note clusters, while trying to achieve his stated goal "of making the guitar sound as unlike a guitar as possible." This he does by parading a host of effects and techniques that dazzle – from Spanish acoustic strumming and minor-key melodies to squawking feedback and space-age screams, Manzanera shapes his sound with a virtuoso's verve and earns his place among his art-rocker peers.

Steve Howe

Steve Howe's credentials as a quintessential art-rock guitarist need no rehearsal: Yes, ASIA, and his own *Steve Howe* solo album have firmly established him. He has been voted best overall guitarist in *Guitar Player* magazine's prestigious Annual Readers Poll no fewer than five times. Clearly, he is a guitar hero to be reckoned with. The secrets of his success? For one thing, he is a very thorough technician. The

Specialty Guitars

It seems that many smaller luthiers think that the development of the guitar will head increasingly toward the unpredictable; and the five examples here serve as an indication—no more—of some innovative leads to the future.

THE FLUTAR

The two-handed playing techniques of such diverse guitarists as Tal Farlow, Allan Holdsworth, and Eddie Van Halen find their technological complement in Gary Ejen's Flutar. (The name is derived from the sound produced, similar to that of a flute or saxophone.) No more picking with the Flutar: designed to be fretted with both hands, the Flutar's thirty-fret, extra-wide fingerboard both enhances its ability to feed back and makes fretting easier because the longer scale length results in reduced string tension. Neck and body are both of ash; electronics are by Ibanez.

TOUCH GUITAR/ORGAN

Like the Flutar, Artisan Instruments' Touch Guitar/Organ is designed primarily to be played by touch rather than picked, although the lower fingerboard can be played conventionally. Both headless maple necks, however, use touch-activated electronics: the four-string neck is played from a standard left-hand position, while the eight-string neck (E and B strings are doubled) is played by the right hand reaching over the fretboard. The special microprocessor control, similar to an electric organ's, provides a choice of up to sixteen registrations of guitar and organ, and is activated by pushbutton.

STEINBERGER

The basic premise behind the Steinberger is the same as for the other guitars featured here: that there is no reason an electric stringed instrument should slavishly imitate the look, feel, or sound of its acoustic relative. Ned Steinberger's all-plastic bass has attracted both design awards and enthusiastic musicians—among them Tim Bogert, John Entwhistle, Tony Levin, Sting, and Bill Wyman. Its unique appearance is based on three principles: first, that the neck is the most important part of a bass guitar; second, that conventional headstocks produce dead spots and unwanted harmonic coloration; and third, that plastic guarantees sustain, brilliance, and clarity of sound. The one-piece body is made from an epoxy resin reinforced with glass and carbon fibers poured into a mold. A clutched plastic strap-holding projection at the center of gravity grips tight at any position, while the plastic knee rest clips on to allow the player to sit comfortably to play. Tuning is accomplished via four knurled knobs that sit behind the bridge and offer a very precise 40:1 ratio, as compared to about 16:1 for conventional heads. The two EMG pickups are specially constructed with their own preamps.

The Steinberger Bass

SARDONYX

It may look like a strange sled, but the Sardonyx Imperial is in fact a solid mahogany guitar with a black semi-gloss lacquer finish. Its stainless steel outriggers counterbalance the neck; the upper one houses a balance arm that is friction-loaded and slides in and out for adjustment. The electronics are incredibly flexible. Two humbucking pickups with coil-splitting capabilities combine with four switches: pickup selection, series/parallel connection, in/out-of-phase routing, and single/dual coil configurations. The tone and volume controls each have selector switches governing choice of pickup(s). And the whole thing weighs in at only seven pounds!

MODULUS GRAPHITE

Modulus has long supplied graphite necks and parts for other manufacturers, as well as making their own graphite guitars; but with the folding guitar, they have created a unique design. Assembled and set up by Larry Robinson, a Modulus employee, this extremely light folding guitar depends on the patented Modulus neck and the patented folding mechanism designed by Leigh Copeland. It folds where the headless neck joins the four and one-half inch thick body (both the body and the neck are graphite). The perimeter of the body consists of flexible polypropylene straps; the instrument when folded is only nineteen inches long. Modulus Graphite has no plans for production—at least, not yet....

The Sardonyx Imperial

generate the sounds he hears. In fact, the very topic of equipment is a turnoff for him. Analog delays, a stereo volume pedal, a routing box to each of two amps patching his custom made White Charvel guitar into separate lead and rhythm channels – that's pretty much his standard setup. The rest is fingerwork.

Even a quick listening to UK's LP with Holdsworth, for example, reveals the range of his unique guitar attack and astonishing technical command of the fretboard as he leaps intervals, rearranges scales, shuffles chord voicings, undermines rhythmic expectations. His astonishing guitar has been undermined by a combination of bad luck, current musical expectations within the industry, and lack of access or visibility – something his connection with Van Halen (and through him, with famed producer Ted Templeman) may remedy. In the meantime, though, he has become a kind of living legend among today's foremost guitarists.

DARK HORSES

Folk musics, especially the blues, are the undercurrent that floats rock music, and especially rock guitar. One of the most haunting qualities of the great old bluesmen was their ability to play call-and-response with their voices and guitars: Robert Johnson, to cite the most obvious example, raised that counterpoint to a new level in his few recordings, where he's playing boogie bass, offbeat slide melodies, and singing in a variety of voices. Sometimes he sounds like a whole band. That special relationship between the guitar and the human voice is the major area the following guitarists avidly explore.

Mark Knopfler

Mark Knopfler formed Dire Straits to play the music he heard in his head, a music that fused twitchy rhythms, bluesy changes, Dylanesque lyrics, and a guitar style that rings out clean and true, melodic to the core. He's learned, as well, how to build a solo in a thematic and textual way. Listen, for example, to the pacing and poise on *Making Movies'* opening cut "Tunnel Of Love." His exquisite fills on the Stratocaster (and later, a Strat-style Schechter) throughout are tasty bits of melody, miniature promises of what is to come; but it is only after the verses are finished that he really opens things up. He pulls the band's dynamic level down to an electronic whisper and lets the Strat's clear treble sing delicately and deliberately through hammer-ons and pull-offs and

trills. The drums back up, the volume pushes up, and Knopfler begins to throw in a triplet here, a wrenched and bent chording there, easing his way out of middle register, until finally the guitar simply arcs out and over the still-pumping beat, soaring into simple moving melodies. It is typical of Knopfler's ear and craft that all the pieces are made to coalesce, and that even at their most syncopated the instruments must sing and float simultaneously, like some shimmering musical crystal.

Richard Thompson

Like Knopfler, Richard Thompson is a guitarist-songwriter whose playing seeks to embody his gifted sense of melody. He comes by it naturally: his roots are in the English folk revival of the 1960s, whence he became a member of Fairport Convention. Leaving in 1974, he moved on to another electric folk group, back into the folk-club scene, and finally teamed up with Linda Peters, later his wife, from whom he is now separated.

Thompson has successfully honed his chops – he plays slide and uses a synthesizer for variety of texture – so that he has a genuinely unique sense of how to make a guitar gently – or not so gently – weep. Listen, on *Shoot Out The Lights*, to how his guitar fills wrap themselves around the vocal lines, overlapping here, doubling a line there, harmonizing fluidly a third place. Sometimes his guitar can sound as stark and pinched as Tom Verlaine's at its most offbeat, sometimes it will snarl and bite with a startling ferocity, but it will always surprise and delight.

FADE OUT

Ideally there should be two things at the closing of a musical excursion like this one: a summation and a forecast of the future. Ideally. But as this survey all too clearly shows, the story of rock guitar is not easy to tell in its entirety – never mind in summary form – too many players have been left out because of space as it is. As far as forecasting the future – well, there's not much point to that. Too many accidents of fate should warn us all that the only constant will be change. Nevertheless, if there is one thing all the players mentioned here share, it's a real working dedication to their instrument and musicianship. This book is meant to be as much as anything else a tribute to as many as possible of the great guitarists of every style. I hope that it is, and a good one. If the past is any indication, the fun has only just begun.

DISCOGRAPHY: ROCK GUITAR

Nowhere is it written that the process of choosing twenty-five albums from literally hundreds of contenders should be an easy one, but it is particularly difficult when you're dealing with a number of prolific and inventive musicians whose approach to their instrument has evolved over time. Eric Clapton is an obvious instance of this in action: his playing ripened even in the short space of time between his stint with the Yardbirds and his joining John Mayall's Bluesbreakers, and has never stopped changing emphasis since. How many Clapton recordings are enough to represent those shifts? How many are too many? The only answer is relative; given the consideration of space, these are the albums that seem to best serve as a basic rock library. Happy listening.

DUANE ALLMAN
The Allman Brothers
Live At The Fillmore
Polydor, two-record set CPN-2-0131

Got the way they should've been got – live, tight, and in front of an admiring audience that eggs them on to better and better things. Everything from "Statesboro Blues" with Duane's slashing, sinuous slide lines to the extravaganza of "Whipping Post" live – twenty plus minutes of belting, blasting, soaring guitar by two of the best in competition. Quite simply, a classic in the annals of rock guitar.

THE BEATLES
Yesterday and Today
Capitol ST-02553

Revolver
Capitol SW-02576

I guess you could figure these as either side of the watershed. On the first, even allowing for the differences between U.S. and U.K. albums, the Fab Four are still performing more or less like a tight touring band in the studio – with the notable exception of Lennon's tune, "I'm Only Sleeping," which features what may well be the first use of a backward-tracked guitar solo. Highlights include "Drive My Car," "Dr. Robert," "And Your Bird Can Sing," and "Day Tripper." *Revolver* marks the beginning of the acceptance of the Beatles as "artists" by the likes of Leonard Bernstein, who spent some U.S. television time going into the strange time and chord changes of "She Said She Said" and "Good Day Sunshine." "Tomorrow Never Knows" is highlighted by a much more developed use of the backward-tracked guitar solo.

JEFF BECK
The Jeff Beck Group
Truth
Epic PE 26413

If Led Zeppelin's first LP opened the era of heavy metal, this is the place where they copped many of their initial ideas. Beck's unpredictable pyrotechnics are at their wildest, wooliest, and most off-the-wall imaginative here. His use of the wah-wah pedal, for example, on "I Ain't Superstitious" mimicks the black cat mentioned in the verse and demonstrates the whiz guitarist's mastery of that effect. The band is an awesome lineup – Rod Stewart on vocals, Ron Wood on bass, Nicky Hopkins on keyboards, Mick Waller on drums – and the music is tight. But from "Greensleeves" to "You Shook Me" and back again, this is truly a showcase album for a guitar hero.

ADRIAN BELEW, ROBERT FRIPP
King Crimson
Beat
Warner Bros/EG 23692

Fripp and Belew together make for some interesting and dynamic contrasts, and the resulting tensions from their stylistic collisions can often drive the too often lackluster tunes on this LP beyond their precious limits. There is plenty of interest here for guitarists. "Neal and Jack and Me" is a good song that shifts time as casually as some people shift lovers, and plays off the disorienting effect with a full panoply of post space–age technology. A promising partnership between two masters.

CHUCK BERRY
The Great Twenty-Eight
Chess, two-record set

Just what it says, starting with "Maybellene" (1955) and finishing up with "I Want To Be Your Driver" (1965). Every tune, every lick on this album has been the recipient of several generations' worth of devoted covers by garage bands and superstars alike. The recording quality is good, the energy level is high, and the cuts are all the originals, so they don't suffer from Berry's later lapses into nonchalance and pickup bands. Personnel include bluesman Willie Dixon on bass, Johnny Johnson on piano, and Fred Below on drums – and on two tracks the Moonglows sing background. A terrific collection.

MICHAEL BLOOMFIELD
The Paul Butterfield Blues Band
East-West
Elektra 7315

If you're even remotely into why and how rock guitarists began to mix up their influences in the late sixties and early seventies, you've got to get this one. All performances – including Butter's harp and vocals, Elvin Bishop's supportive rhythm and occasional lead work, Mark Naftalin's fluid and idiomatic keyboards – are simply outstanding. Above it all, though, soars Michael Bloomfield's guitar, now searing, now weeping, here droning Eastern modalities, there smoothing out changes to the famed Nat Adderly composition, "The Work Song." There is nothing as exciting as hearing a virtuoso who has just come into his full powers; and the title track has it all.

ERIC CLAPTON, PETER GREEN, MICK TAYLOR
John Mayall's Bluesbreakers
Looking Back
London 562

A good compilation that allows you to meditate on the differences between the young Clapton, Peter Green, and the very young Mick Taylor, as they play their way through Mayall's ever-shifting line-up. Clapton rears back and punches out a fine solo in "Stormy Monday," recorded live. Green's carefully constructed lines appear on "Looking Back" and "Double Trouble," the old Otis Rush tune. Like Clapton, Taylor appears only on one cut, "Suspicions," but his style is already formed beautifully here.

ERIC CLAPTON
Cream
Wheels of Fire
Atco, two-record set RSO 3802

The advantage of this double LP one side live, the other studio, is that it captures both aspects of this seminal band's work. Live cuts include "Crossroads," on which Clapton's solo work shines with a sharp brilliance, and the legendary if disorganized "Spoonful," where Clapton, bassist Jack Bruce, and drummer Ginger Baker alternate between high points of real musical intensity and blank patches of uncertain wandering. Studio cuts include "White Room" (Clapton on wah-wah), "Sitting On Top Of The World" (a tasty blues solo), and "Politician" (triple-tracked

guitar lines throughout). An earful of the best.

ERIC CLAPTON
Derek and the Dominoes
Layla And Other Love Songs
RSO, two-record set 3801

Eric Clapton learned how to really sing the blues as well as play them for this LP, and Duane Allman came out of the studio shadows to become a guitar hero in his own right. The title cut is, to put it bluntly, one of the most moving sonic tapestries ever created on a rock recording, with Allman and Clapton wrapping guitar lines around each other's and the melody. Other high points include "Key To The Highway," "Nobody Knows You When You're Down And Out," and rocker "Keep On Growing" – all of which feature some great guitar exchanges as the two heroes push each other to their limits and still make it all work as a whole sound.

EDDIE COCHRAN
The Very Best of Eddie Cochran
Liberty FA 3019

This reissue of a reissue (it first appeared in 1970 to mark the tenth anniversary of Cochran's death) has been remastered into what the liner notes describe as "total mono" and includes virtually all of the important tunes – "C'mon Everybody," "Three Steps To Heaven," "Summertime Blues," and "Twenty Flight Rock." But the real sleeper is Cochran's blistering version of his own "Eddie's Blues," which features heavy use of vibrato, of echo, and some very unusual phrasing. It smokes, 32nd notes and all.

RY COODER
Bop Til You Drop
Warner Bros. 3358

Cooder makes amiable music that displays an intimate if seemingly effortless familiarity with a staggering array of styles, beats, sonorities, and overall feels. This is one of his best LPs, and the one that

netted him the broad public appreciation to match the consistent critical praise he had won. Highlights: "Little Sister" and "Down In Hollywood." (N.B. – Cooder's fellow junk-guitar aficionado and session master David Lindley appears on eight of the nine cuts, often doubling the angry mosquito sound of Cooder's favored Japanese Strat imitations.)

BO DIDDLEY
Bo Diddley
Teldec/Chess LC 0156

The man who gave rock'n'roll one of its basic beats performs his original versions, courtesy this Telefunken-Decca reissue of his Chess recordings. "You Can't Judge A Book By The Cover," "Who Do You Love," "Bo Diddley," "I'm A Man," others. Not subtle, but steady.

JERRY GARCIA
The Grateful Dead
The Grateful Dead
Warner Bros. 1689

Their very first album, and one of the finest moments of San Francisco psychedelia. Intense and continuous energy propels the playing through a really eclectic range of material, from the blues of "Good Morning Little Schoolgirl" to the folkier "Morning Dew," and the combination creates a truly mesmerizing LP. Tough and tight, the music rocks in a way that leaves no room for the noodling which characterizes the later Dead. You can feel everybody head full-throttle for a music revolution.

JIMI HENDRIX
The Jimi Hendrix Experience
Electric Ladyland
Warner/Reprise, two-record set 6307

Nobody has ever made a rock record quite like this, even in the decade-plus since its release. From the wah-wah gurglings of the opening cut "And The Gods Made Love," followed by the shift into the underwater underworld of "Have You Ever Been (To Electric Ladyland)," then the sudden explosion of pent-up energy into "Crosstown Traffic," which modulates into a "live" (in the studio) recording of a beautifully paced blues called "Voodoo Chile," which features Traffic's Steve Winwood on organ and Jefferson Airplane's bassist Jack Casady – with all that, this LP puts you on notice that you are hearing a mixture of musical styles, textures, techniques, and directions that is, quite simply, unique. And that's only side one! This album was the most ambitious project Hendrix completed before his early death, and it still holds secrets that other guitarists have yet to unlock. A must-have.

BUDDY HOLLY
Buddy Holly and the Crickets
20 Golden Greats
MCA/MCTV-1 3040

No home should be without one. There are no liner notes, the sound is decently reprocessed in electronic stereo, and the music includes some of the best things rock has ever produced: "That'll Be The Day," "Peggy Sue," "Words Of Love," "Every Day," "Not Fade Away,." "Oh Boy," "Maybe Baby" – to name a few of the classics on here. Holly's guitar work, especially his tight interaction with drummer Jerry Allison, comes across very well; there's still a lot to learn from him.

STEVE HOWE
The Steve Howe Album
Atlantic 19243

A bit overblown in spots, but some first-class guitar work as well. "Cactus Boogie" features some fine chicken-pickin'; "Meadow Rag" shows off Howe's playful familiarity with ragtime fingerpicking; "The Continental" offers affectionate homage to Django Rheinhardt and Stephane Grappelli, with a side glance at Western swing steel. A virtuoso's showcase.

DAVID LINDLEY
El Rayo-X
Elektra/Asylum 524

An easygoing, unpretentious album that shows off both Lindley's musicianship and his encyclopedic array of musical influences. From the opening cut, "She Took Off My Romeos", with its puns and reggae-ish beat, to the raunch of "Mercury Blues" or the black humor of "Quarter of a Man," a rare and tasty treat that is offbeat, fun, and instructive.

JIMMY PAGE
Led Zeppelin
Led Zeppelin
Atlantic 19126

Here it is – the LP that made heavy metal a marketable commodity. Jimmy Page assembled his ersatz New Yardbirds in the studio for seventeen hours and made rock history. "Dazed And Confused," "Good Times, Bad Times," "Communication Breakdown," "How Many More Times," all shaped the mold that heavy metalists would fit and refit for over ten years after this album's release in 1969. Unlike many of his followers, though, Page drew the strength of succinctness from his studio experience, and kept his guitar work from flailing all over the song without reason: the music is tight and powerful.

CARL PERKINS
Original Golden Hits
Sun 111 E

"Honey Don't," "Matchbox," "Everybody's Trying To Be My Baby," and of course "Blue Suede Shoes" are the greats here. Reprocessed for stereo, the sound still approximates the famed Sun sound – echo, echo, and more echo with a big beat. Perkins's specialty was walking bass runs behind his vocal, alternating with sharp broken chordings and trebly picking. It's all here.

BRUCE SPRINGSTEEN
Born to Run
Columbia JC-33795

The Boss in his moment of breakthrough glory. The Phil Spector-ish "wall of sound" sometimes degenerates into a sonic wall of mud, but Springsteen's guitarwork here is tasty, disciplined, and laden with references to some of the greatest names in rock guitar, including Keith Richards and Roy Buchanan.

ANDY SUMMERS
The Police
Zenyatta Mondatta
A&M 3720

A powerhouse recording of fantastic songs, widely varied textures, and spectacular musicianship. Who could ask for anything more? "Don't Stand So Close To Me" kicks off with spacey guitar weaving around Sting's breathy vocal, and it's all over the place from then on. "Canary In A Coalmine," "Da Do Do Do, De Da Da Da" (one of rock's more memorable nonsense lyrics – with a point), the good-natured parody of "Bombs Away," the highly syncopated searching of "Man In A Suitcase," all showcase this band's fine blend of virtuoso and ensemble techniques. They deserve every bit of their success.

EDDIE VAN HALEN
Van Halen
Diver Down
Warner Bros. 3677

Give him a little more time and young Eddie Van Halen is bound to really shake up the ways of rock guitarists. This album features almost every technique he stores in his impressively varied arsenal, from finely filigreed acoustic work ("Little Guitars") to mumbling and screeching feedback raunch ("Pretty Woman") to splashy tone-painting ("Cathedral"). There's more to come.

Acknowledgements
I'd like to thank Allan Kozinn, Peter Welding, Dan Forte, Noe Goldwasser, and David Lindley for their help and guidance.

MAIL ORDER SOURCES

A-1 RECORD FINDERS
P.O. Box 75071-M
Los Angeles, CA 90075
Specializes in early jazz.

ARHOOLIE RECORDS
Box 9195
Berkeley, CA 94709
Blues, jazz, country, rock'n'roll.

AUDIO SOURCE
1185 Chess Drive
Foster City, CA 94404
Early music.

BERKSHIRE RECORD OUTLET
428 Pittsfield-Lenox Road
Lenox, MA 01240

CHEAPO
645 Massachusetts Ave.
Cambridge, MA 02139
Blues, early jazz.

COUNTRY MUSIC SALES
Box 866
Hot Springs, AR 71901

DENVER FOLKLORE CENTER
608 E. 17th Ave.
Denver, CO 80218
Blues, early jazz, country.

THE DISCOPHILE
26 W. 8th St.
New York, NY 10036
Classical.

DOBELL'S FOLK AND BLUES SHOP
21 Tower St.
London WC2H 9N5, England

DOWNHOME MUSIC
10341 San Pablo Ave.
El Cerrito, CA 94530
Blues, jazz, country, rock'n'roll.

FARRINGDONS
28 Holborn Viaduct
London, EC1, England

FOLKWAYS RECORDS
43 W. 61st St.
New York, NY 10023
Blues and jazz.

HARMONIA MUNDI USA
2351 Westwood Blvd.
Los Angeles, CA 90064
Classical.

HOUSE OF OLDIES
35 Carmine St.
New York, NY 10014
Everything since 1950.

INTERNATIONAL BOOK AND
RECORD DISTRIBUTORS
40-11 24th St.
Long Island City, NY 11101

J&F SOUTHERN RECORD SALES
4501 Risinghill Road
Altadena, CA 91001
A variety of specialist fields.

JAZZ AND BLUES RECORD STORE
893 Yonge St.
Toronto, Ontario, Canada

JAZZ RECORD MART
11 West Grand
Chicago, IL 60610
Jazz and blues.

MUSICAL HERITAGE SOCIETY
14 Park Road
Tinton Falls, NJ 07724
Classical.

OUT OF PRINT RECORD LOCATOR
6114 Grist Ave.
Baltimore, MD

RECORD HUNTER
507 Fifth Ave.
New York, NY 10017

ROUNDER RECORDS
186 Willow Ave.
Somerville, MA 02144
Blues, country, folk.

ROUND UP
Box 147
Cambridge, MA 02141
Blues, jazz.

SOHO MUSIC GALLERY
26 Wooster St.
New York, NY 10013

STRIDER RECORDS
29 Cornelia St.
New York, NY 10011
Oldies.

TANDY'S RECORDS
24 Islington Row
Birmingham, B15, 1LJ, England

TEMPLAR RECORD SHOPS LTD.
9a Irving St.
London WC2, England

TOWER RECORDS
692 Broadway
New York, NY 10012

YAZOO RECORDS
245 Waverly Place
New York, NY 10014
Blues and jazz.

INDEX

Newman, Jerry, 108
Newman, Michael, 48
Newport Folk Festival, 145, 171
Newport Jazz Festival, 142
new wave, 192–195, 198
Nichols, Red, 93, 98
Nichols, Roy, 147, 148
Nighthawk, Robert, 71, 80
Nitty Gritty Dirt Band, 138, 147
Norman, Philip, 164
North, Nigel, 48
Norvo, Red, 112, 113, 135

O

odd-stringed guitars: *Chitarra tiorbata*, 38; *Doppelgitarre*, 38; Enharmonic guitar, 38; *Guitarpa*, 38; Lyre-guitar, 38; seven-string, 39; ten-string, 40
Odum, Howard, 51
OKeh Records, 65, 96
Old Homestead Records, 130
"old" tuning, 15
Oliver, Paul, 61, 69
Ophee, Montanya, 23
Origin Jazz Library, 86
Original Dixieland Jazz Band, 53
Osborne, Mary, 109
Otto, Jacob Augustus, 24
Owens, Buck, 127, 147, 148–149, 151, 153, 156

P

Pablo Records, 116
Pacific Jazz Records, 116
Paganini, 28, 29, 46, 49
Page, Jimmy, 159, 161, 167, 168–169, 170, 175, 181, 184
Palmer, Robert, 80
Palumbo, Francisco, 15
pandoura, 8, 9
Pappalardi, Felix, 180
Paramount Records, 64, 66, 69, 86
Parkening, Christopher, 43
Parker, Charlie, 108, 116, 175
Parsons, Gene, 145
Parsons, Gram, 143
Pass, Joe, 115, 116, 121, 124
Patton, Charley, 56–57, 77, 132
Paul, Les (person), 6, 138, 140, 141, 144, 150, 151, 159
Paul, Les (guitar), 164, 167. *See also* Gibson guitars
pavan, 15, 16
Peabody, Charles, 51
Pearl, Minnie, 136
Pedrell, Felipe, 12
Peer, Ralph, 130
Pekar, Harvey, 110
Pellegrini, Domenico, 21
Penny, Hank, 134, 135
Perfect Records, 145
Perins, Bill, 92
Perkins, Al, 152
Perkins, Carl, 142, 143, 144, 161, 173
Perkins, Luther, 143
Persip, Charlie, 152
Peter, Paul & Mary, 144
Peterson Trio, 110
Petties, Arthur, 77
Petway, Robert, 77
Phalèse, Pierre, 16
Piccolo Pete, 70
Pickett, Dan, 70
Pickett, Wilson, 188
p'ip'a, 9
Pisador, Diego, 13
Pizzarelli, Buck, 99
pizzicato, 95. *See also* punteado
Plant, Robert, 183
Playford, John, 16
Poco, 152, 185
Police, The, 194
Ponce, Manuel, 36–37, 47, 49
Ponty, Jean-Luc, 195
pop, 78, 79, 85, 142, 143, 145, 151, 185. *See also* country and western; jazz; rock
portamento, 46
Poulton, Diana, 11
Powell, Louis, 99
powerchord, 169, 170, 176, 181, 189, 193, 195
Prat, Domingo, 30
Pratten, Madame Sidney, 32
Presley, Elvis, 140, 142–143, 145, 156, 159, 161–162, 163, 190
Presti, Ida, 40, 45, 48
Previn, Andre, 42, 49
progressive jazz, 42. *See also* jazz
psychedelia, 167, 168, 169, 172, 173, 183. *See also* rock
Pujol, Emilio, 7, 12, 13, 33, 47, 48
pull-offs, 140, 144, 173, 189, 195, 198. *See also* hammer-ons
punk. *See* new wave
punteado, 14, 22, 23

Q

Quarrymen, The, 169
Quicksilver Messenger Service, 173, 175
Quine, Robert, 192
Quintet of the Hot Club, 104

R

"race records," 97, 130
Rager, Mose, 137
ragtime, 62, 66, 68–70, 86, 172, 187
Rainey, Gertrude "Ma," 51, 69, 71
Rainwater, Cedric, 133
Ramey, Hurley, 106
Ramones, The, 192, 193
Randolph, Boots, 140, 142
Raney, Doug, 113, 118
Raney, Jimmy, 113, 115, 116
rasgueado, 14, 15, 21
Ravel, Maurice, 49
Raven (Chicago), 173
Rawsthorne, Alan, 41
Raye, Martha, 65, 96
R & B (rhythm and blues), 61, 79, 80, 81, 159, 163, 166, 167, 169. *See also* blues
RBF Records, 87
RCA Records, 137, 140, 151, 161
Record, 144
recording techniques, 92
Red, Tampa, 62, 66, 68, 69, 70, 88
Redding, Noel, 176
Redding, Otis, 161
"redneck rock." *See* country and western
Reed, Jerry, 128, 140, 150, 151, 156
Reed, Jimmy, 77, 80
Reed, Lou, 192
Reeves, Jim, 141
reggae, 194
Reinhardt, Django, 6, 40, 65, 78, 101, 104, 105, 115, 116, 121, 125, 141, 147, 148, 174
Remington, Herb, 134
Remler, Emily, 109
Reno, Don, 133, 144
resumen, 23
Reuss, Allen, 100
Rhodes, David, 48
rhythm and blues. *See* R&B
Rice, Tony, 133, 151, 153
Rich, Charlie, 143
Rich, Don, 147, 148
Richards, Keith, 161, 163, 166, 178, 185
Richardson, Jerome, 153
Rickenbacker guitars, 134, 178, 185
Rinzler, Ralph, 144, 145
Ritz Cafe (Oklahoma City), 106
Robertson, Robbie, 171
Robinson, Alex, 69
Robinson, Larry, 197
Roca, Pepita, 33
rock, 158–201; acid, 173; art, 192–195, 198; folk, 185; heavy metal, 181, 189–192; in England, 165, 180–185; in Los Angeles, 185–188, 193; skiffle, 166, 169; southern, 188–189; surf, 165. *See also* new wave; psychedelia; rockabilly; San Francisco
rock 'n' roll, 43, 110, 142–143, 147, 148, 159–161, 163, 166, 171, 173–174, 176, 183
Rock 'N' Roll Trio, 142, 143
rockabilly, 133, 142–144, 148, 152, 161, 163–164, 178, 183
Rockpile, 144
Rockwell, John, 194
Rogers, Jimmie, 130–131, 137
Rodrigo, Joaquín, 36, 37, 47, 49
Rogers, Roy, 147
Rollini, Adrian, 93, 98
Rolling Stone, 172
Rolling Stone Illustrated History of Rock & Roll, The, 142, 194
Rolling Stones, The, 166, 168, 183, 184, 187
Rollins, Sonny, 115, 152
romances, 13
Roncalli, Ludovico, 21
Ronstadt, Linda, 152, 187
Rose Tim, 173
Ross Gorman's Earl Carroll Orchestra, 98
Rossington, Gary, 188
Rounder Records, 145
Roussel, Albert, 35
Rowbotham, James, 16
"Roxy Music," 194
RPM Records, 78, 79
rubato 35
Rubio, Juan Manuel Garcia, 24
Rundgren, Todd, 189
Rush, Otis, 80, 81, 86, 183
Rushing, Jimmy, 78
Russell, David, 45
Russell, Leon, 116, 148

S

Saint-Saens, Camille, 28
Sallis, James, 171
Salvador, Sal, 112
Sam, "Magic," 81, 86
samisen, 9
San Francisco, CA, 173, 174, 175, 180, 188
Sane, Dan, 59, 69
Santana, 175
Satie, Erik, 194
Sanz, Gaspar, 8, 15, 22–23, 37, 42, 47, 49
Saunders, Fernando, 192
Scarlatti, 35, 44, 46, 47
Scene, The (New York City), 172
Schon, Neal, 189
Schubert, Franz, 28–29, 36, 46
Schuller, Gunther, 96
Schumann, 35, 37
Schwartz, Jim, 195
Scoefield, John, 121
Scott, Bobby, 152
Scranton Sirens, 93
Scruggs, Earl, 133, 147
Seals, Son, 85
Searcy, DeLoise, 96
Sebastian, John, 152, 187
Seeger, Pete, 171
Segovia, Andrés, 6, 7, 31, 33–35, 40, 41, 43, 46, 47, 49, 98, 148
Setzer, Brian, 144
Sex Pistols, 192
Shamblin, Eldon, 135, 148
Shank, Bud, 116
Shaw, Artie, 113
Shaw, Robert, 61
Shearing, George, 112, 113
Shindig, 163
Shines, Johnny, 73, 77
Sholes, Steve, 140
Short, Jimmy, 136
Shott's Cafe (Philadelphia), 93
Shout, 164
Shuffler, George, 144
Sims, Zoot, 113
Sinatra, Frank, 135
sitar, 9
six-string guitar, 24, 39
Skaggs, Ricky, 153
Skillet Lickers, 129, 130, 137
Sky, 42
Skynyrd, Lynyrd, 188, 189
Slack, Freddie, 74
Slevin, Dick, 93
Slick, Grace, 174
slide, 70–72, 73, 76, 77, 168, 173, 174, 181, 195, 198
Smith, Arthur, 132, 141
Smith, Bessie, 65, 93, 96
Smith, Clara, 96
Smith, Fay "Smitty," 136
Smith, Floyd, 106
Smith, J.T., 63
Smith, Johnny, 113, 148, 151, 164